Healthy One-Dish *Cooking*

Beef in beer casserole, page 244

Healthy
One-Dish
Cooking

230 healthy, fuss-free recipes for Canadian cooks

Reader's
Digest

Contents

Beef in ale with horseradish dumplings, page 246

Vegetable pies with cheese and herb pastry, page 307

Creamy vegetable fricassee, page 256

Mexican vegetable bake, page 291

One-dish cooking

Healthy one-dish cooking is all about creating
all-in-one balanced meals with the minimum
of fuss. In this section you'll find lots of
information to help you. There's guidance on
how to prepare veggies and fruit, how to joint
a chicken, how to use herbs and spices to add
flavour, as well as recipes for making stocks.
If you want to know when to add different
ingredients or how to modify your recipes with
easy variations, it's all here, along with ideas
for boosting your meals with simple, healthy
accompaniments and ways to achieve Canada's
Food Guide's recommended seven to ten
vegetable and fruit servings per day.

How to use this book

Healthy one-dish cooking includes a wide variety of recipes; some cooked in just one pot, others involving a little preparation before coming together in one dish. From hearty soups and stews, tempting roasts and oven-bakes, creamy risottos and satisfying pasta dishes to speedy stir-fries, main-meal salads, nutritious sandwiches and healthy pizzas, there are delicious dishes for all tastes and occasions.

About the recipes

All the recipes in this book are designed to provide a healthy balance of energy and nutrients, while restricting saturated fats, salt and added sugars. At the same time, the recipes will help you towards your goal of eating seven to ten servings of vegetables and fruit every day. In general, the recipes emphasize:
• **Fresh ingredients** over packaged or processed foods.
• Liberal use of **vegetables and fruits**.
• **Whole grains** over refined grains.
• **Extra salt** has not been included, but we suggest seasoning to taste where appropriate.

The analyses

Every recipe has a *nutritional analysis* per serving. The analysis is based on the following standards unless otherwise stated on individual recipes.

• **Vegetables and fruit** are medium-sized.
• **Potatoes and legumes** are included in the vegetable count.
• **Eggs** are medium-sized.
• **Milk** is 1% (switch to skim or fortified soy beverage if you prefer).
• **No optional ingredients** have been included in the nutritional analysis for each recipe.

• **Simple, no-cook serving ideas**, such as bread or salad, are sometimes suggested in the recipe introductions, but these are not included in the nutritional analyses. Bread may be recommended to boost the carbohydrate or fibre value of a meal, and a salad may be suggested to provide extra fruit or vegetables.
• **Certain foods**, such as sausages, ham, bacon, cheese, olives and some sauces are high in sodium, which makes the recipes that include them higher than is ideal. But it's fine to enjoy these dishes once in a while.
• **Stocks are diluted**, salt-reduced commercial stock, using half water, half stock. If you use a homemade stock (pages 28–29), your sodium intake will be lower.
• **Where appropriate**, readily available, reduced-fat dairy products have been used – such as light sour cream, light cream cheese and low-fat yogourt.
• **You can now buy** an increasing range of salt-reduced products, such as salt-reduced soy sauce, tomato sauce, tomato paste and canned vegetables. Using them will help to reduce sodium content further. Some recipes specify to use salt-reduced products so that the sodium level of the recipe falls within acceptable levels, but others let you choose.
• **Meat products**, such as ground meat, have been analyzed based on good-quality lean meat, trimmed of

excess fat. Poultry is generally skinned, unless otherwise stated.

About grilling

Recipes that instruct you to use the grill will work equally well with the broiler, barbecue or a grill pan.

ADDED FEATURES

Some of the recipes in this book have added information, such as being ideal for freezing or preparing ahead or being suitable for vegetarians. These recipes are clearly labelled with a green strip on the side of the page so you can identify them easily.

Great to freeze Many dishes, such as soups, stews, curries and casseroles usually freeze well, so why not make a double quantity of these recipes and freeze one for a later date? Or simply prepare the dish ahead when you have time to cook, then pop it in the freezer for eating another day.

Vegetarian For strict vegetarians, check the packaging on cheeses to make sure they are suitable. Most are, or you can buy vegetarian varieties. Some cheeses, made by traditional methods, use animal rennet. Parmesan is one example, but you can choose other varieties of hard cheese instead.

Prepare ahead Some recipes are suited to being prepared ahead. These are suitable for either cooking completely and then chilling or freezing, or cooking elements of the dish in advance. When reheating a cooked dish that has been chilled or frozen, make sure it is piping hot all the way through.

*H*ealthy eating

It is neither difficult nor time-consuming to eat healthily. You just need a good variety of foods in the right proportions. So include plenty of grain products, a wide variety of fruit and vegetables, and a little good-quality protein, 1% milk and other dairy foods for essential fatty acids, vitamins and minerals. And restrict foods that are high in saturated fats, salt and sugar.

Grain products

Aim to include six to eight servings of grain products each day. In general, one Food Guide serving is a slice of bread, half a small bagel, pita or tortilla, ½ cup (125 ml) of cooked rice or pasta or 30 grams of cold cereal. Ideally, make at least half your grain products whole grain, as these offer three benefits:
• They are rich in fibre, which can help to prevent constipation, bowel disease, heart disease and many other health problems.
• They contain higher levels of nutrients, such as B group vitamins.
• Most are a good source of slowly digested carbohydrates, which provide slow-release energy to keep you satisfied longer.

Glycemic index

Glycemic Index (GI) is a classification of carbohydrate foods according to their effect on blood sugar levels. Foods with a low GI such as pumpernickel bread, whole grain rye bread, oatmeal, oat bran, barley, sweet potato, legumes, apples, pears and yogourt are digested and absorbed slowly, producing more gradual rises in blood sugar levels. Foods with a high GI such as white bread and refined breakfast cereals are digested and absorbed quickly, which causes a more rapid increase in blood sugar levels.

Choosing low or medium GI foods helps moderate blood sugar levels and may help regulate appetite and weight.

> The recipes in this book include a good selection of carbohydrates with an emphasis on the low- to medium-GI types.

Vegetables and fruit

Adults should aim to eat seven to ten servings of vegetables and fruit each day. Fresh is best, but frozen, canned and dried are good, too. Vegetables and fruit are packed with vitamins, minerals and other antioxidant nutrients that help to protect against illness, and they offer vital dietary fibre, needed for healthy digestion. Try to eat a wide variety, as each type contains different combinations of nutrients.
• Orange, yellow and red fruit and vegetables, such as carrots, peppers, orange sweet potatoes, mangoes and strawberries are rich in vitamin C, beta-carotene and other powerful antioxidants that are thought to help fight against cancer, heart disease, cataracts, arthritis and general aging.
• Tomatoes are a good source of vitamin C and also lycopene, another powerful antioxidant.
• Brassicas, including cabbage, cauliflower, broccoli, Brussels sprouts and kale contain antioxidants and are a good source of vitamin C, folates and minerals.
• Onions, garlic and others of the onion family contain allicin, a phytochemical believed to lower risk of cancer and heart disease.

What counts as a portion of vegetables and fruit?

You can get your seven to ten in a variety of ways. Add extra vegetables to a soup, casserole or pizza topping, add seasonal salads and fruit on the side and choose more vegetarian-style dishes. The following is a general guide to portions:
• 1 small glass (1/2 cup/125 ml) of fruit or vegetable juice
• 1 medium-sized piece of fruit, such as an apple, orange, pear, peach or banana
• 2 small pieces of fruit, such as plums or small mandarins
• a handful of very small fruit such as cherries, grapes or berries
• 1/2 cup (125 ml) dried fruit such as apricots or figs
• 1/2 cup (125 ml) fresh, frozen or canned vegetables or fruit
• 1/2 cup (125 ml) cooked vegetables
• 1 cup (250 ml) salad or raw vegetables
• 1/2 cup cooked legumes

Daily guidelines for nutrients are based on average calorie needs, depending on age, sex and activity levels. The recommendations for vegetables, fruits and grains are based on Canada's Food Guide. The following figures are based on the intakes for an average adult man or woman who is not overweight or totally sedentary. Those who are overweight should aim to reduce their calories by approximately 500 calories per day to lose about 1 pound/week.

FOOD GROUP	WOMEN	MEN
Calories	1800 – 2200	2200 – 2800
Veggies and fruit	7 to 8 servings	7 to 10 servings
Fibre	21 to 25 grams	30 to 38 grams
Total fat	45 to 75 grams	50 to 105 grams
Saturated fat (maximum. No more than 10% of daily calories)	20 g (16 g)	27 g (20 g)
Sodium (daily upper limit)	2300 mg	2300 mg
Grains (3+ whole)	6 to 8 servings	6 to 8 servings

Meat and alternatives

Meat, poultry, fish, dairy, eggs and vegetarian alternatives like tofu, legumes and nuts, contain protein, which is essential for growth and cell repair. These foods also provide minerals like iron, zinc and magnesium and B vitamins (B_{12} is found only in sources of animal protein).

Protein foods can be high in fat so choose lean meat products, trim visible fat and skin poultry. Eat fish at least twice a week. Fish, especially the fatty ones like salmon, trout, herring, mackerel and sardines, are rich in omega-3 fatty acids, which are believed to lower risk of heart attack and stroke. Legumes are naturally low in fat, a great source of vegetable protein, high in fibre and rich in vitamins and minerals. Nuts, although high in fat, contain mainly the healthier, unsaturated type.

Ways of restricting fat, such as removing skin, are usually applied to the protein foods in this book.

Milk and alternatives

Milk, yogourt, cheese and fortified soy beverage are all excellent sources of calcium, needed for strong bones and teeth, blood clotting, muscle contraction and a healthy nervous system. These foods are particularly important for young children, for adolescent girls – to prevent osteoporosis later – and for women in general. Dairy products can be high in saturated fat, so try to choose low fat varieties. These foods also provide protein, vitamins A and B_{12}, riboflavin, magnesium, zinc and potassium. Fluid milk, fortified soy beverages and some yogourts contain vitamin D.
• Aim to include 2–3 portions of dairy foods per day.

• A serving could include: one cup (250 ml) milk or fortified soy beverage; ¾ cup (175 ml) yogourt; 50 g (1½ oz.) of cheese. (For a healthy dairy-free diet, include almonds, dark greens, fortified soy beverage and canned fish, eaten with the bones.)

Fats

A small amount of the right kind of fat is essential for a healthy diet, providing valuable fat-soluble vitamins and essential fatty acids. Some fat also makes food taste good. However, no more than one-third of your daily calorie intake should come from fat. Fats can be divided into three main groups:

• Saturated fats (found in meat, poultry, full-fat dairy foods, coconut and palm oil). A high intake of these fats increases cholesterol levels, which raises the risk of heart disease. It is recommended to cut down on these fats as much as possible.

- **Mono-unsaturated fats**, found in olive, canola and peanut oils, as well as avocado, some margarines, and nuts like almonds and pecans, lower heart disease risk by lowering cholesterol levels.

- **Trans fats**, found in many cookies, pastries, snacks and fast foods, are linked to a higher risk of heart disease.

- **Polyunsaturated fats** (found mainly in liquid vegetable oils). Certain essential polyunsaturated fatty acids must be supplied by food. There are two groups: omega-3s from oily fish such as salmon, trout and sardines as well as flaxseed oil, canola oil and walnuts; and omega-6s from vegetable oils like corn, safflower and sunflower. Both are essential for good health.

> **Most of the recipes contain less than 30 g total fat and a maximum of 8 g saturated fat per serving.**

Salt

A small amount of sodium (available from foods or salt) is needed for healthy body function but most people in the developed world eat far too much salt. Overconsumption can lead to health problems, such as high blood pressure and an increased risk of heart disease, stroke and kidney failure.

Adults 19 to 50 need only 1500 mg of sodium per day with an upper limit of 2300 mg. Eating processed, fast and premade foods, and adding salt to food lead to over-consumption.

There is also salt in bread, cheese, cured meat and smoked meats or fish. Other high-salt foods include condiments like ketchup, soy sauce, barbecue sauce, dressings, pickles, olives and canned or packaged foods, so always check the label and try and buy salt-reduced alternatives if they are available.

Sugar

Added sugars contain no vitamins, minerals or fibre and simply provide the body with empty calories. Pure glucose has a GI value of 100 and may cause rapid fluctuations in blood glucose. However, a small amount of sugar adds to the enjoyment of food, so you can include occasional sweet foods as part of a well-balanced diet, as long as you don't overdo it.

Remember that fruit contains fructose (a natural fruit sugar) and fruit can frequently be used for sweetening dishes rather than using added sugar. There is an added benefit to using fruit as it provides fibre, vitamins, minerals and plant chemicals, all linked to good health.

Drinking enough

Drinking plenty of liquid is essential for healthy body function, and you should aim to drink at least 2 litres of non-alcoholic liquid each day. Water is the best choice because it has no calories or sugar but soda water, fruit juice, milk, soy beverages, sport drinks, soft drinks and even tea and coffee can keep you hydrated. In hot, humid weather and during exercise, your fluid needs increase.

Consuming moderate amounts of alcohol has been linked to a reduced risk of heart disease. If you do drink, limit yourself to one drink a day for women and two for men. One drink is 145 ml (5 oz) wine, 45 ml (1½ oz.) spirits or 341 ml (12 oz) beer.

Preparation techniques

Don't be put off using unfamiliar vegetables when they're available because you don't know how to use them. Preparation is usually very simple; it's just a case of following the right routine.

Asparagus Young spears need no preparation but if the stems seem coarse, snap off or trim away the woody ends. (The ends are great for adding flavour to homemade stock so don't throw them away.) Asparagus is best steamed, microwaved with a splash of water or chargrilled. For stir-frying, slice the stems and cook them for a little longer than the delicate tips.

Avocado A ripe avocado should yield slightly when gently pressed in the palm of your hand. If bought hard, put in a paper bag and ripen at room temperature. Store ripe avocados in the refrigerator for up to 2 days. To halve, cut lengthwise through to the stone, using a stainless steel knife, then twist the two halves in opposite directions to separate. Remove the stone, then peel. To prevent the flesh from turning brown, sprinkle with lemon juice.

Fava beans are best when young and should be eaten as fresh as possible. Remove beans from the pods, then boil or steam them for 5–10 minutes, depending on size and age. Very young fava beans (up to 7 cm long), can be cooked whole in their pods for about 5 minutes. Mature (late-season) beans are best peeled after cooking.

Butternut squash Peel off the tough skin using a vegetable peeler, then cut in half lengthwise and scoop out the seeds and fibrous pulp using a teaspoon. Cut the flesh into chunks or as required for the recipe. It's good boiled, then mashed, roasted or cooked in soups or casseroles. The squash can also be pricked with a fork and baked whole. These cooking methods apply to all varieties of squash.

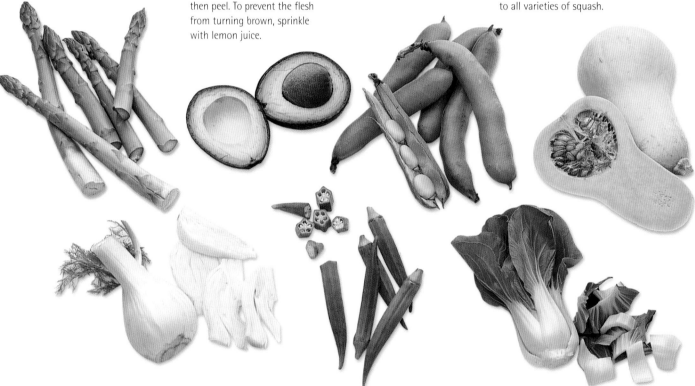

Fennel Reserve the feathery fronds for garnishing and remove any tough outer ribs, then thinly slice the bulb as you would for celery. It can be eaten raw in salads or cooked – but should be put in acidulated water (water with a little lemon juice or vinegar) once sliced to prevent the cut surfaces turning brown.

Okra Wash okra just before using it. Remove fine fuzz on the surface with a soft brush. Trim away the stalks but don't tear the pods and expose the seeds, which can give a slightly gloopy texture to dishes. However, if this is what you want – for a gumbo, for example – slice thickly or thinly according to the recipe.

Bok choy Roughly chop the leaves into wide strips and the stalks into slightly smaller pieces or simply separate the stems and leave whole. The smaller the plant, the more tender the vegetable will be. It is ideal for stir-fries or steaming and should always be quickly cooked.

Peppers To grill peppers, cook halved or quartered peppers, skin-side up, for about 10 minutes under a hot grill, until the skins are charred. Put the hot peppers in a plastic bag and leave for about 10 minutes until cool enough to handle. The steam created in the bag will help to loosen the skins so that they slip off easily. The peppers will have a sweet and slightly smoky flavour.

Celeriac Remove the tough knobbly skin using a vegetable peeler, then slice or dice using a large sharp knife. Immerse the cut flesh in a bowl of acidulated water (water with lemon juice or vinegar added) to prevent discolouration. It can be added to soups and stews or boiled for about 20 minutes until tender, then mashed or briefly blanched for salads.

Corn Trim the ends with a sharp knife, then remove the husks and silks. Cook whole cobs in boiling water for about 10 minutes, without salt as this may toughen the kernels. They can then be roasted or barbecued, or just eaten as they are. Baby corn can be used whole or sliced lengthwise and is ideal for cooking in stir-fries and other Asian dishes. Do not overcook them as they can become tough and lose their sweetness.

Eggplant It was once recommended to degorge eggplants (sprinkling them liberally with salt and leaving them to stand for about 20 minutes) to draw out the bitter indigestible juices. New varieties are rarely bitter although salting may help the fibrous flesh to absorb less oil when cooked. Rinse off the salt and pat the eggplant dry before cooking. Slices can be lightly brushed with oil and grilled rather than fried in oil.

Spinach (and kale) Remove any tough stalks before cooking. Always wash spinach thoroughly, then cook very briefly in just the water clinging to the leaves. A large quantity wilts down to a small heap, so always prepare plenty. Baby spinach leaves need no preparation and are ideal for salads.

Sweet potato There are two main types of sweet potato – white fleshed or orange fleshed. Peel and cook in chunks, or boil or bake in their jackets, peeling off the skins after cooking. Deliciously sweet and wonderfully versatile, use them as you would normal potatoes for soups and casseroles.

Tomatoes To peel tomatoes, cut a cross in the base of each tomato and place in a bowl. Pour boiling water over them and leave them to stand for about 30 seconds. Drain, refresh in cold water to cool quickly, then drain again and peel. The skins will slip off easily. (This blanching technique is also useful for peeling shallots quickly and easily. Stand in the boiling water for 10 minutes.)

Preparing a chicken

Here are six easy steps to jointing a chicken.

1 Place the chicken, breast-side up, on a board. Gently pull one leg away from the body and use a heavy cook's knife to cut through the skin between the body and leg. Bend the leg outwards until the ball pops out of the socket joint, then carefully cut through the flesh under the joint. Repeat with the second leg.

2 To separate the drumstick from the thigh, stand one leg on the board so that it forms a natural V-shape. Firmly hold the end of the drumstick in one hand and cut through the joint where the two bones meet at the centre of the V. Repeat with the second leg.

3 To separate the wings from the body of the chicken, make a deep cut into the breast meat near to the inside of each wing. As you do this, angle the knife diagonally across the neck end of the bird so that the uncut breast forms a diamond shape. Cut down into the meat far enough to expose the bones.

4 To free the wings from the carcass, use a pair of poultry shears or strong kitchen scissors to cut between the ball and socket joints and through the remaining flesh and bone. Make sure there are no sharp splinters of bone embedded in the cut portions.

5 To remove the breast meat, lay the carcass on its side then use shears or scissors to cut through the thin rib cage on either side of the backbone.

6 Divide the breast into two, cutting crosswise or lengthwise through the bird's flesh using a knife and then through the bones and cartilage with the shears or scissors. Use the carcass to make stock (page 28).

Preparation terms

Have you ever wondered what exactly is meant by "dice" or "cube"? Here are some chopped vegetables showing relative sizes.

- **Dice** cut into small squares.
- **Cube** cut into bite-sized chunks.
- **Julienne** cut into fine sticks, about 4 cm long.
- **Ribbons** peel lengthwise into wide strips using a vegetable peeler.
- **Zest** (pare) thinly remove outer rind and not the bitter white pith, from citrus fruits using a vegetable peeler, or use a grater or citrus zester tool to take off fine shreds.

Healthy flavourings

There is a wealth of wonderful and exciting flavours to be found in herbs, spices and other seasonings. It is worthwhile becoming familiar with the variety available and how best to use them. You will not only be able to reduce the amount of salt in your food, you will add a whole new flavour dimension to your cooking.

Herbs

Fresh herbs are widely available in greengrocers, supermarkets and Asian food stores. It's also easy to grow your own, in a herb bed in the garden, in pots on a deck or in a window box. They are great for imparting flavour to all kinds of dishes. Herbs can be divided into two groups, listed below.

• Robust herbs, such as rosemary, thyme, sage, oregano and bay leaves, are particularly good used in slow-cooked dishes, such as stews and casseroles, as well as marinades and stuffings. They are usually added at the start, because long, slow cooking mellows their powerful taste. Because of the strength of their flavour, they should be used sparingly. They're best removed before serving as woody twigs, stalks and leaves are not palatable.

• Tender herbs, such as basil, mint, tarragon, cilantro, chives, dill and parsley, have a much fresher flavour than the robust herbs and are usually added to dishes at the last minute. Prolonged cooking will generally spoil their delicate flavour and appearance. Use liberally in soups, salads and stir-fries, and for pretty garnishes.

Herbs can be chopped with a sharp knife or mezzaluna on a board, but it can be quicker to put them in a jug then snip with scissors. Basil should be torn into rough pieces or can be rolled up tightly, then shredded with a sharp knife. For chives, simply snip using scissors.

HERB	ESPECIALLY COMPLEMENTS	IDEAL FOR
Basil	tomatoes, green vegetables, soft cheeses, lamb and eggs	salads, soups, pasta sauces and Mediterranean dishes
Bay leaf	meat, poultry, fish and vegetables	soups, stews, casseroles and pot-roasts
Chives	eggs, cheese, potatoes, fish and chicken	soups, salads and omelettes
Cilantro	chicken, fish, seafood, rice and tomatoes	Thai, Indonesian, Indian, Chinese and Middle Eastern stir-fries and curries
Dill	chicken, fish, eggs, cheese and potatoes	soups, salads, sauces and marinades
Mint	lamb, potatoes, peas and tomatoes	salads and vegetable dishes
Oregano	pork, poultry, game, fish and vegetables (especially tomatoes)	pasta sauces, stuffings and Italian dishes
Parsley	lamb, chicken, ham, fish, vegetables, eggs and cheese	soups, salads, sauces and casseroles
Rosemary	lamb, pork and game	stuffings, casseroles and for spiking joints
Sage	pork, duck, offal and tomatoes	stuffings and casseroles
Tarragon	eggs, fish, chicken and vegetables	salads and sauces
Thyme	fish, chicken, beef and game	stuffings, casseroles, marinades and pasta sauces

Spices

Spices add fragrant scents and exotic flavours to a wide range of dishes. They are best bought in small quantities and whole if possible, to be ground when required, to retain their freshness. A mortar and pestle or an electric coffee grinder is ideal for grinding your own. Store in airtight containers, in a cupboard, away from direct heat and sunlight and use within 6 months.

• **For general seasoning** Pepper complements all savoury dishes. It has a warm, pungent taste and brings out the flavour of other ingredients. White pepper has a more delicate flavour than black.

• **Hot spices** For a spicy kick, use chili flakes or powder (sold in mild and hot varieties). Pure chili powder (and cayenne pepper) is extremely hot, so just a pinch, or $1/2$ teaspoon, is plenty. Chili seasoning blends can be used much more freely – up to 1–2 tablespoons to flavour a typical

dish. Paprika is far milder with a sweet, earthy aroma that's ideal for stews and sauces.

• **Warm spices** include coriander, cumin, star anise and turmeric and impart an aromatic flavour to dishes. They are usually included early in the cooking process to allow their flavours to mellow. Turmeric is ideal for many Indian and vegetarian dishes, but choose saffron for a subtle and distinctive honey-like colour and flavour in risottos, paellas

and seafood dishes. It can be bought either as powder or threads.

• **Sweet spices** Cinnamon, ginger, cardamom and nutmeg, and other sweet spices, add fragrant, spicy undertones to stews and simmered dishes. A cinnamon stick is better than ground for savoury dishes. Nutmeg is best freshly grated. Cardamom pods can be added whole for a subtle flavour (the pod is not edible) or crushed before using and just the seeds added to the dish.

SPICE	ESPECIALLY COMPLEMENTS	IDEAL FOR
Cardamom	fish, meat, rice, vegetables and yogourt	curries, stews and pilafs
Chili	meat, poultry, fish, tomatoes and peppers	Indian, Mexican and South-East Asian dishes
Cinnamon	meat, rice and spinach	curries, stews and spicy casseroles
Coriander	meat and vegetables	spicy meat and vegetable stews
Cumin	meat, poultry, rice, legumes and vegetables	curries, Mexican and Moroccan dishes and tomato sauces
Fennel seed	fish, pork, potatoes and rice	oily fish dishes, salads and risottos
Ginger	fish, poultry and root vegetables	curries, stir-fries and marinades
Nutmeg	beef, milk, cheese and vegetables, especially spinach, carrots and mushrooms	Italian pasta dishes and sauces
Paprika	pork, chicken and vegetables, especially potatoes	soups and stews
Saffron	chicken, fish, seafood, rice and potatoes	paellas, risottos, couscous and fish soups
Star anise and five-spice powder	fish, chicken and meat, especially pork	Chinese braised dishes and stir-fries
Turmeric	fish, vegetables, rice and eggs	curries, pilafs and vegetarian dishes

Fresh aromatics

The health benefits of garlic are now widely recognized and it has become a favourite and essential flavouring for everyday cooking. However, how familiar are you with other aromatics, such as fresh ginger, lemon grass and chili peppers? These too are readily available from supermarkets and greengrocers and can add an exotic and distinctive note to a variety of dishes.

Lemon grass is widely used in South-East Asian dishes to provide a heady, citrus accent. To prepare, remove any wrinkled outer leaves and discard the root end of the stalk, then finely chop the bulbous base and about the first 10 cm of the stem.

Fresh chili peppers There are many varieties of chili pepper, ranging from fiery to mild. Care must be taken when preparing chili peppers because the oily compound, capsaicin, found in the ribs near the seeds, can irritate the eyes and skin. Cut the chili pepper in half lengthwise, scrape out the seeds and ribs using a sharp-pointed knife, then slice widthwise. For the full chili heat, leave in the seeds or, for a milder flavour, add the whole uncut chili pepper, then remove before serving.

Fresh ginger has a hot, yet refreshing flavour and is essential for Chinese stir-fries and Thai-style dishes. To prepare, peel off the brown knobbly skin using a vegetable peeler, then grate or finely chop. The unpeeled ginger root will keep well for about a month, covered in plastic wrap, stored in the refrigerator.

More flavourings

• **Citrus juices and zests** can pep up spicy soups, fish, stews and stir-fries. Add just before serving to get the full, fresh flavour impact.
• **Flavoured oils and vinegars** can be used in cooking in place of regular ones or drizzled over cooked dishes, salads and vegetable accompaniments.
• **Red or white wine**, used to replace part of the stock or cooking liquid, will boost the flavour of stews, casseroles, sauces and stocks. Wine is usually added at the start of the cooking process and may be reduced to concentrate the flavour.
• **Condiments**, such as mustard, pesto, fish sauce, soy sauce, mirin, tomato paste and Worcestershire sauce are all great flavour enhancers, but they are also generally high in salt, so taste the meal before adding any extra salt.

The question of salt

Dishes that are well flavoured with herbs and spices are likely to not need any extra salt. Generally, it's best to season a dish towards the end of cooking when all the other flavouring ingredients have had a chance to impart their flavour, and to add salt only if necessary. The rule is simply to taste and to trust your own judgment.

Marinades and rubs

These are a great way to add flavour to meat, fish, poultry, tofu and vegetable dishes before cooking.
• **A marinade** is a seasoned liquid used to flavour and tenderize as well as add moisture, especially to foods that are to be grilled or barbecued. It can also be used for basting while cooking. Marinades generally include an acidic ingredient (such as lemon juice, vinegar, wine or yogourt) to tenderize, oil to add succulence, and herbs or spices to add flavour. Fish needs only brief marinating (about 30 minutes), whereas red meat is best marinated for several hours or even overnight.
• **Rubs** are the dry equivalent of marinades and are a means of adding flavour by rubbing a mixture of dried herbs and spices into raw food before cooking. They can add instant flavour or be applied ahead for a longer, more intense flavouring time. On cooking, the flavour of the rub is absorbed into the food, leaving a coating of the rub mixture on the outside.

Getting the timing right

All ingredients have different cooking times, so you need to add them at the right stage to make sure they are all cooked to perfection when the dish is complete. This basic guide groups ingredients according to whether they need long, medium or quick cooking. Size also affects the cooking time, so small pieces will cook much faster than larger pieces of the same ingredient.

Meats on the bone and tougher cuts of meat require longer cooking times to allow the meat to tenderize. This is why you'll often see these cuts used as the basis of casseroles, braises or roasts while tenderloin and steaks are more often briefly grilled, stir-fried or pan-fried.

It may seem obvious, but harder vegetables need long cooking to soften them. For instance, root vegetables require longer cooking than crisp vegetables, such as broccoli. And some salad vegetables and leafy greens require no cooking at all.

The secret with herbs is to use pungent, tough herbs in dishes that require long cooking, otherwise their flavour can be overwhelming. But delicate herbs should be added at the last minute or their fresh flavour will be destroyed.

Longer-cooking

• Joints of meat, braising and stewing cuts (casserole meat) and whole birds. It is important that pork and poultry are cooked right through.

• Dried legumes require overnight soaking, then simmering in liquid for about 1 hour until tender. All dried legumes should be cooked to destroy natural toxins. Once cooked, legumes are safe, healthy foods.

• Brown rice takes longer to cook than white rice, so allow about 30 minutes in boiling liquid.

• Onions, garlic and fresh ginger are pungent flavourings and are usually added at the beginning of cooking to help to flavour the whole dish.

• Root vegetables, including potatoes, carrots, turnips, parsnips, celeriac and fresh beets need to be steamed, boiled, baked, roasted or slowly cooked in a soup or casserole with liquid.

• Squash have cooking properties similar to root vegetables and need to be steamed, boiled, baked or roasted until tender.

• Tomatoes, when used as the base of a sauce, usually require long, slow cooking to bring out their flavour.

• Dried fruits are usually added to stews and casseroles at the beginning of cooking to allow them to plump up and sweetly flavour the dish.

• Robust herbs, such as sage, rosemary, bay leaf, oregano and thyme, and warm and hot spices, including chili, are usually added at the start of long cooking times to provide a subtle, balanced flavour to foods.

Medium-cooking

• Ground meats, chicken portions, chops and uncooked sausages.
• Whole fish, fish steaks and fillets.
• Rice (white, basmati, risotto, wild), pasta and dried lentils. The cooking times vary, depending on the type of rice and the size and shape of pasta, so be sure to follow the package instructions. Cook rice, pasta and lentils in a large pot of boiling or simmering water or stock.
• Crisp vegetables, such as fennel and celery, and brassicas, such as broccoli, cauliflower, Brussels sprouts and cabbage. Cook until just tender and take care not to overcook. (A flat skewer is useful for testing.)
• Peppers, eggplant and zucchini are especially delicious stuffed, grilled or chargrilled and roasted. (They can also be quickly cooked by stir-frying.)
• Corn on the cob and baby corn need to be cooked in boiling water, then grilled, barbecued or roasted. Baby corn need a shorter boiling or steaming time and can also be sliced and stir-fried.
• Beans, such as fava beans, runner beans and green beans, need to be cooked until just tender.
• Leeks are more subtle in flavour than onions and simply need to be cooked until they are soft, but still retain some shape and colour.
• Dried mushrooms should be soaked first, then cooked for 15–20 minutes. They give a great flavour boost to many types of foods.

Quick-cooking

• Steaks, escalopes, pork tenderloin, lean cubes of meat or poultry for kebabs and thin slices/strips for stir-fries.
• Cured meats, such as bacon, ham and chorizo sausage.
• Shellfish, such as cooked shrimp, just require a quick heat through or they'll toughen.
• Tofu (soy bean curd).
• Noodles, couscous, bulgur and instant polenta.
• Canned legumes should simply be drained and rinsed, before adding to the pot. Heat through for a hot dish.
• Tender fresh pods, shoots and sprouts, such as peas, snow peas, asparagus and bean sprouts.
• Fresh mushrooms are best cooked briefly to retain their appearance and texture.
• Tender leafy vegetables, such as spinach and Asian greens, should be only very briefly cooked until just wilted.
• Frozen and canned vegetables are best if cooked quickly, to retain their nutrients.
• Salad vegetables, such as scallions, avocado, cucumber, celery and watercress, do not require cooking but may be briefly cooked for hot dishes, such as soups.
• Fresh fruits generally don't need cooking but are added for flavour, colour and appeal. They only need to be warmed through gently to retain their shape.
• Tender, delicate herbs should be tossed in at the last minute to retain their fresh, aromatic flavour.
• Nuts should be added at the end of the recipe and cooked only briefly, to retain their crunch.

Creating your own dishes

One-dish meals are highly adaptable. It's a simple matter to vary the ingredients and flavourings according to personal taste and dietary requirements, what you have available at home and what's in season at the time.

Good swaps

Most ingredients can be replaced by other foods that fall into the same "family group," or those with similar taste, texture and cooking properties. For example, different white fish, such as cod and sole, or sweet root vegetables, such as carrots and parsnips, are mostly interchangeable. You can also swap lean meat for poultry or even tofu to make a vegetarian dish. Here are some simple suggestions:

- leeks in place of onions or shallots
- Swiss chard in place of spinach
- napa cabbage in place of bok choy
- peas in place of fava beans
- fennel in place of celery
- butternut squash in place of other varieties of squash
- snow peas in place of asparagus
- pears in place of apples
- peaches in place of mango or papaya
- dried apricots in place of prunes or figs
- swordfish in place of fresh tuna
- trout in place of salmon
- chicken or turkey in place of pork
- tangy goat's cheese in place of blue cheese
- couscous in place of bulgur
- almonds in place of pine nuts.

Making more

You can also boost dishes with extra ingredients, either to make a dish more substantial or to feed more people. Most recipes can be easily doubled, or you can stretch a dish with extra vegetables, beans, pasta or rice, or an extra portion of meat or fish.

Stock up

Keep your pantry, refrigerator and freezer well stocked with staple foods and you'll always be able to rustle up delicious meals on short notice. The following list is not meant to be exhaustive, but includes the essential ingredients you need to have available for healthy, tasty cooking.

- Condiments: salt-reduced soy sauce, ketchup, honey, cranberry sauce, pesto sauce, Dijon mustard, mayonnaise and horseradish sauce
- Canned vegetables: whole roma and chopped tomatoes and corn
- Canned fish: tuna in water, sardines and salmon
- Salt-reduced stock
- Pasta: various varieties

- Legumes: canned (or dried) beans, lentils and chickpeas
- Rice (different types), couscous, polenta and bulgur
- Rolled oats
- Dried fruits, nuts and seeds
- Dried herbs, spices, sea salt and black pepper mills
- Oils and vinegars
- Flour, cornstarch and sugar

Healthy options

Here is how to vary ingredients according to when they are available or in season. Peppers stuffed with beef and tomatoes (page 269) could be made with any number of different ingredients. It makes a great main meal for two, or can be served as a light meal for four with crusty bread and a simple side salad. The recipe can easily be doubled.

Any kind of ground meat could be used, such as lamb, pork, turkey or chicken.

Replace the breadcrumbs with some cooked rice, bulgur or couscous to bind the stuffing together and add carbohydrate.

Use large green or red peppers instead of yellow ones or replace the peppers with large zucchini or large tomatoes.

Good alternative cheeses to cheddar are any well-flavoured hard or semi-hard cheese, such as Gruyère or Parmesan.

Omit the cheesy topping and sprinkle the stuffing mixture with a few roughly chopped nuts instead.

Canned tomatoes in the stuffing mixture could be replaced with three large peeled and chopped fresh tomatoes.

Fennel is braised in the dish with the peppers, but sliced celery would work equally well.

Boosting your meals

The recipes in this book have been designed to give a healthy balance of nutrients and to be complete lunch or dinner dishes, served with good bread or a simple salad. But allowing for variation in appetites and the fact that some recipes are naturally lighter than others, you may sometimes want to boost the recipe to provide a more substantial meal or to feed unexpected guests.

Boosting carbs

Adding lots of filling starchy carbohydrates is one of the best ways to stretch a meal for lots of hungry people.

• **Bulgur** is a delicious alternative to rice, with a wholesome, nutty flavour. Pour boiling water over it, leave to soak for about 20 minutes, then drain. Enjoy it plain, or toss with a little olive oil and lemon juice to moisten and add plenty of chopped fresh herbs. It is good with grilled meats and fish, roasts and casseroles.
• **Couscous** goes particularly well with saucy stews and casseroles (called tagines in North Africa, where couscous is a staple).
• **Pasta and noodles** come in all kinds of shapes, sizes and flavours and are a perfect low-fat accompaniment. For those following a wheat-free diet, choose rice and buckwheat (soba) noodles and wheat-free varieties of pasta.
• **Rice** is great with stews, casseroles, curries and stir-fries. Whole grain rice varieties, such as brown or wild rice (not a true rice but a whole grain), are especially healthy options.
• **Beans and lentils** are a tasty, high-fibre carbohydrate option to serve with roasts or braised and grilled dishes. Mashed or crushed, they make a healthy alternative to mashed potatoes.

SIMPLE ACCOMPANIMENTS

Bread

Bread is the simplest accompaniment, as it requires no cooking and there are so many different varieties. Choose from:
• whole wheat, multigrain (or seeded) or rye bread
• French bread, ciabatta or focaccia (plain or flavoured)
• crumpets, bagels, English muffins, pita, bread sticks (grissini), potato scones or oat cakes
• nan or chapattis
• Irish soda bread
• oatmeal or walnut bread.

Bread is best freshly baked or served warm. Some stores sell partly-baked breads that you can keep in the freezer and finish baking just before serving; these are ideal.

Potatoes

Try these quick ideas.
• Toss steamed or boiled baby new potatoes with a little olive oil, lemon zest and chopped fresh mint.
• Make a warm new potato salad by tossing sliced, boiled new potatoes with a little vinaigrette dressing, snipped chives and/or chopped fresh parsley.
• For healthy oven fries, cut scrubbed potatoes (with the skin) into thick wedges, then brush lightly with olive oil on a baking tray and bake for 30–40 minutes in a hot oven. If you like, you can sprinkle with dried herbs or fennel seeds or, for a spicy flavour, sprinkle with paprika or Cajun seasoning.
• Add a little pesto, mustard or horseradish sauce to mash.
• For a mixed root mash, boil 2–3 root vegetables together (choose from carrots, turnip, parsnips, celeriac, potatoes or sweet potatoes), then mash with yogourt and chives.

Potatoes make a popular accompaniment to stews, casseroles, roasts and grills. Here they have been roasted in a little olive oil and rosemary.

Beans and lentils can be a little bland served plain, so jazz them up by tossing them with a little extra virgin olive oil and crushed garlic, lemon juice or light sour cream with chopped fresh herbs, or a little pesto or tomato sauce.

Mediterranean roasted lamb (page 212)

EXTRA CARBS

Couscous To prepare, put the couscous in a bowl, pour over boiling water or stock, leave to soak for about 5 minutes until the couscous has absorbed the liquid, then drizzle with olive oil and fluff up with a fork. To add flavour, stir in a handful of chopped dried fruit, nuts, sun-dried tomatoes or olives and plenty of chopped fresh herbs.

Pasta and noodles couldn't be simpler to cook in a pot of boiling water, following the package instructions for timings, then served plain or tossed with a little olive or sesame oil, plus garlic, fresh herbs, lemon zest, parmesan or freshly ground black pepper. Noodles are especially good with Asian-style stir-fries, but you can really choose any type you fancy.

Peas and beans (fresh or frozen) combined look more interesting than a single vegetable. Steam or gently boil, then toss with some chopped parsley or snipped chives.

Spinach and oranges Fresh baby spinach leaves or watercress, tossed with orange or pink grapefruit segments, make a zingy salad. Sprinkle with a little olive oil, citrus juice and black pepper.

EXTRA VEGETABLES AND FRUIT

Zucchini and pine nuts Stir-fry some diagonally sliced zucchini with a handful of pine nuts, almonds or unsalted cashews, until they are lightly golden.

Peppers and squash Chunks of sweet red pepper and butternut squash can be roasted in the oven at the same time as the main dish.

Boosting your 7 to 10 a day

A side salad adds refreshing flavour to a meal and boosts your intake of essential vitamins and minerals. Here are some tempting, quick ideas – but be adventurous and experiment with your own combinations.

- **Lamb's lettuce** with sliced tomatoes and kiwis.
- **Mixed greens** tossed with sliced mushrooms and toasted hazelnuts.
- **Thinly sliced fennel and oranges** with black olives.
- **Chickpeas** tossed with arugula and halved cherry tomatoes.
- **Grated carrot** with thinly sliced apple and celery.
- **Sliced avocado** sprinkled with lemon juice and chopped walnuts.
- **Zucchini ribbons** tossed with sun-dried tomatoes, a little olive oil and lemon juice, and snipped chives.
- **Carrot and cucumber julienne** combined with snow peas, bean sprouts and toasted peanuts, sprinkled with a spicy chili dressing.
- **Finely shredded carrots** and white cabbage mixed with sliced radishes, chopped scallions and sultanas, with a little light mayonnaise stirred into plain low-fat yogourt.
- **Red kidney beans**, diced onions and tomatoes combined with red or green pepper and corn, and a little finely chopped red chili pepper if you like.

Hot vegetable ideas

If you prefer a hot vegetable side dish to a salad, here are some simple ideas. The healthiest ways to cook vegetables are to steam, stir-fry or microwave them.

- **Dress up** steamed cauliflower florets with a sprinkling of garlicky breadcrumbs or some chopped hard-boiled egg.
- **Serve steamed green beans** topped with a fresh tomato salsa and torn basil leaves.
- **Cook carrot sticks in orange juice** with a little finely chopped fresh ginger.
- **Sprinkle steamed broccoli** with a pinch of chili flakes.
- **Stir-fry spinach briefly** with garlic, then toss in a handful of pine nuts.
- **Toss steamed zucchini** with a little extra light sour cream and plenty of chopped fresh dill or tarragon for herby flavour.
- **Toss cooked baby fava beans** with arugula, chopped fresh mint and lemon zest.
- **Stir-fry** any selection of mixed vegetables (whatever you happen to have) with chopped fresh ginger and minced garlic.

THREE EASY EXTRAS

Here are some dips and dressings to boost a one-dish meal. Guacamole and raita make great quick-and-easy side dishes, and a homemade dressing perks up any salad.

ZESTY GUACAMOLE

Serves 4

1 large ripe avocado, pitted and mashed

2 tomatoes, chopped

1 lime, zest grated and juiced

2 scallions, chopped

1 garlic clove, crushed

1 tablespoon chopped cilantro

Combine all the ingredients together shortly before serving. (Add 1/2 fresh green chili pepper, deseeded and finely chopped or a dash of Tabasco for a spicy kick.)

VINAIGRETTE DRESSING

Makes about 2/3 cup (150 ml)

1/2 cup extra virgin olive oil

2 tablespoons red wine vinegar or lemon juice

1 teaspoon Dijon or whole-grain mustard

1/2 teaspoon honey or pinch of sugar

freshly ground black pepper

Put all the ingredients in a screw-top jar, put on the lid and shake. This will keep well in the refrigerator to be used when required. Add crushed garlic, finely chopped ginger or chopped fresh herbs, if you like. Shake well before using.

BANANA MINT RAITA

Serves 4

1 large banana, sliced

1/2 cup plain low-fat yogourt

1 tablespoon chopped fresh mint

1 teaspoon honey

pinch of paprika

Stir the sliced banana into the yogourt and add the mint and honey. Sprinkle with ground paprika. (For a cucumber raita, use 1/3 English cucumber, diced, in place of the banana and add 1 crushed garlic clove.)

Make your own stock

Homemade stock is a far cry from salty, over-seasoned premade cubes, and cheaper than fresh chilled stock. After chilling and removing the fat, you can boil the stock until it is reduced and concentrated in flavour, then cool and freeze it in icetrays. The frozen stock cubes can then be packed in a freezer bag and used individually – add them frozen to hot liquids in soups, stews and casseroles and they will melt almost instantly.

Beef, veal or lamb stock

You can use fresh, raw or cooked bones for this stock, plus any lean meat scraps. Trim fat or fatty skin from meat or bones before using for the stock. For a richer stock, first roast the bones at 450°F (230°C) for 40 minutes.

Makes **about 1.5 litres**

Preparation time **20 minutes**

Cooking time **2–3 hours**

1 kg (2 lb) meat bones (beef, veal or lamb)

8 cups water

2 sprigs of fresh thyme

2 sprigs of fresh parsley

1 large bay leaf

2 onions, roughly chopped

2 celery stalks, roughly chopped

2 carrots, roughly chopped

6 peppercorns

1 Place the bones in a large pot or stockpot and add the water, or enough to cover the bones. Bring to a boil, skimming off the scum as it rises to the surface.

2 Tie together the thyme, parsley and bay leaf and add to the pot with the onions, celery, carrots and peppercorns. Cover and simmer gently for 2–3 hours.

3 Strain the stock through a sieve into a bowl, discarding the bones and vegetables. Leave to cool, then chill. Skim any fat from the surface and discard before using the stock.

Chicken stock

This stock, made with the leftovers from a roast chicken, can be used as a great base for soups, casseroles, sauces and gravies.

Makes **about 1.5 litres**

Preparation time **10 minutes**

Cooking time **1 hour**

1 chicken carcass or the bones from 4 chicken pieces (or fresh chicken wings, browned first)

1 onion, roughly chopped

1 large carrot, roughly chopped

1 celery stalk, roughly chopped

1 large bay leaf

6 black peppercorns

8 cups water

1 Break up the chicken carcass or bones and put into a large pot or stockpot. Add the vegetables, bay leaf and peppercorns. Pour over the water.

2 Bring to a boil over a high heat, then turn the heat down so the liquid is simmering gently. Cover the pot and leave to bubble for 1 hour.

3 Strain the stock through a sieve into a bowl, discarding the bones and vegetables. Skim any fat from the surface with a spoon, if using the stock right away. Alternatively, chill the stock first, which will make it easier to remove the fat.

Vegetable stock

Use this light stock as a base for delicate soups and sauces, and in risottos and similar dishes.

Makes **about 1.75 litres**
Preparation time **15 minutes**
Cooking time **1 hour**

1 tablespoon butter

250 grams ($^1/_2$ lb) leeks, roughly chopped

250 grams ($^1/_2$ lb) onions, roughly chopped

1 large bay leaf

several sprigs of fresh thyme

several sprigs of fresh parsley

250 grams ($^1/_2$ lb) carrots, roughly chopped

150 grams (5 oz) celery, roughly chopped

5 black peppercorns

8 cups water

1 Melt the butter in a large pot or stockpot over a medium heat. Stir in the leeks and onions, then reduce the heat to low. Cover with a tight-fitting lid and leave the vegetables to cook gently for 20 minutes without lifting the lid.

2 Tie the herbs together into a bouquet garni. Add it to the pot with the carrots, celery, peppercorns and water. Increase the heat and bring slowly to a boil, skimming the surface if necessary to remove any scum. As soon as the water boils, reduce the heat to low and simmer for 35 minutes.

3 Strain the stock into a large heatproof bowl and set aside to cool. Keep chilled or freeze.

Fish stock

Fish trimmings – the head, skin and bones – from any white fish with a good flavour can be used. (Oily fish are not suitable for making stock as they give it a strong, fatty flavour.)

Makes **about 1.25 litres**
Preparation time **10 minutes**
Cooking time **30 minutes**

1 kg (2 lb) trimmings from white fish, including skin, bones and heads without gills

1 onion, thinly sliced

4 sprigs of fresh parsley

2 bay leaves

2 carrots, thinly sliced

2 celery stalks, thinly sliced

4 black peppercorns

$5^1/_3$ cups water

1 Rinse the fish bones and heads thoroughly, then place them in a large pot or stockpot. Add the onion, parsley, bay leaves, carrots, celery, peppercorns and water. Bring to a boil, then reduce the heat and simmer gently for about 30 minutes, skimming the froth from the surface as it appears.

2 Remove from the heat and leave to cool, then strain the stock through a fine sieve into a heatproof bowl. Discard the fish trimmings and vegetables. Use the stock at once or cool and chill or freeze.

COOK'S TIP
• *Fresh stocks will keep in the refrigerator for 3–4 days or in the freezer for up to 6 months.*

VARIATIONS
• *For special-occasion fish dishes, use $1^1/_4$ cups white wine and just 4 cups of water.*
• *Make a shellfish stock using shrimp, crab, lobster or mussel shells, instead of the white fish trimmings.*

Soups and salads

Nourishing, easy to make and incredibly versatile, soup is the ultimate one-dish meal. The ingredients—fresh seasonal produce, satisfying carbohydrates and vital protein —are simmered together in a nutritious stock, retaining all of their goodness. Like soups, salads are a great way to enjoy healthy meals with little effort. Salads are generally served cold, but some are good warm, which makes them suitable for all seasons. What's more, the fruit and vegetables are normally included raw, or just slightly cooked, so lots of vitamins and minerals are retained. Soups and salads make a healthy choice for family meals or fuss-free dining with friends.

Onion soup with Gruyère croûtes

The secret of this rich, warming soup lies in the slow cooking of the onions and leeks, in just a little butter and oil, until lightly caramelized. Thinly sliced potatoes add extra carbohydrate and help to thicken the stock.

Step 1

Step 2

Step 3

Serves 4

Preparation time 10 minutes

Cooking time 1 hour

1 tablespoon unsalted butter

1 tablespoon olive oil

3 large onions, halved and thinly sliced

2 leeks, trimmed, halved lengthwise and thinly sliced

1 teaspoon water

1 garlic clove, crushed

2 teaspoons fresh thyme

½ teaspoon superfine sugar

1 tablespoon sherry vinegar

3 small potatoes (about 300 grams/⅔ lb in total)

6 cups diluted salt-reduced or homemade beef stock (page 28)

4 fresh chives, snipped

GRUYÈRE CROÛTES

3 thick slices whole wheat bread

1 garlic clove, halved

2 teaspoons Dijon mustard

½ cup coarsely grated Gruyère cheese

⅓ cup walnut pieces

1 Heat the butter with the oil in a large pot. Add the onions, leeks and water. Cook over a medium heat for 7–8 minutes, stirring frequently until they begin to soften. Turn down the heat to very low, cover and cook gently for 20–25 minutes, stirring occasionally. Increase the heat slightly, add the garlic, thyme and sugar and cook, stirring, for 1 minute. Then add the vinegar and continue cooking, stirring frequently, for 3–4 minutes until the onions and leeks are light golden.

2 Peel the potatoes, cut in half lengthwise and thinly slice. Add to the onion mixture with the stock. Bring to a boil, then reduce the heat, cover and cook for 15–20 minutes until the potatoes are tender and just beginning to break down and thicken the soup. Season to taste.

3 Meanwhile, prepare the croûtes. Preheat the broiler. Trim the crusts off the bread and cut each slice into four triangles. Place on a grill rack and toast very lightly on both sides. Gently rub one side of each croûte with the cut surface of the garlic, then spread with a thin layer of mustard. Top with the cheese and walnuts, pressing down gently.

4 Put the cheese-topped croûtes back under the broiler and toast until the cheese is just starting to bubble and brown and the walnuts are lightly toasted.

5 Sprinkle the soup with snipped chives, then serve with the Gruyère croûtes on top of the soup.

EACH SERVING

17 g protein • 23 g fat of which 7 g saturates • 29.5 g carbohydrate • 7 g fibre • 408 Calories

COOK'S TIP

• *Sherry vinegar is matured in wooden barrels by methods similar to those used for sherry itself. It has a rich, mellow flavour that makes it popular in cooking. If sherry vinegar is unavailable, you can use red wine vinegar instead.*

VARIATION

• *For a vegetarian soup, use a good vegetable stock instead of beef stock and stir in ¹/₂ teaspoon yeast extract for a richer flavour and colour. For the croûtes, use a Swiss-style non-animal rennet cheese as Gruyère is not suitable for strict vegetarians.*

Bacon and lentil soup

A satisfying and comforting soup packed with a good mix of healthy vegetables that take you well on the way to your 7 to 10 a day. Enjoy chunks of warm whole-grain bread with this winter warmer.

Serves 4

Preparation time 20 minutes

Cooking time 50 minutes

1 tablespoon olive oil

2 garlic cloves, crushed

2 slices back bacon, chopped

1 large onion, chopped

2 carrots, peeled and diced

½ large rutabaga, peeled and diced

4 cups diluted salt-reduced or homemade chicken or vegetable stock (pages 28–29)

²/₃ cup green lentils

1 lemon, zest grated

4 parsnips, peeled and diced

2–3 tablespoons chopped fresh parsley

1 Heat the oil in a large pot. Add the garlic, bacon, onion, carrots and rutabaga and mix well. Cook over a medium heat, stirring frequently, for 5 minutes until the bacon has changed colour and the onion has softened.

2 Stir in the stock, lentils and half the lemon zest. Bring to a boil, then reduce the heat, half cover the pot and cook gently for 10 minutes.

3 Stir in the parsnips, cover and continue to cook gently for 25–30 minutes until the lentils and vegetables are tender.

4 Use a vegetable masher or hand-held blender to crush some of the lentils and vegetables into the soup, leaving the majority chunky. Stir in half of the parsley and season to taste. Serve sprinkled with the remaining chopped parsley and grated lemon zest.

EACH SERVING

14 g protein • 7 g fat of which 1.5 g saturates • 25.5 g carbohydrate • 9 g fibre • 241 Calories

VARIATIONS

• For a vegetarian soup, omit the bacon and use vegetable stock. Serve sprinkled with mixed lightly toasted sunflower seeds and pumpkin seeds along with the lemon and parsley.

• Celeriac makes a good alternative to parsnips.

Vegetable and pasta soup

This classic pistou from the south of France, topped with a rich-tasting garlic and basil paste, called aïllade, and a sprinkling of Parmesan, makes a nourishing main meal. Serve with crusty bread.

Serves 4

Preparation time 20 minutes

Cooking time 25 minutes

5$\frac{1}{3}$ cups diluted salt-reduced or homemade vegetable stock (page 29)

2 small leeks, trimmed and thinly sliced

3 carrots, peeled and diced

2 zucchini, diced

$\frac{1}{2}$ a 796 ml can chopped tomatoes (no added salt)

200 grams (7 oz) green beans, cut into short lengths

540 ml can white kidney beans, drained and rinsed

100 grams (3$\frac{1}{2}$ oz) pasta vermicelli, broken into short lengths

$\frac{1}{3}$ cup shaved Parmesan cheese

AÏLLADE

3 garlic cloves

1 cup roughly chopped fresh basil

1 tomato, peeled, deseeded and chopped

COOK'S TIP

• Both the soup and the aïllade can be prepared ahead of time. Add the aïllade to the soup when ready to serve.

VARIATION

• Depending on the season, almost any fresh, diced vegetables can be added to the soup and, if supplies are short, you can use frozen vegetables.

1 Bring the stock to a boil in a large pot and add the leeks, carrots, zucchini and canned tomatoes with their juice. Bring back to a boil, then reduce the heat slightly, cover and simmer for 15 minutes.

2 Stir in the green beans, white kidney beans and vermicelli, bring back to a boil, then reduce the heat slightly and simmer for 5 minutes or until all the vegetables and pasta are tender. Season to taste.

3 Meanwhile, to make the aïllade, use a mortar and pestle to pound the garlic, basil and tomato until smooth. Season to taste.

4 Ladle the soup into wide bowls and add a spoonful of aïllade and some thin shavings of cheese to each serving.

EACH SERVING

13 g protein • 4 g fat of which 1.5 g saturates • 34 g carbohydrate • 12 g fibre • 243 Calories

Mixed bean chili soup

This heart-warming soup is perfect for a chilly evening. It's packed full of vegetables and mixed legumes, making it an excellent source of fibre. Enjoy it with some crusty French bread to mop up the delicious liquid.

*Serves **4***

*Preparation time **20 minutes***

*Cooking time **25 minutes***

2 tablespoons canola oil

1 onion, chopped

2 garlic cloves, crushed

1 red pepper, deseeded and chopped

1 green pepper, deseeded and chopped

³/4 cup sliced button mushrooms

¹/2 teaspoon chili powder, or to taste

1 teaspoon ground cumin

540 ml can mixed beans, drained and rinsed

¹/2 a 796 ml can can chopped tomatoes

2¹/2 cups tomato juice

1¹/4 cups diluted salt-reduced or homemade vegetable stock (page 29)

2 tablespoons chopped cilantro

¹/3 cup light sour cream

4 sprigs of cilantro

1 Heat the oil in a large pot. Add the onion, garlic and red and green peppers and fry them gently, stirring constantly, for 2–3 minutes until softened. Add the mushrooms, chili powder and ground cumin and cook gently, stirring, for about 30 seconds.

2 Tip the mixed beans and tomatoes with their juice into the pot. Add the tomato juice, stock and chopped cilantro. Stir well, bring to a boil, then reduce the heat. Partially cover the pot with a lid and simmer gently for 20 minutes until all the vegetables are tender.

3 Ladle the soup into bowls and garnish each portion with a dollop of sour cream and a coriander sprig.

EACH SERVING

10 g protein • 15 g fat of which 4 g saturates • 24.5 g carbohydrate • 9.5 g fibre • 293 Calories

Mushroom and fennel soup

Sweet anise-flavoured fennel and earthy mushrooms make a delicious combination in this smooth vegetable soup, topped with a cheesy garnish. Serve with chunks of rustic bread to make a satisfying meal.

Serves **6**   *Preparation time* **25 minutes**   *Cooking time* **35 minutes**

2 fennel bulbs

1/2 lemon, zest grated and juiced

1 tablespoon olive oil

1 large onion, roughly chopped

4 potatoes, peeled and diced

250 grams (1/2 lb) mushrooms, halved

1/2 cup dry sherry

2 1/2 cups diluted salt-reduced or homemade vegetable stock (page 29)

1 1/4 cups 1% milk

175 grams (6 oz) cheddar cheese, finely crumbled or grated

1 Trim any feathery tops from the fennel and reserve for garnishing the soup. Cut the bulbs into quarters. Finely chop one-quarter of the fennel bulb and place in a bowl with the lemon juice. Stir well and set aside for topping the cooked soup. Roughly chop the rest of the fennel.

2 Place the olive oil in a large pot. Add the onion and roughly chopped fennel, cover and cook over a medium heat for 5 minutes, shaking the pot occasionally. The vegetables should be slightly softened but not well browned.

3 Add the potatoes and mushrooms, stir well, then pour in the sherry and stock. Bring to a boil, reduce the heat, cover and simmer for 30 minutes, stirring once or twice, until the potatoes are tender and falling apart.

4 Purée the soup in a blender or food processor until smooth, or in the pot using a hand-held blender. Stir in the milk and lemon zest, season with freshly ground black pepper, then reheat if necessary. (If you are freezing the soup, do it at this stage.) Mix the reserved chopped fennel with the cheese. Ladle the soup into bowls, top with this mixture and garnish with the feathery fronds.

VARIATIONS
• *Use Jerusalem artichokes instead of the potatoes or a head of celery instead of the fennel. Leeks would also be delicious with the potatoes and mushrooms as an alternative to fennel.*
• *For a hearty meal, spread the cheese and fennel mixture onto thick slices of French bread, then toast until golden. Serve with the soup.*

EACH SERVING

15.5 g protein • 14 g fat of which 7 g saturates • 23 g carbohydrate • 6 g fibre • 308 Calories

COOK'S TIPS
• *Rinse canned beans thoroughly in a sieve under cold running water to remove as much salt as possible.*
• *Add chili powder according to taste — it is very fiery so you only need a little.*
• *If you are freezing the soup, add the coriander sprig and sour cream just before serving — they do not freeze well.*

Tomato and lentil soup

This simple soup is flavoured with warm spices, then blended to a velvety smooth texture and topped with yogourt. Serve it as a fast and sustaining lunch with nan bread or other lightly toasted bread of your choice.

Serves **4**

Preparation time **20 minutes**

Cooking time **45 minutes**

1 tablespoon olive oil

1 onion, roughly chopped

2 celery stalks, roughly chopped

1 carrot, peeled and roughly chopped

1 garlic clove, crushed

1 teaspoon ground cumin

1/2 teaspoon ground coriander

1 cup split red lentils

5 1/3 cups diluted salt-reduced or homemade vegetable stock (page 29)

1/2 a 796 ml can Roma tomatoes

2 teaspoons tomato paste

1 bay leaf

YOGOURT TOPPING

2 tablespoons chopped cilantro

1/3 cup Greek-style yogourt

COOK'S TIP

• *If you are preparing the soup ahead of time, add the cilantro yogourt just before serving.*

VARIATION

• *For a spicy lentil and parsnip soup, stir in 1/4 teaspoon chili flakes with the spices and add 250 grams (1/2 lb) roughly chopped parsnips instead of the celery.*

1 Heat the oil in a pot. Add the onion and cook over a low heat for about 8 minutes, stirring occasionally, until beginning to soften. Stir in the celery and carrot and cook for 3 minutes, stirring frequently. Add the garlic, cumin and coriander and cook for a further minute, stirring constantly.

2 Add the lentils, stock, tomatoes with their juice, tomato paste and bay leaf. Bring to a boil, reduce the heat, then half cover the pot with a lid and simmer for 25–30 minutes until the lentils and vegetables are very soft.

3 Meanwhile, to make the yogourt topping, stir the chopped cilantro into the yogourt.

4 Remove the bay leaf from the soup. Blend the soup in the pot using a hand-held blender, or tip into a blender or food processor, process until smooth, then return the soup to the pot. Check the consistency; it will be fairly thick, so if you prefer it thinner, dilute with a little more stock or some water. Season to taste, then reheat until just bubbling. Serve drizzled with some of the yogourt topping.

EACH SERVING

7 g protein • 7 g fat of which 2 g saturates • 17.5 g carbohydrate • 5 g fibre • 173 Calories

Beet and orange soup

A luscious, flavourful soup packed with vibrant vegetables and topped with beet salsa.

Serves **4**

Preparation time **20 minutes**

Cooking time **45 minutes**

1 tablespoon olive oil

2 carrots, peeled and sliced

2 celery stalks, roughly chopped

1 onion, chopped

1 fennel bulb, sliced

3 tomatoes, roughly chopped

300 grams (²/₃ lb) cooked beets, peeled and sliced

2 oranges, zest grated and juiced

4 cups diluted salt-reduced or homemade vegetable stock (page 29)

BEET SALSA

1 teaspoon olive oil

¹/₂ cup cooked beets, peeled and finely chopped

1 tomato, finely chopped

2 scallions, thinly sliced

BAGELS

4 bagels, halved

³/₄ cup low-fat cream cheese

1 tablespoon horseradish sauce

COOK'S TIP

• *The soup is suitable for freezing but it's best to prepare the accompaniments just before serving to maintain freshness.*

1 Heat the olive oil in a heavy pot over a medium heat. Add the carrots, celery, onion and fennel. Reduce the heat to low and gently cook the vegetables, with the pot covered, for 10–15 minutes until they are all softened but not browned.

2 Add the tomatoes to the pot with the beets and cook for about 3 minutes longer. Stir in the orange zest with the stock. Bring the mixture to a boil, stirring occasionally, then cover the pot, reduce the heat and simmer for about 25 minutes until all the vegetables are tender.

3 Meanwhile, prepare the salsa and bagels. For the salsa, simply combine the ingredients together in a bowl. Then, for the bagel topping, blend the cream cheese with the horseradish sauce until well mixed. Toast the bagels, then spread the cheese mixture over the toasted bagel halves.

4 Remove the soup from the heat, blend in a blender or food processor until completely smooth, then return to the pot. Alternatively, blend the soup in the pot using a hand-held blender. Stir in the orange juice, and a little extra stock if too thick, then reheat gently and season to taste.

5 Serve the soup topped with a little of the beet salsa and accompanied by the bagels.

EACH SERVING

8.5 g protein • 7.5 g fat of which 1 g saturates • 38 g carbohydrate • 9 g fibre • 269 Calories

COOK'S TIPS
• Freeze the three elements of the meal separately
and combine just before serving.
• If you prefer, a generous dash of chili sauce can
be added to the soup instead of the chili flakes.

VARIATION
• For a vegetarian version, replace the chicken stock
with vegetable stock and use toasted pumpkin
seeds to sprinkle over the soup in place of the
pepperoni. You'll also need 1 tablespoon olive oil to
fry the onion.

Chili-spiced squash soup

This golden, velvet-textured soup is very satisfying and perfect for a warm light lunch on a chilly day. Green apple adds a sweet-sour tang to the flavour, with added zip from chili peppers, and the croutons provide a satisfying crunch.

Step 2

Step 3

Step 4

Serves **4**

Preparation time **30 minutes**

Cooking time **1 hour**

2 slices whole wheat bread

90 grams (3 oz) pepperoni sausage, diced

1 large onion, chopped

1 butternut squash or small pumpkin, peeled, deseeded and chopped

1 green apple, peeled, cored and chopped

1 garlic clove, crushed

1 sprig of fresh thyme or ½ teaspoon dried thyme

½ teaspoon chili flakes

2½ cups diluted salt-reduced or homemade chicken stock (page 28)

1 To make the croutons, cut the bread into small cubes, then gently cook in a large, dry, heavy-based pot until golden brown. Remove from the pot.

2 Put the pepperoni in the pot and fry gently for about 4 minutes until the fat runs off and the pieces are browned. Lift out and drain on paper towel, leaving the fat in the pot. Reserve the pepperoni for garnish.

3 Add the onion to the pot and fry gently in the pepperoni-flavoured oil for 4–5 minutes, stirring occasionally, until softened.

4 Stir in the squash or pumpkin, apple, garlic, thyme and chili flakes, cover and leave to cook on a very low heat for 45 minutes, stirring occasionally, until the pumpkin is tender when tested with the point of a knife.

5 Remove the sprig of thyme and tip the contents of the pot into a food processor or blender. Add about half the stock and process to a smooth purée. (You may need to do this in two batches.) Return to the pot and add the remaining stock. Reheat gently and season to taste. Sprinkle with pepperoni and croutons before serving.

EACH SERVING

11 g protein • 9 g fat of which 3 g saturates • 22 g carbohydrate • 4 g fibre • 219 Calories

Chilled melon soup with shrimp and avocado

Fresh fruit soups can be prepared ahead and are light and cooling on a hot summer's day. Serve with grissini (Italian bread sticks) for a light lunch.

Serves 4

Preparation time 15 minutes, plus at least 1½ hours chilling

Cooking time 5 minutes

2 English cucumbers

2 cantaloupes

1 lemon, juiced

2 tablespoons chopped fresh mint

1 cup water

250 grams (½ lb) cooked peeled shrimp, thawed and drained if frozen

1 ripe but firm avocado

2 tablespoons fresh mint

VARIATION
• *For a vegetarian version of this soup, omit the shrimp and add an extra avocado.*

1 Peel the cucumbers and cut in half crosswise. Divide each half lengthwise, then use a teaspoon to scoop out the seeds. Chop the flesh roughly. Drop into a pot of lightly salted boiling water and cook gently for 2 minutes. Drain in a sieve, then refresh under cold running water.

2 Halve the cantaloupes and remove the seeds. Scoop out the flesh using a tablespoon and put into a blender or food processor. Add the cucumber, lemon juice and chopped mint, then whizz together until blended. Turn out the mixture into a bowl. Pour the water into the blender or processor and whizz briefly, then stir this liquid into the melon and cucumber mixture.

3 Stir in the shrimp and season lightly with freshly ground black pepper. Chill for at least 1½ hours and up to 12 hours.

4 Just before serving, peel, pit and dice the avocado and add the diced flesh to the soup. Snip in some mint leaves to garnish and season to taste with more pepper if needed.

EACH SERVING
16.5 g protein • 11 g fat of which 2.5 g saturates • 14 g carbohydrate • 4 g fibre • 231 Calories

Corn chowder with crab

Leeks, corn and potatoes make this chunky seafood chowder a satisfying main meal soup. Serve garnished with a swirl of sour cream and some crusty whole-grain bread to accompany.

Serves 4

Preparation time 15 minutes, plus 5 minutes standing

Cooking time 30 minutes

1 tablespoon olive oil

28 grams (1 oz) fresh ginger, peeled and finely chopped

2 slices back bacon or 3 strips bacon, chopped

1 onion, chopped

1 small carrot, peeled and diced

2 celery stalks, chopped

2 leeks, trimmed and thickly sliced

3 cups boiling water

170 grams canned white crab meat

3 potatoes, peeled and cut into small chunks

1 1/3 cups frozen corn kernels, thawed

2 tablespoons chopped fresh dill (optional)

1/4 cup light sour cream

1 small red chili pepper, deseeded and finely diced (optional)

COOK'S TIP

• *The soup is suitable for freezing without the sour cream.*

VARIATION

• *Instead of crab, use 350 grams peeled raw shrimp, adding them with the corn, or add 250 grams peeled cooked shrimp, thawed and drained if frozen, at the end of cooking.*

1 Heat the oil in a large pot. Add the ginger, bacon, onion, carrot and celery and stir over a high heat for 1 minute. Add the leeks, reduce the heat to medium and cook for a further 4 minutes, stirring occasionally. Pour in the water and bring to a boil. Reduce the heat, cover the pot with a lid and simmer for 5 minutes.

2 Drain the crab, reserving the liquid, and set it aside. Stir the potatoes and reserved crab liquid into the soup. Bring back to simmering point, cover again and cook for about 10 minutes until the potatoes are tender.

3 Stir in the corn. Heat again to simmering point, then cover the pot and simmer for 5 minutes until the potatoes break up slightly and thicken the liquid. Lightly stir in the crab and dill (if using), cover the pot and remove it from the heat. Leave to stand for 5 minutes to allow the flavours to infuse. Season with freshly ground black pepper to taste.

4 Serve the chowder in warmed bowls topped with a spoonful of sour cream and a sprinkling of diced chili pepper, if you like.

EACH SERVING

17 g protein • 12 g fat of which 4 g saturates • 36 g carbohydrate • 6 g fibre • 334 Calories

Fish soup

Mixed seafood combined with white fish, simmered with chunks of potato, tomatoes and some handy frozen vegetables, make a main course soup that is bursting with flavour and goodness. It is delicious served with bread.

Serves **4**

Preparation time **10 minutes**

Cooking time **20 minutes**

1 tablespoon olive oil

2 shallots, finely chopped

1 garlic clove, crushed

4 cups diluted salt-reduced or homemade fish or chicken stock (pages 28–29)

pinch of saffron threads

1 bay leaf

250 grams (½ lb) potatoes, peeled and cut into 1 cm cubes

3 cups frozen mixed vegetables

3 tomatoes, peeled, deseeded and diced

200 grams (7 oz) firm white fish fillet, cut into 2.5 cm chunks

350 grams (12⅓ oz) mixed seafood (mussels, squid rings and shrimp), thawed if frozen

1 Heat the oil in a large pot and fry the shallots and garlic gently for about 5 minutes, to soften but not brown. Add the stock, saffron and bay leaf and bring to a boil.

2 Add the potatoes to the pot, reduce the heat, cover and simmer gently for about 10 minutes until tender.

3 Increase the heat to high and add the frozen mixed vegetables. Bring back to a boil, then stir in the tomatoes, fish fillet and mixed seafood. Reduce the heat and simmer gently, without stirring, for about 3 minutes until the fish is white and firm. Season to taste, then serve immediately.

EACH SERVING

33 g protein • 7 g fat of which 1.5 g saturates • 19 g carbohydrate • 2.5 g fibre • 288 Calories

Vegetable soup with meatballs

Adding little meatballs to a vegetable soup turns it into a satisfying meal that will appeal to the whole family. Caraway seeds and ginger add a delicious flavour to the meatballs, as well as being great aids to digestion. Serve with some tasty rye bread.

Serves **4**   *Preparation time* **30 minutes**   *Cooking time* **15 minutes**

MEATBALLS

400 grams (14 oz) ground pork

15 grams (½ oz) fresh ginger, peeled and grated

½ teaspoon caraway seeds, lightly crushed

1 garlic clove, crushed

½ beaten egg

SOUP

200 grams (7 oz) new potatoes, scrubbed

2 carrots, peeled

1 large or 2 small leeks

6 cups diluted homemade vegetable stock (pages 28–29), hot

¼ savoy cabbage, finely shredded

1 To make the meatballs, place the ground pork, ginger, caraway seeds, garlic and beaten egg into a bowl, season with a little salt and pepper, then mix together until thoroughly combined. Roll the mixture into small walnut-sized balls (about 24 altogether) and set aside.

2 Cut the potatoes and carrots into small cubes. Trim and clean the leeks, removing most of the dark green part. Cut in half lengthwise and slice thinly.

3 In a large pot, bring the stock to a boil. Add the potatoes, carrots and leeks and simmer for 5 minutes until almost tender. Add the meatballs and simmer gently for 6–8 minutes until cooked through.

4 Finally, add the shredded cabbage and cook for 1 minute until just wilted. Serve immediately.

COOK'S TIP

• *The meatballs can be prepared a day ahead of time and stored, covered, in the refrigerator.*

EACH SERVING

27 g protein • 8 g fat of which 3 g saturates • 14 g carbohydrate • 5 g fibre • 246 Calories

VARIATION

• *For a special occasion, replace about ½ cup of the stock with dry white wine and replace the mixed seafood with whole mussels in the shell. Cook until the mussel shells open (discarding any that stay closed), and add a handful of cooked whole shrimp to each bowl.*

Beef pho

Pho (pronounced fur) is a Vietnamese fragrant beef noodle soup. It is perfect for lunch or dinner with friends because each person can add their own accompaniments to taste.

Serves **4**

Preparation time **15 minutes**

Cooking time **20 minutes**

4 cups beef consommé

4 cups water

1 cm piece fresh ginger, julienned

1 cinnamon stick

2 star anise

2 green cardamom pods, bruised

½ teaspoon coriander seeds, toasted

1–2 tablespoons fish sauce, to taste

250 grams (½ lb) dried rice vermicelli

200 grams (7 oz) piece beef sirloin, thinly sliced

ACCOMPANIMENTS

handful of cilantro

handful of Vietnamese mint

1 cup bean sprouts

1 red chili pepper, sliced

1 lime, cut into wedges

⅓ cup hoisin sauce

COOK'S TIPS

• *Some people like to make the bean sprouts look neater by trimming off the little "tails" at the end.*
• *This soup is traditionally served with raw beef placed into the serving bowls. When the hot stock is added, it cooks the beef.*
• *If you would prefer less heat, remove the seeds and membrane from the chili pepper.*

1 Place the consommé, water, ginger, cinnamon stick, star anise, cardamom pods, coriander seeds and fish sauce in a pot. Bring to a boil, reduce the heat to a simmer and cook for 10–15 minutes or until aromatic.

2 Meanwhile, place the noodles in a heatproof bowl, pour boiling water over them and allow to sit for 5 minutes, or until cooked. Drain.

3 Place separate piles of the herbs, bean sprouts, chili and lime onto a platter or large plate, and the hoisin sauce in a small bowl.

4 Once the fragrant stock is ready, strain, then return to the pot and bring back to a boil. Place the meat into the hot stock, stir and remove from the heat as soon as it is cooked — this will happen quickly. Divide the noodles among four large bowls, piling the beef on top. Ladle over the hot stock. Allow each guest to help themselves to the accompaniments. Serve immediately.

EACH SERVING

22.5 g protein • 7.5 g fat of which 2.5 g saturates • 53 g carbohydrate • 6.5 g fibre • 381 Calories

South American beef and pepper soup

This main meal soup is sure to appeal to the heartiest of appetites. Lean pieces of beef are simmered slowly in a rich, spicy tomato and red pepper broth that's studded with golden corn and creamy lima beans. Serve with warm tortillas to complete the meal.

Serves 4

Preparation time 10 minutes

Cooking time 45 minutes

50 grams (1³/₄ oz) chorizo sausage, skinned and diced

500 grams (1 lb) lean stewing beef, cut into 1 cm strips

796 ml can chopped tomatoes

125 grams (4 oz) chargrilled red peppers, drained and thinly sliced

2 cups water

¹/₂ a 796 ml can lima beans, drained and rinsed

2 cups frozen corn kernels

1 teaspoon dried oregano

1 teaspoon paprika

2 tablespoons roughly chopped fresh flat-leaf parsley

1 Fry the chorizo in a heavy pot or flameproof casserole dish over a medium heat for about 5 minutes until some of the fat is released and the chorizo is slightly crispy. Using a slotted spoon, transfer the chorizo to a bowl, leaving the flavoured oil in the pot. This will add flavour to the soup with no need to add any extra oil.

2 Return the pot to the heat and add the beef. Cook, stirring occasionally, for about 10 minutes until evenly browned.

3 Return the chorizo to the pot with the tomatoes and their juice, peppers and water. Bring to a boil, then stir in the lima beans, corn, oregano and paprika. Reduce the heat, cover and simmer over a low heat for 30 minutes until the beef is tender. Season to taste and serve scattered with parsley.

EACH SERVING

37 g protein • 9.5 g fat of which 3.5 g saturates • 33 g carbohydrate • 10 g fibre • 381 Calories

COOK'S TIPS
• *The soup can be made up to 1 day ahead. Allow to cool completely, then keep in the refrigerator until needed. Reheat gently, taste for seasoning and sprinkle with chopped parsley.*
• *Chargrilled red peppers can be bought from delicatessens and supermarkets. They are usually stored in oil, so make sure to drain them well.*

VARIATION
• *To lighten the soup, you could replace the beef with the same weight of chicken thigh meat.*

Creole-style chicken and shrimp gumbo

From the deep south comes this piquant gumbo with rice, chicken, shrimp and vegetables, a cross between a soup and a stew — a feast in a bowl.

Step 1

Step 3

Step 4

Serves **4**

Preparation time **30 minutes**

Cooking time **about 1 hour**

100 grams (3½ oz) chorizo sausage, skinned and finely diced

2 tablespoons canola oil

3½ tablespoons all-purpose flour

2 celery stalks, finely chopped, leaves reserved for garnish

2 onions, finely chopped

2 green peppers, deseeded and chopped

3 garlic cloves, crushed

½ a 796 ml can chopped tomatoes (no added salt)

4 cups salt-reduced or homemade chicken or vegetable stock (pages 28–29)

200 grams (7 oz) okra, thinly sliced

2 tablespoons chopped fresh parsley

1 teaspoon dried thyme

1 bay leaf

pinch of cayenne pepper

1 cup basmati and wild rice, rinsed

3 skinless boneless chicken thighs

250 grams (½ lb) peeled large raw shrimp

Tabasco (optional)

1 Put the chorizo in the base of a heavy-based pot or flameproof casserole dish over a medium heat. Fry, stirring frequently, until it has rendered some fat and is crisp at the edges. Drain on paper towel and set aside.

2 Add the oil to the sausage fat remaining in the pot. Reduce the heat to low and sprinkle in the flour, stirring constantly, until well blended. Cook very gently, stirring occasionally, for 5 minutes until the mixture turns a rich brown.

3 Increase the heat slightly, stir in the celery, onions, green peppers and garlic and continue frying, stirring frequently, for 5 minutes or until soft. Add the tomatoes with their juice, the stock, okra, parsley, thyme, bay leaf and cayenne pepper. Bring to a boil, then reduce the heat, half cover the pot and simmer for 30 minutes, stirring frequently, until the okra thickens the soup. While the soup is simmering, cut the chicken into bite-sized pieces.

4 Increase the heat and bring the liquid to a boil. Stir in the rice, then reduce the heat to low, add the chicken and simmer for 15–20 minutes until the rice is tender and the chicken is cooked through. Pour in a little extra stock if needed. Add the shrimp and reserved chorizo and simmer for 1 minute or until the shrimp turn pink and the sausage is heated through.

5 Remove the bay leaf. Season to taste, then ladle into bowls and garnish with the reserved celery leaves. Serve with Tabasco, if you like.

EACH SERVING

43 g protein • 22.5 g fat of which 5.5 g saturates • 61 g carbohydrate • 7 g fibre • 633 Calories

• The combination of peppers, onions and celery is called the "holy trinity" by Cajun cooks, and is used to flavour many dishes; red or yellow peppers can be substituted for the green.

• Okra is thought to have originated in Africa. When cut, it releases a sticky substance with thickening properties, which makes it popular in this kind of dish. Okra can now be found in many supermarkets and grocery stores.

Spicy chicken soup

Chicken soup is often credited with being a panacea for all kinds of ills, and this version — with its warming Indian spices and vibrant colour — should perk up anyone. Serve with whole wheat chapattis or nan bread.

Serves **4**

Preparation time **15 minutes**

Cooking time **25 minutes**

2 tablespoons canola oil

2 onions, finely chopped

2 large garlic cloves, crushed

1 teaspoon ground coriander

1 teaspoon ground cumin

¼ teaspoon cayenne pepper, or to taste

¼ teaspoon ground cloves

¼ teaspoon ground ginger

¼ teaspoon ground turmeric

4 cups diluted salt-reduced or homemade chicken or vegetable stock (pages 28–29)

½ a 796 ml can chopped tomatoes

500 grams (1 lb) skinless boneless chicken breasts, cut into 5 mm strips

250 grams (½ lb) green beans, trimmed and chopped

¾ of a 540 ml can chickpeas, drained and rinsed

2 tablespoons chopped cilantro

⅓ cup low-fat plain yogourt

pinch of cayenne pepper

12 sprigs of cilantro

VARIATIONS

• *Extra vegetables can be added if you'd like a chunkier soup. Sliced carrots, zucchini or corn are ideal.*

• *If you don't have a can of chickpeas, use canned white or red kidney beans. Green lentils would also work well.*

1 Heat the oil in a large, heavy-based pot or flameproof casserole dish over a medium heat. Add the onions and fry for 3 minutes, stirring. Add the garlic and continue stirring for about 2 minutes longer until the onions are softened, but not brown.

2 Reduce the heat slightly and stir in the spices. Continue stirring over a gentle heat for a few minutes so the spices release their aroma. Take care not to let the mixture burn.

3 Stir in the stock and tomatoes with their juice, increase the heat and bring to a boil. Then reduce the heat to a gentle simmer.

4 Add the chicken, beans and chickpeas to the pot, bring back to a boil, then reduce the heat, cover and leave the soup to cook gently for about 10 minutes until the chicken is cooked through and the beans are just tender. Taste a bean to test if it is cooked and cut a piece of chicken in half to make sure it is no longer pink in the centre. Stir in the chopped cilantro and season. (If freezing the soup, add the coriander and remaining ingredients after reheating.)

5 Ladle the soup into individual bowls, then add a dollop of yogourt to each serving, sprinkle with a little cayenne pepper and garnish with cilantro.

EACH SERVING

39 g protein • 19 g fat of which 3.5 g saturates • 25 g carbohydrate • 9 g fibre • 441 Calories

Chicken noodle soup

This is one of the simplest soups to make with wonderful exotic flavours provided by lemon grass, coconut, ginger and chili pepper. The addition of thin noodles makes it quick and easy to prepare in one pot.

Serves 4

Preparation time 20 minutes

Cooking time 25 minutes

6 cups diluted salt-reduced or homemade chicken stock (page 28)

2 lemon grass stalks, white part only, finely chopped

2 teaspoons finely chopped fresh ginger

1 red chili pepper, deseeded and finely chopped

2 garlic cloves, finely chopped

3 skinless boneless chicken breasts

150 grams (5 oz) instant thin rice noodles

175 grams (6 oz) fresh baby corn, sliced on the diagonal

150 grams (5 oz) small button mushrooms, thinly sliced

1 tablespoon salt-reduced soy sauce

414 ml can light coconut milk

1 lime, zest grated and juiced

200 grams (7 oz) bok choy, sliced

3 scallions, thinly sliced on the diagonal

small handful of cilantro, roughly chopped

1 Pour the chicken stock into a large pot, add the lemon grass, ginger, chili pepper and garlic and bring to a boil. Add the chicken, reduce the heat and simmer for about 15 minutes until the chicken is cooked.

2 Lift out the chicken with a slotted spoon, put onto a chopping board and allow to cool. Leave the pot of stock on the heat.

3 Break or cut the noodles into the hot stock, then add the baby corn, mushrooms, soy sauce and coconut milk. Bring the pot back to simmering temperature, then cook for 3 minutes.

4 Meanwhile, cut the chicken into fine shreds. Stir the chicken into the soup with the lime zest and juice and the bok choy and simmer gently for 2 minutes until the bok choy has wilted.

5 Ladle the soup into four soup bowls and scatter with scallions and cilantro. Provide a spoon and fork for ease when eating.

EACH SERVING

36 g protein • 13 g fat of which 4.5 g saturates • 41 g carbohydrate • 3 g fibre • 441 Calories

Warm new potato salad with beets and pastrami

Beets add vivid colour to this lovely warm salad, and are combined with a light, low-fat yogourt and dill dressing. For a more substantial meal, serve with thin slices of rye or pumpernickel bread.

Serves **4**

Preparation time **30 minutes**

Cooking time **15 minutes**

700 grams (25 oz) new potatoes

3 cooked beets, peeled

¾ cup frozen peas

6 scallions, thinly sliced

90 grams (3 oz) pastrami

6 radishes, thinly sliced

DILL DRESSING

⅓ cup low-fat plain yogourt

1 tablespoon light mayonnaise

2 teaspoons whole-grain mustard

2 tablespoons chopped fresh dill

1 tablespoon bottled capers, rinsed and chopped

1 Cook the potatoes whole in their skins in a pot of lightly salted, boiling water for about 15 minutes until tender.

2 Meanwhile, mix together all the ingredients for the dressing and cut the beets into thin julienne strips about 3 cm long. Cook the peas for 2–3 minutes in a dish in the microwave or in the pot of boiling water with the potatoes until tender, then drain well.

3 Drain the potatoes and thickly slice, then put them in a large serving bowl with the peas, half the scallions and the pastrami, loosely folded.

4 Just before serving, very lightly stir the beets into the salad and drizzle with the dressing. Scatter the remaining scallions and the radishes over the top. Serve warm.

EACH SERVING

12.5 g protein • 2.5 g fat of which 0.5 g saturates • 35 g carbohydrate • 8 g fibre • 231 Calories

Thai lamb salad

Try this delicious variation on the traditional Thai beef salad. Lean lamb tenderloin work beautifully with the fresh vegetables, fragrant herbs and crunchy salad greens.

Serves 4–6   Preparation time 25 minutes   Cooking time 10 minutes, plus 5 minutes standing

115 grams (4 oz) fresh baby corn, halved lengthwise

100 grams (3½ oz) Asian salad mix

1 small red onion, sliced

150 grams (5 oz) cherry tomatoes, halved

1 Lebanese cucumber, deseeded and sliced

2 pieces lamb tenderloin

cooking spray

DRESSING

2 limes, juiced

2 tablespoons fish sauce

1 tablespoon water

1 lemon grass stalk, white part only, finely chopped

2 garlic cloves, chopped

1–2 red chili peppers, chopped

2 tablespoons soft brown sugar

1 teaspoon sesame oil

2 tablespoons chopped cilantro

2 tablespoons chopped fresh mint

1 Place the corn in a heatproof bowl, pour some boiling water over it and blanch for 2–3 minutes. Drain, then transfer to a large bowl. Add the salad mix, onion, tomatoes and cucumber and toss together.

2 To make the dressing, combine all the ingredients in a bowl and set aside until ready to use.

3 Heat a non-stick frying pan over a medium–high heat. Spray the lamb with cooking spray, then cook for 2–3 minutes each side or until cooked to your liking. Transfer to a sheet of foil, wrap tightly, and allow to sit for about 5 minutes. Slice the meat into 1 cm thick slices, place into a large bowl, pour over some of the dressing and toss well. (The heat of the meat will help to absorb the flavours of the dressing.) To serve, toss the meat and salad together, drizzling over any remaining dressing, if you like.

COOK'S TIPS
• *Many supermarkets and grocers sell packages of mixed Asian salad greens. Alternatively, use your favourite salad leaves.*
• *Most of the heat from chili peppers is contained in the seeds and membrane. If you would like to tone down the heat of this salad, deseed the chili peppers before using them.*

EACH SERVING (6)

29 g protein • 12.5 g fat of which 6 g saturates • 8 g carbohydrate • 1.5 g fibre • 265 Calories

VARIATIONS
• *For vegetarians, omit the pastrami and add 2–3 hard-boiled eggs, cut into quarters, to the salad just before adding the salad dressing.*
• *For a different flavour, swap the pastrami for 200 grams (7 oz) of herring fillets in tomato sauce — you may like to cut the herrings into strips to make them easier to eat.*

Pasta, ham and fava bean salad

This quick and easy pasta salad is just right for busy people. It is appealing and sustaining and the watercress and walnut pesto dressing adds a great flavour.

Serves **4**

Preparation time **15 minutes**

Cooking time **about 15 minutes,**
  plus 5 minutes standing

300 grams (²/₃ lb) fusilli

2¹/₂ cups fresh or frozen shelled baby fava beans, thawed if necessary

400 grams (14 oz) cherry tomatoes, halved

150 grams (5 oz) lean cooked ham, diced

¹/₄ cup snipped fresh chives

1 tablespoon extra virgin olive oil

50 grams (1³/₄ oz) watercress leaves, roughly chopped

WATERCRESS AND
WALNUT PESTO

50 grams (1³/₄ oz) watercress leaves

¹/₃ cup walnut pieces

1 garlic clove, peeled

¹/₄ cup extra virgin olive oil

¹/₂ lemon, zest grated and juiced

¹/₄ cup low-fat plain yogourt

1 Cook the pasta in a large pot of lightly salted boiling water for 10 minutes. Add the fava beans and bring back to a boil, then reduce the heat slightly and cook for a further 2–3 minutes until the pasta is tender and the beans are lightly cooked.

2 Meanwhile, mix together the tomatoes, ham, chives and oil in a large serving bowl. Set aside. To make the pesto, process the watercress, walnuts and garlic together in a food processor or blender until finely ground. Add half the oil and pulse until combined, then add the remaining oil, lemon zest and juice and the yogourt and blend again. Season to taste.

3 Drain the pasta and beans and immediately add them to the tomato mixture. Mix well, then cover and leave to stand for 5 minutes. Stir the pesto and chopped watercress into the salad, then serve immediately.

COOK'S TIP
• *If prepared ahead, add the pesto and watercress just before serving. Until then, keep the rest of the salad and the pesto, covered separately, in the refrigerator.*

EACH SERVING

24.5 g protein • 29 g fat of which 4 g saturates • 53 g carbohydrate • 11 g fibre • 596 Calories

VARIATIONS
• *For a vegetarian salad, omit the ham and add 4 chopped, hard-boiled eggs to the salad with the watercress.*
• *Instead of fava beans, use 250 grams (¹/₂ lb) small broccoli florets. Cook with the pasta in the same way.*

Smoked trout niçoise

A variation on a colourful Provençale favourite, this hearty salad is just perfect for an early summer lunch, making the most of baby new potatoes and asparagus at the peak of their season.

Serves **4**

Preparation time **10 minutes**

Cooking time **30 minutes**

600 grams (1⅓ lb) baby new potatoes, scrubbed

250 grams (½ lb) asparagus, trimmed and cut into short lengths

250 grams (½ lb) cherry tomatoes, halved

⅓ cup pitted black olives

2 large eggs

175 grams (6 oz) smoked trout, flaked

90 grams (3 oz) arugula

PARSLEY DRESSING

2 tablespoons extra virgin olive oil

1 tablespoon lime juice

1 teaspoon Dijon mustard

1 tablespoon chopped fresh flat-leaf parsley

VARIATIONS
• The smoked trout can be replaced by canned tuna or salmon.
• Quail's eggs make a pretty alternative if they're available – use 4 quail's eggs to replace the 2 hen's eggs and boil for 2–3 minutes. Cut in half.

1 First make the parsley dressing by putting the oil, lime juice, mustard and parsley in a screw-top jar, then shake thoroughly until combined. Season to taste.

2 Cook the potatoes in a pot of lightly salted, boiling water for about 15 minutes until just tender. Lift out the potatoes with a slotted spoon; leave whole if they are small or slice thickly if they are larger. Toss the potatoes in the dressing and set aside to allow the potatoes to absorb the flavours.

3 Bring the pot of water back to a boil and add the asparagus, then reduce the heat and simmer for 4–5 minutes until tender. Remove with a slotted spoon, refresh briefly under cold water, then drain. (This cools the asparagus quickly and helps to retain the bright green colour.) Stir the asparagus into the potatoes, along with the tomatoes and olives.

4 Add the eggs to the pot of water and simmer for 7 minutes. Remove, run under cold water until cool enough to handle, then peel away the shells and cut the eggs into quarters.

5 Add the eggs, flaked trout and arugula to the potatoes and toss lightly to coat evenly in the dressing. Serve slightly warm or cold.

EACH SERVING

24 g protein • 15.5 g fat of which 3 g saturates • 66.5 g carbohydrate • 8.5 g fibre • 527 Calories

Warm teriyaki salmon salad

The technique of cooking salmon in foil captures all the succulent juices of the fish that, together with the teriyaki baste, makes a superb dressing for a mixed leaf and bean sprout salad. The fat in oily fish such as salmon contains omega-3 fatty acids, which have been shown to boost heart health. Serve with warm bread.

Serves **4**

Preparation time **10 minutes**

Cooking time **20 minutes**

1 tablespoon teriyaki marinade

1 tablespoon canola oil

2 teaspoons rice vinegar

4 skinless, boneless salmon steaks

2 large red peppers, deseeded and thinly sliced

100 grams (3½ oz) baby spinach leaves

90 grams (3 oz) watercress leaves

²/₃ cup bean sprouts

COOK'S TIP

• You can buy bottles of ready-made teriyaki marinade in most supermarkets.

VARIATIONS

• Instead of salmon, use skinless boneless chicken breasts. Increase the cooking time to about 20 minutes or until tender.
• Canned sliced water chestnuts, drained, would provide an alternative crunchy texture in place of the bean sprouts.

1 Preheat the oven to 400°F (200°C). Cut out four pieces of foil, each measuring about 25 x 30 cm. Mix together the teriyaki marinade, oil and vinegar in a small bowl.

2 Place a salmon steak on each piece of foil. Top each steak with one-quarter of the pepper slices and spoon over one-quarter of the teriyaki mixture. Bring two sides of the foil together to make loose parcels, then crimp the edges to seal so that none of the juices can escape.

3 Place the foil parcels on a baking tray and bake for 15–20 minutes. To test if the salmon is cooked, carefully open one of the parcels and cut into the centre of the salmon. The flesh should be pale pink and flake easily.

4 While the salmon is cooking, toss together the spinach, watercress and bean sprouts and divide evenly among four plates.

5 Top each salad with a salmon steak and pepper strips, then drizzle the cooking juices over the top and serve at once.

EACH SERVING

31.5 g protein • 15.5 g fat of which 3 g saturates • 2.5 g carbohydrate • 2.5 g fibre • 281 Calories

Egg mayonnaise salad with smoked salmon

This variation on the classic egg mayonnaise salad uses little quail's eggs with a creamy yet light mayonnaise and yogourt dressing. It is combined with mixed greens, cucumber and slivers of succulent smoked salmon. All you need to accompany the dish is some brown or whole wheat bread.

Serves **4**

Preparation time **20 minutes**

Cooking time **5 minutes**

12 quail's eggs

100 grams (3½ oz) watercress leaves

1 small oak leaf lettuce, separated into leaves

¼ English cucumber, halved lengthwise and thinly sliced

125 grams (4 oz) smoked salmon, sliced

2 teaspoons lime juice

MAYONNAISE YOGOURT DRESSING

2 tablespoons bottled capers, rinsed and roughly chopped

2 tablespoons light mayonnaise

1 tablespoon low-fat plain yogourt

COOK'S TIP
• If you would prefer the dressing to have a thinner consistency, add some lime juice.

1 Put the eggs into a pot of cold water. Bring to a boil and cook for 3 minutes. Lift out of the pot using a slotted spoon and plunge into cold water to cool. Peel off the shells and cut each egg in half.

2 To make the dressing, put the capers in a small bowl and mix with the mayonnaise and yogourt.

3 Arrange the watercress, lettuce leaves and sliced cucumber on a serving plate or in a large shallow salad bowl. Scatter over the eggs, then drizzle with the dressing.

4 Sprinkle the smoked salmon with the lime juice, grind over a little black pepper, then scatter the salmon over the salad.

EACH SERVING

14 g protein • 6.5 g fat of which 1.5 g saturates • 5.5 g carbohydrate • 3.5 g fibre • 144 Calories

Seafood salad

A ready-to-use mixed seafood selection provides the base for this tasty and attractive salad, perfect for an easy summer meal. Seafood is an excellent source of zinc, which is essential for a healthy immune system but often lacking in the diet. Serve with a loaf of crusty French bread.

Serves **4**   *Preparation time* **20 minutes**   *Cooking time* **5 minutes**

175 grams (6 oz) green beans

250 grams (¹/₂ lb) mixed prepared and cooked seafood, such as mussels, clams, squid and shrimp, thawed and drained if frozen

5 gherkins, finely chopped

12 pimento-stuffed green olives

2 heads Belgian endive

TOMATO SALSA DRESSING

2¹/₂ tablespoons olive oil

1 small lemon, juiced

¹/₂ small red onion, finely diced

250 grams (¹/₂ lb) large tomatoes, peeled and diced

¹/₂ Lebanese cucumber, finely diced

1–2 green chili peppers, deseeded and finely chopped

¹/₄ cup chopped fresh flat-leaf parsley

1 First make the dressing. Whisk together the oil and lemon juice in a bowl with a little freshly ground black pepper to taste. (No salt is needed for seasoning as both the gherkins and olives will add salt to this dish.) Add the red onion and stir to coat, then add the remaining dressing ingredients. Mix together and set aside.

2 Cook the beans in lightly salted boiling water for 3 minutes or until just tender. Drain in a sieve, then refresh under cold running water to prevent further cooking. Cut the beans in half, then put them in a large serving bowl with the seafood, gherkins and olives. Spoon over the salsa dressing and gently mix everything together.

3 Separate the Belgian endive into individual leaves and tuck them around the edge of the salad. Serve right away.

VARIATION

• *For a Thai seafood salad, make a mango salsa by mixing 2 thinly sliced shallots, 1 finely diced mango, ¹/₂ finely diced English cucumber, 2 deseeded and finely chopped red chili peppers, 1 finely chopped 5 cm piece of lemon grass, 1 tablespoon fish sauce, 2 tablespoons lime juice, 1 tablespoon rice vinegar, 2 tablespoons chopped cilantro and a pinch of superfine sugar. Toss with the seafood, 1¹/₂ cups bean sprouts and 150 grams (5 oz) lightly cooked sliced snow peas.*

EACH SERVING

16 g protein • 14 g fat of which 2.5 g saturates • 7 g carbohydrate • 7.5 g fibre • 234 Calories

VARIATION

• *If you prefer, regular hen's eggs can be used. Cook in a pot of simmering water for 7 minutes so the yolks will be set but still lightly creamy. Plunge into cold water and leave to cool, then crack the shells, peel and roughly chop. Gently stir the chopped eggs into the mayonnaise dressing, then pile on top of the salad greens.*

Tunisian fattoush with tuna

Versions of this fresh-tasting, crunchy vegetable and bread salad are popular throughout the Middle East, where it is often served as an accompaniment to roast lamb. Here, it is transformed into a filling meal with grilled tuna steaks.

Serves 4

Preparation time 25 minutes

Cooking time 10 minutes

4 large tomatoes

1 English cucumber, halved, deseeded and diced

6 scallions, chopped

2 baby romaine lettuces

40 grams (1½ oz) fresh flat-leaf parsley, chopped

⅓ cup chopped fresh mint

2 tablespoons bottled capers, rinsed

12 pitted black olives, sliced

4 large whole wheat pita breads

4 tuna steaks

SPICY DRESSING

⅓ cup extra virgin olive oil

2 garlic cloves, crushed

2 large lemons, zest finely grated and juiced to yield ⅓ cup plus 2 tablespoons juice

¼ teaspoon harissa

1 First prepare the salad dressing. Put the olive oil, garlic, lemon zest and juice and harissa in a large serving bowl and whisk together.

2 Cut the tomatoes in half, scoop out and discard the seeds and chop the flesh, then add to the bowl with the dressing. Add the cucumber and scallions.

3 Cut the lettuces in half lengthwise and shred the leaves. Add to the salad bowl with the chopped herbs, capers and olives, toss to mix, then set aside. Preheat the grill to medium.

4 Place the pita breads under the broiler and toast for about 1–2 minutes on each side until crisp and puffed up. Allow to cool slightly, then tear into bite-sized pieces and add to the salad.

5 Sprinkle the tuna steaks with a little freshly ground black pepper. Place on the grill rack and cook for 2–3 minutes. Turn the steaks over and cook for a further 2–3 minutes until just tender.

6 As soon as the tuna is cool enough to handle, flake it into the salad in large pieces. Gently toss everything together and serve immediately.

EACH SERVING

46 g protein • 29.5 g fat of which 6 g saturates • 62.5 g carbohydrate • 11.5 g fibre • 733 Calories

Rice salad with shrimp

A colourful, crunchy vegetable salad tossed in a tastebud-tingling, Asian-style dressing, this dish gives a great vitamin boost. Soy sauce is high in salt, so no extra seasoning is needed for the dressing.

Serves **4**

Preparation time **15 minutes**

Cooking time **Nil**

1 red pepper, deseeded and thinly sliced

1 yellow pepper, deseeded and thinly sliced

1 orange pepper, deseeded and thinly sliced

4 cups bean sprouts

6 scallions, thinly sliced

½ English cucumber, julienned

250 grams (½ lb) cooked, peeled jumbo shrimp

1¾ cups cooked long-grain white rice

1 tablespoon sesame seeds, toasted

SWEET CHILI DRESSING

2 tablespoons salt-reduced soy sauce

1 tablespoon sesame oil

1 tablespoon canola oil

2 tablespoons sherry vinegar or rice vinegar

1 tablespoon sweet chili sauce or 1 red chili pepper, deseeded and finely chopped

1 tablespoon honey

15 grams (½ oz) fresh ginger, peeled and finely grated

1 First make the dressing. Put all the ingredients for the dressing into a large salad bowl and whisk together to combine.

2 Just before serving, add all the salad ingredients, apart from the sesame seeds. Toss everything together to coat in the dressing, then sprinkle the sesame seeds on top. Serve at once.

EACH SERVING

21 g protein • 12 g fat of which 1.5 g saturates • 35.5 g carbohydrate • 5 g fibre • 348 Calories

COOK'S TIPS

• _Rice absorbs roughly three times its weight in water when you cook it, so you'll need to cook about ½ cup long-grain rice to give you 2 cups cooked rice. Keep it chilled until ready to add to the salad._

• _To save time, you could use a bag of stir-fry vegetables._

COOK'S TIP
• If the avocado is bought hard, place it in a paper bag and ripen at room temperature. Store ripe avocados in the refrigerator for up to 2 days.

VARIATION
• If fresh crab meat is unavailable or hard to find, you can replace it with canned crab meat, drained, or the same weight of peeled cooked shrimp.

Avocado and crab salad

This is a salad that is ideal for a special summer occasion. Crabmeat is a good source of low-fat protein and goes beautifully with juicy papaya and creamy avocado. Serve with light rye bread.

Step 1

Step 2

Step 3

Serves **4**

Preparation time **20 minutes**

Cooking time **Nil**

2 baby romaine lettuces, shredded, or 1 mature romaine lettuce, outer leaves removed, shredded

1 ripe papaya

1 large avocado, ripe but firm

398 ml can pinto beans, drained and rinsed

200 grams (7 oz) fresh white crab meat

½ lime, zest cut into thin strips

CREAMY LIME AND GINGER DRESSING

⅓ cup natural low-fat yogourt

2 tablespoons light mayonnaise

1 lime, zest grated and juiced

15 grams (½ oz) fresh ginger, peeled and finely chopped

1 First make the dressing. Whisk together the yogourt, mayonnaise, lime zest and juice and ginger in a bowl, then set aside.

2 Spread the lettuce on a large serving platter. Cut the papaya in half lengthwise and remove the seeds, then peel off the skin and slice the flesh. Arrange over the lettuce.

3 Cut the avocado in half lengthwise, remove the stone, then peel and slice the flesh. Arrange on the platter, alternating the slices with the papaya.

4 Fork the pinto beans and crab meat together. Spoon the mixture on top of the salad, then drizzle on the dressing, garnish with the strips of lime zest and serve immediately.

EACH SERVING

15 g protein • 16.5 g fat of which 3.5 g saturates • 27 g carbohydrate • 6 g fibre • 336 Calories

Chili-lime chicken salad

In this salad, chicken is gently poached in stock to give an almost melt-in-the-mouth texture and is then mixed with salad greens and vegetables and topped with a chili-lime dressing.

Serves **4-6**

Preparation time **25 minutes**

Cooking time **25 minutes**

2 skinless boneless chicken breasts

1½ cups diluted salt-reduced or homemade chicken stock (page 28)

1 cup water

1 carrot, peeled and finely julienned

3 shallots, sliced on the diagonal

1 red pepper, deseeded and sliced

1 radicchio treviso or radicchio lettuce, shredded

100 grams (3½ oz) watercress leaves

CHILI-LIME DRESSING

2 tablespoons dried coconut, lightly toasted

2 limes, juiced

2 garlic cloves, roughly chopped

1 bird's eye chili pepper, deseeded and roughly chopped

½ cup Greek-style yogourt

15 grams (½ oz) watercress leaves

1 Place the chicken breasts, stock and water into a pot, ensuring the chicken is just covered. Gently bring the chicken to a boil while covered. Once the stock comes to a boil, remove the pot from the heat, keeping the lid on tight. Leave for 20–25 minutes or until the chicken is fully cooked when tested. Drain and allow to cool.

2 In a large bowl, toss together the carrot, shallots, pepper, radicchio and watercress. Once the chicken is cooled, gently shred or, if you prefer, slice. Add to the salad.

3 To make the dressing, place the coconut, lime juice, garlic, chili, yogourt and the reserved watercress into a small food processor bowl and gently whiz together until creamy. Alternatively, place into a small jug and blend with a hand-held blender.

4 To serve, pour the dressing over the salad and gently toss together. Divide onto serving plates.

EACH SERVING (6)

23 g protein • 8.5 g fat of which 4 g saturates • 7 g carbohydrate • 4 g fibre • 208 Calories

Chicken and beet salad

Roast chicken and ruby red beets are a mouth-watering combination, and white kidney beans and fresh mixed salad greens add fibre and vitamin value to this appealing salad dressed with tangy lime and horseradish.

Serves **4**   *Preparation time* **20 minutes**   *Cooking time* **Nil**

350 grams (12 oz) skinless roast chicken, cubed

2 x 398 ml cans white kidney beans, drained and rinsed

100 grams (3½ oz) mixed salad greens

1 red onion, thinly sliced

400 grams (14 oz) cooked beets, peeled and cubed

4 lime wedges

HORSERADISH DRESSING

¾ cup reduced-fat ricotta cheese

1 lime, zest grated and juiced

2 teaspoons horseradish sauce, or to taste

¼ English cucumber, diced

1 To make the dressing, mix the ricotta, lime zest, half the lime juice and the horseradish sauce in a bowl, then stir in the diced cucumber. Add the chicken to the bowl with the white kidney beans. Mix lightly to combine the chicken and beans with the dressing.

2 Toss the salad greens with the onion and remaining lime juice, then spread on a large shallow serving platter, reserving a few pretty leaves for garnishing. Pile the chicken and bean mixture on top, then scatter with the beets and reserved leaves. Garnish with lime wedges and serve immediately.

VARIATION

• *For a vegetarian salad, omit the chicken and add 2 peeled, pitted and diced avocados. Sprinkle with toasted sesame seeds before serving.*

EACH SERVING

8 g protein • 2.5 g fat of which 1 g saturates • 6 g carbohydrate • 2.5 g fibre • 79 Calories

COOK'S TIPS

• *You'll need to use about 1 bunch of watercress for this recipe — choose a bunch that weighs about 370 grams (13 oz), then trim off the stems and any straggly-looking leaves.*
• *If you like, you can serve the dressing in a jug and allow each diner to add their own dressing.*

Spiced chicken and mango salad

Here is a modern, lighter version of the traditional Coronation chicken. The familiar curry flavours and vegetables are still present but they have a South-East Asian flavour, with spicy Thai curry paste and juicy fresh mango pieces added. This is the perfect salad for a refreshing summer lunch, accompanied by toasted nan or pita bread.

Serves **4**   *Preparation time* **25 minutes**   *Cooking time* **Nil**

3 cooked skinless boneless chicken breasts, cubed

4 celery stalks, sliced

3/4 cup dried apricots, thinly sliced

100 grams (3 1/2 oz) arugula

1 mango, peeled, pitted and sliced

1/3 cup unsalted cashews, lightly toasted and chopped

CURRY DRESSING

1/3 cup low-fat plain yogourt

2 tablespoons light mayonnaise

2 teaspoons mango chutney

1/2 teaspoon tomato paste

1/2 teaspoon Thai red curry paste

15 gram (1/2 oz) piece stem ginger in syrup, finely chopped, or 1 1/2 tablespoons finely chopped candied ginger

1 lime, zest grated

1 In a large bowl, make the dressing by mixing together the yogourt, mayonnaise, chutney, tomato paste, curry paste, ginger and lime zest.

2 Add the chicken, celery and apricots to the bowl and lightly toss together until coated with the dressing.

3 Spread the arugula leaves and mango slices on a serving dish. Spoon the chicken mixture on top, then serve scattered with the cashews.

COOK'S TIP
• *The dressing can be made 2 days ahead and stored in the refrigerator.*

VARIATION
• *To turn this salad into a wonderful sandwich filling, dice the chicken, celery, mango and apricots, then add the dressing and mix well. Pile onto multigrain bread with some arugula leaves.*

EACH SERVING

30.5 g protein • 15.5 g fat of which 3.5 g saturates • 31 g carbohydrate • 5.5 g fibre • 394 Calories

Mediterranean roast chicken salad

Save time and effort on hot days with a wonderfully easy salad. It uses ready-roasted chicken, and the pasta and sugar snap peas can be cooked ahead. Feta cheese, arugula and sweet juicy grapes — rich in antioxidants — all add to the feast of flavours.

Serves 4   Preparation time 15 minutes   Cooking time 10 minutes

400 grams (14 oz) pasta shells

300 grams (²/₃ lb) sugar snap peas, trimmed and halved on the diagonal

¼ cup extra virgin olive oil

400 grams (14 oz) skinless roast chicken, torn into bite-sized pieces

125 grams (4 oz) arugula

1 tablespoon balsamic vinegar

250 grams (½ lb) black or red seedless grapes, halved

¼ cup chopped fresh mint

100 grams (3½ oz) feta cheese, drained

1 Cook the pasta in a large pot of boiling water according to the package instructions. About 3 minutes before the pasta is ready, add the sugar snap peas to the pot and continue boiling until the pasta is al dente and the peas are tender but crisp. Drain both into a colander, then tip them into a large serving bowl.

2 Drizzle with 1 tablespoon of the oil and stir. Add the chicken and season to taste with freshly ground black pepper. At this point, the salad can be completed for serving warm, or the ingredients can be left to cool to serve later.

3 Just before serving, stir the arugula leaves into the bowl. Mix together the remaining olive oil and the balsamic vinegar, pour over the salad and toss all the ingredients together.

4 Gently stir in the grapes and chopped mint, then crumble the feta cheese over the top. Taste and adjust the seasoning if necessary, but the feta cheese is quite salty so there should be no need to add extra salt.

VARIATION

• *This is a versatile recipe so you can make changes, depending on what's available. Well-drained canned tuna chunks, chopped lean ham or turkey breast could be used in place of the roast chicken; juicy, vine-ripened cherry tomatoes used rather than grapes; and frozen peas or trimmed snow peas used as an alternative to sugar snap peas. Other good pasta shapes would be fusilli or penne.*

EACH SERVING

42 g protein • 27.5 g fat of which 7.5 g saturates • 70 g carbohydrate • 7 g fibre • 715 Calories

Duck, rice, mushroom and orange salad

In this attractive salad, full-flavoured shiitake and brown mushrooms are combined with slices of tender grilled duck, juicy orange segments, crunchy water chestnuts and rice, with a fresh ginger and honey dressing.

Step 2

Step 3

Step 4

Serves **4**

Preparation time **30 minutes**

Cooking time **15 minutes**

½ cup basmati and wild rice, rinsed

400 grams (14 oz) boneless duck breasts, skinned

2 tablespoons canola oil

125 grams (4 oz) brown mushrooms, sliced

125 grams (4 oz) fresh shiitake mushrooms, sliced

3 oranges

1 pomegranate

230 gram can water chestnuts, drained and thinly sliced

50 grams (2 oz) lamb's lettuce or baby salad greens

GINGER AND HONEY DRESSING

½ teaspoon orange zest and 1 tablespoon orange juice (from 1 of the oranges)

1 tablespoon fresh ginger, peeled and finely chopped

1 teaspoon Dijon mustard

2 teaspoons honey

1½ tablespoons walnut oil

1 teaspoon white wine vinegar

1 Cook the rice in a pot of boiling water according to the package instructions, until tender. Drain, then transfer to a large bowl.

2 Meanwhile, heat a cast-iron, ridged grill pan. Brush the duck breasts on both sides with 2 teaspoons of the canola oil, then cook over a medium heat for 3 minutes on each side, or longer for medium or well-done. Transfer the duck to a board and leave to cool. Brush the pan with half of the remaining oil and add half the mushrooms. Cook for 3–5 minutes until tender, turning occasionally. Remove and set aside, then repeat with the remaining oil and mushrooms.

3 Grate ½ teaspoon of zest from 1 of the oranges and set aside for the dressing. Cut away all the peel and pith from the 3 oranges, then, cutting between and close to the membranes, remove the segments, holding the fruit over a bowl to catch the juices. Reserve 1 tablespoon of the juice for the dressing.

4 Cut the pomegranate in half and carefully remove the seeds, leaving the pith behind. Add half the pomegranate seeds to the rice with the orange segments, mushrooms, water chestnuts and lamb's lettuce or salad greens.

5 To make the dressing, whisk together the orange zest and juice, ginger, mustard, honey and walnut oil in a small bowl. Season to taste. Add 1 tablespoon of dressing to the rice mixture, toss well, then transfer to a serving platter. Thinly slice the duck and arrange over the rice. Drizzle with the remaining dressing and sprinkle with the remaining pomegranate seeds just before serving.

EACH SERVING

14 g protein • 18.5 g fat of which 2 g saturates • 54.5 g carbohydrate • 7 g fibre • 453 Calories

Summer fruity cottage cheese salad

This salad tastes as great as it looks. With its colourful mixture of fruit and salad greens, it is packed with vitamins and fibre and transforms plain cottage cheese into an exciting salad. Serve with rice cakes for a low-fat accompaniment.

*Serves **4***

*Preparation time **20 minutes***

*Cooking time **Nil***

1 orange, zest finely grated and juiced to yield ⅓ cup juice

2¼ cups cottage cheese

2 red apples

1¼ cups blueberries

16 dried apricots, finely chopped

2 celery stalks, finely chopped

150 grams (5 oz) mixed salad greens

2 kiwis, peeled and sliced

2 nectarines, pitted and sliced

1 tablespoon sesame seeds, toasted (optional)

COOK'S TIP

• If some of the fresh fruits are not in season, use fruits canned in juice, such as pineapple chunks, peach slices or apricots to make up a good variety.

1 Mix the orange zest into the cottage cheese. Core and dice the apples and mix with the blueberries, apricots and celery in a large bowl.

2 Divide the salad greens onto four serving plates. Top each mound of leaves with equal portions of kiwi and nectarines and sprinkle each one with 1 tablespoon orange juice.

3 Share out the cottage cheese and fruit mixture onto the plates and sprinkle with sesame seeds, if you like.

EACH SERVING

22 g protein • 7.5 g fat of which 4.5 g saturates • 34.5 g carbohydrate • 7 g fibre • 309 Calories

Pear and Roquefort salad

Pears and creamy blue cheese are natural partners in this light and easy salad. Poppy seeds and crunchy toasted pecans add extra interest and mineral value.

Serves **4**   *Preparation time* **20 minutes**   *Cooking time* **Nil**

1 celery stalk

3 ripe pears (preferably red or pink-flushed)

1 head Belgian endive, separated into leaves

50 grams (2 oz) lamb's lettuce or baby salad greens

¼ cup pecans or walnuts, lightly toasted

90 grams (3 oz) Roquefort cheese

4 slices pumpernickel or walnut bread, toasted

POPPY SEED DRESSING

2 tablespoons walnut oil

1 tablespoon sherry or balsamic vinegar

1 teaspoon Dijon mustard

1 teaspoon honey

2 teaspoons poppy seeds

1 First make the dressing by placing all the ingredients in a screw-top jar and shaking until well combined. As the Roquefort is quite salty, there is no need to add any salt.

2 Cut the celery into 5 cm lengths, then slice again lengthwise into thin strips.

3 Core and thinly slice the pears lengthwise and place in a large bowl with the Belgian endive leaves, salad greens, nuts and celery. Add the dressing and toss well to coat evenly. Crumble the Roquefort over the salad.

4 Place a slice of the toasted pumpernickel or walnut bread on each plate and pile the salad evenly over the top. Serve immediately.

VARIATIONS
• *Other blue cheeses would also work well. For a lower-fat alternative, try feta cheese.*
• *For a more tropical flavour, you could replace the pears with 2 sliced mangoes.*
• *For a lighter-flavoured dressing, replace half the walnut oil with a light olive or sunflower oil.*

EACH SERVING

11.5 g protein • 22 g fat of which 6 g saturates • 40 g carbohydrate • 9.5 g fibre • 419 Calories

VARIATION
• *The variations to this are only limited by your imagination – cherries, grapes, mangoes, orange segments, peaches, raspberries, strawberries and dried fruits, such as figs, raisins and sultanas, are all suitable.*

Vietnamese tofu and noodle salad

An exciting layered salad combining crisp vegetables flavoured with fresh herbs, noodles and marinated grilled tofu. The tofu is best prepared several hours in advance as longer marinating will enhance the flavour.

Serves **4**

Preparation time **45 minutes, plus at least 30 minutes marinating**

Cooking time **15 minutes**

2 x 250 gram packages firm tofu, drained

3½ cups bean sprouts

200 grams (7 oz) mustard greens, napa cabbage or bok choy, finely shredded

¼ cup roughly chopped cilantro

½ cup roughly chopped fresh basil

2 limes, juiced (use the zest for the marinade)

2 teaspoons superfine sugar

200 grams (7 oz) snow peas

250 grams (½ lb) medium rice noodles

2 tablespoons olive oil

¾ cup unsalted peanuts, chopped

½ English cucumber, halved lengthwise and cut into sticks

MARINADE

2 green chili peppers, deseeded and finely diced

2 garlic cloves, thinly sliced

6 scallions, thinly sliced

⅓ cup salt-reduced soy sauce

grated zest of 2 limes

1 teaspoon sesame oil

⅓ cup dry sherry

1 Slice the blocks of tofu in half horizontally and lay flat in a non-metallic, heatproof dish. Mix together all the ingredients for the marinade and sprinkle evenly over the tofu. Turn the slices so that both sides are coated, then cover and leave to marinate for at least 30 minutes.

2 Meanwhile, combine the bean sprouts, shredded greens, cilantro and basil in a large, deep serving dish. Sprinkle with the lime juice and half the sugar. Add the snow peas to a pot of boiling water. Bring back to a boil and cook for just 1 minute, then remove with a slotted spoon, drain in a colander and refresh under cold running water. Scatter over the bean sprout mixture.

3 Add the noodles to the pot of water. Bring back to a boil, then remove the pot from the heat, cover with a lid and leave to stand for 4 minutes or until the noodles have softened. Drain in a colander and rinse under cold running water, then tip them back into the pot.

4 Preheat the broiler. Drain the marinade from the tofu onto the noodles, toss and set aside. Leave the tofu lying flat in the dish.

5 Sprinkle half the oil over the tofu, then broil for 4–6 minutes until beginning to brown and forming a skin on the surface. Use a large spatula to turn the pieces of tofu over. Sprinkle with the remaining sugar and oil and broil for a further 4 minutes. Sprinkle the nuts over the tofu and cook for a final 2 minutes or until the nuts are browned.

6 Tip the noodles on top of the bean sprout mixture to make a separate layer. Slice the tofu into 2 cm thick fingers and arrange on top of the salad with the cucumber sticks and toasted nuts. Serve immediately while the tofu is warm.

VARIATION

• Instead of tofu, use thin fillets of chicken breast or lean steak. Boil the marinade for 2–3 minutes in a small bowl in the microwave before adding it to the noodles.

EACH SERVING

4 g protein • 4.5 g fat of which 0.5 g saturates • 8.5 g carbohydrate • 1.5 g fibre • 94 Calories

Mixed leaf and peach salad with brie crostini

A delicious way to enjoy the delights of summer, with rust-red salad greens, currants and peaches all bursting with vitamin C. The addition of crostini with creamy brie makes this a satisfying salad to serve as a light lunch.

Serves **4**

Preparation time **15 minutes**

Cooking time **10 minutes**

1 large radicchio, separated into leaves

50 grams (2 oz) arugula

50 grams (2 oz) watercress leaves

8 radishes, sliced

3 large ripe peaches, pitted and cut into thick slices

³/₄ cup currants or blueberries

2 tablespoons olive oil

2 teaspoons balsamic vinegar

¹/₄ cup hazelnuts, toasted and roughly chopped

BRIE CROSTINI

1 small baguette, trimmed and cut into 12 slices

125 grams (4 oz) ripe brie, cut into 12 slices

1 To make the crostini, preheat the broiler. Lightly toast the bread slices on both sides under the broiler. Top each toast with a slice of brie and cook until the cheese has melted and is just bubbling. Set aside.

2 Combine the salad greens in a large salad bowl. Add the radishes, peaches and about ²/₃ cup of the currants or blueberries.

3 Put the remaining currants or blueberries in a small bowl, add the oil and, using a fork, lightly crush the fruit. Stir in the vinegar and season to taste.

4 Pour the dressing over the salad and toss together well to mix. Scatter with the toasted hazelnuts and arrange the brie crostini on top. Serve immediately.

EACH SERVING

17 g protein • 25.5 g fat of which 7.5 g saturates • 55.5 g carbohydrate • 9 g fibre • 540 Calories

VARIATIONS

• *In place of the brie you could use the same weight of a creamy blue cheese for the crostini.*
• *If any of these salad greens are not available, replace them with other salad greens, such as curly endive, red-leaf lettuce or lamb's lettuce.*

Goat's cheese and watermelon salad

Juicy watermelon makes the perfect partner to tangy goat's cheese in this easy-to-assemble pasta salad. Flavour and texture are provided by crunchy Belgian endive, peppery arugula and toasted pine nuts, which combine to give a Mediterranean flair.

*Serves **4** Preparation time **25 minutes** Cooking time **15 minutes***

200 grams (7 oz) penne, preferably whole wheat

125 grams (4 oz) firm goat's cheese

1/2 small watermelon, peeled, cubed and deseeded

100 grams (3 1/2 oz) arugula

1/4 cup pine nuts, toasted

2 small heads Belgian endive

4 slices prosciutto, trimmed of all excess fat and cut into strips

MINT DRESSING

2 1/2 tablespoons mild olive oil

1 tablespoon lime juice

1 tablespoon balsamic vinegar

1 tablespoon chopped fresh mint

1 Cook the pasta in boiling water for 11–13 minutes or according to the package instructions. Drain and rinse under cold running water, then drain thoroughly and set aside to cool.

2 Put all the ingredients for the dressing in a screw-top jar and shake together well. Season to taste with freshly ground black pepper. Both the cheese and prosciutto are quite salty, so no extra salt should be needed.

3 Crumble the cheese into the cooled pasta and add the watermelon. Pour the dressing over and lightly toss together, then add the arugula and pine nuts.

4 Separate the Belgian endive into individual leaves and arrange on a serving platter or shallow salad bowl. Arrange the salad on top and scatter with the prosciutto.

VARIATIONS

• *Feta cheese may be used instead of goat's cheese. Reduce the salt content slightly by soaking in a bowl of cold water for 2–3 minutes, then draining. Crumble or cut into small cubes.*
• *Instead of the watermelon, try cubed honeydew melon or diced ripe mango. Add the squeezed juice of 2 tablespoons freshly grated ginger to the dressing.*

EACH SERVING

20.5 g protein • 25.5 g fat of which 6.5 g saturates • 42 g carbohydrate • 11.5 g fibre • 501 Calories

Red cabbage, Edam and walnut salad

This crunchy, colourful winter salad provides an excellent nutritional mix. The vegetables and apple are rich in vitamin C and fibre, Edam cheese adds protein and calcium, and walnuts contain essential fatty acids. Serve with oatcakes.

Serves **4**

Preparation time **20 minutes**

Cooking time **10 minutes**

1 small celeriac, peeled and cut into eighths

½ lemon, juiced

1 small red cabbage, core removed, then quartered

1 red onion, thinly sliced

⅓ cup chopped walnuts

100 grams (3½ oz) Edam cheese

1 crisp red apple

DRESSING

1½ tablespoons walnut oil

1 tablespoon canola oil

2 teaspoons balsamic vinegar

1 Shred the wedges of celeriac using the grating disc of a food processor, or thinly slice using a sharp knife. Put into a pot of boiling water with half the lemon juice, cook for 5 minutes until tender, then drain well and put into a large bowl. Shred the cabbage in the same way as the celeriac, then add to the bowl with the celeriac, along with the onion.

2 In a screw-top jar, shake together the ingredients for the dressing and season to taste. Spoon two-thirds of the dressing over the celeriac, cabbage and onion and toss lightly. Set aside.

3 Heat a small non-stick frying pan over a moderate heat, dry-fry the walnuts for 2 minutes, stirring, then take off the heat and reserve. Cut the Edam into matchsticks. Core the apple, cut it into thin slices, then put on a plate and sprinkle with the rest of the lemon juice to prevent it discolouring.

4 Just before serving, toss the Edam, apple slices and toasted walnuts into the salad. Spoon over the rest of the dressing, toss and serve immediately.

EACH SERVING

13 g protein • 26 g fat of which 6 g saturates • 14 g carbohydrate
• 10.5 g fibre • 354 Calories

Feta and orange tabouli

A fabulous main meal salad based on bulgur, generously flavoured with fresh herbs.
It is best prepared ahead to give time for all the wonderful flavours to mingle.

Serves 4

Preparation time 40 minutes,
*   plus at least 30 minutes chilling*

Cooking time Nil

1 1/3 cups bulgur

500 grams (1 lb) ripe but firm
tomatoes, diced

1 red onion, finely chopped

50 grams (2 oz) pitted black olives,
halved (optional)

1 green or red chili pepper,
deseeded and diced (optional)

1/4 cup chopped fresh
herbs, such as mint, basil and
cilantro

1 garlic clove, crushed

1/2 teaspoon superfine sugar

2 tablespoons extra virgin olive oil

2 oranges

175 grams (6 oz) feta cheese,
drained and diced

1/4 cup flaked almonds, toasted

200 grams (7 oz) romaine lettuce
or young spinach leaves

VARIATIONS
• *Omit the feta cheese and*
instead add 2 small diced
avocados to the salad.
• *Instead of almonds, use*
chopped walnuts or lightly
toasted pine nuts.
• *Add some chopped dried*
apricots to the salad.

1 Put the bulgur in a bowl, pour over enough boiling water to cover and stir
well. Leave to soak for 20–30 minutes.

2 Meanwhile, combine the tomatoes, onion, olives and chili pepper (if using),
herbs, garlic and sugar in a large serving bowl and stir in the olive oil.

3 Using a zester, remove the zest from 1 orange in fine shreds and add them
to the tomato mixture. Slice the top and bottom off both oranges, cut off all
the peel and pith, then halve and chop the fruit, removing the seeds and any
large pieces of membrane from the middle. Add the oranges to the tomato
mixture with any juice on the board.

4 Drain the bulgur in a sieve, pressing out excess water, then add it to the
tomato mixture. Cool, then cover and refrigerate for at least 30 minutes.

5 Just before serving, stir the feta cheese and almonds into the tabouli. Season
to taste. Serve with salad greens, crisp enough to use as scoops or large
enough to wrap around forkfuls of tabouli.

EACH SERVING

18 g protein • 24 g fat of which 8.5 g saturates • 47 g carbohydrate • 11.5 g fibre • 499 Calories

Hummus salad

Homemade hummus only takes a few moments to whizz together and makes a perfect light lunch, served simply with pita. But for a balanced meal, turn it into this more substantial salad with the addition of crisp salad vegetables.

Serves **4**   *Preparation time* **25 minutes**   *Cooking time* **Nil**

HUMMUS

1¹/₂ 540 ml cans chickpeas

¹/₃ cup tahini

2 tablespoons olive oil

2 tablespoons lemon juice

2 large garlic cloves, crushed

2 tablespoons chopped fresh flat-leaf parsley, cilantro or mint

SALAD

¹/₂ English cucumber, pared into ribbons with a vegetable peeler

2 carrots, peeled and pared into ribbons with a vegetable peeler

1 red onion, thinly sliced

90 grams (3 oz) radishes, sliced

90 grams (3 oz) mixed salad greens,

2 tablespoons rice vinegar

¹/₂ cup hazelnuts, toasted and chopped

4 lemon wedges (optional)

4 sesame pita breads, warmed

1 Reserve ¹/₄ cup of the liquid from 1 can of chickpeas, then drain and rinse all the chickpeas and put them into a blender or food processor with the reserved liquid. Add the tahini, olive oil, lemon juice, garlic and herbs. Process for about 30 seconds or until well mixed. Season to taste.

2 Put the cucumber, carrots, red onion, radish and salad greens into a large salad bowl. Sprinkle with the rice vinegar and hazelnuts and toss together.

3 Heap the salad onto individual plates and spoon the hummus on top. Serve with lemon wedges to squeeze over, if you like, and warmed pita bread.

COOK'S TIPS

• *For speed, you can use a ready-made hummus – choose a reduced-fat version if you can.*

EACH SERVING

6 g protein • 8.5 g fat of which 1 g saturates • 17 g carbohydrate • 4.5 g fibre • 177 Calories

Couscous, orange and date salad

Couscous makes a brilliant base for a quick salad, as it needs only a brief soaking in hot stock (or water). Here it is combined with chickpeas, dates, oranges and pistachios for a Middle Eastern-style vegetarian dish.

Serves **4**   *Preparation time* **25 minutes, plus 1 hour standing**   *Cooking time* **Nil**

1 cup couscous

¾ cup plus 2 tablespoons diluted salt-reduced or homemade vegetable stock (page 29), hot

2 oranges

¾ of a 540 ml can chickpeas, drained and rinsed

¾ cup roughly chopped pitted dried dates

½ cup shelled pistachios, roughly chopped

¼ cup chopped fresh mint

CITRUS DRESSING

½ teaspoon grated orange zest

2 tablespoons extra virgin olive oil

2 tablespoons lemon juice

1 teaspoon paprika

1 Put the couscous into a large bowl, pour over the hot vegetable stock and set aside for 10 minutes until all the stock is absorbed.

2 Meanwhile, to make the dressing, put the grated orange zest into a bowl, add the rest of the dressing ingredients and whisk together. Season to taste.

3 Fluff the couscous with a fork and drizzle the dressing over the top while the couscous is still warm.

4 Cut the pith away from the oranges, then cut out the segments between the membranes, placing the fruit on a plate to catch all the juices. Cut each segment in half.

5 Stir the oranges, their juice, the chickpeas, dates, pistachios and 2 tablespoons of the mint into the couscous. Season to taste, then leave to stand at room temperature for at least 1 hour to allow the flavours to mingle. Scatter the remaining mint over the top just before serving.

EACH SERVING

10.5 g protein • 18 g fat of which 2.5 g saturates • 39 g carbohydrate • 9.5 g fibre • 378 Calories

Moroccan lamb and couscous salad

Enjoy the fragrant flavours of cilantro and mint in this North African-inspired salad, which can be largely prepared ahead. Lamb is a good source of protein, as well as B vitamins, iron and zinc.

Serves **4**

Preparation time **about 30 minutes, plus 10 minutes resting**

Cooking time **1 hour**

2 zucchini, quartered and cut into chunks

2 red peppers, deseeded and cut into chunks

2 yellow peppers, deseeded and cut into chunks

2 red onions, each cut into six wedges

2 tablespoons olive oil

500 grams (1 lb) lamb, trimmed of fat

2 cups couscous

2 tablespoons chopped cilantro

1 tablespoon chopped fresh flat-leaf parsley

1 tablespoon chopped fresh mint

8 pitted black olives, sliced

6 scallions, sliced on the diagonal

MARINADE

¼ cup lemon juice

1 tablespoon olive oil

3 garlic cloves, crushed

1 teaspoon ground cumin

1 teaspoon ground coriander

pinch of cayenne pepper

TOMATO DRESSING

7 tablespoons tomato juice

2 tablespoons balsamic vinegar

1 teaspoon chili sauce, or to taste

1 Preheat the oven to 400°F (200°C). Put the zucchini, peppers and red onions in a roasting pan, spoon over the olive oil and toss together to coat the vegetables. Put the pan in the oven and roast for 30 minutes, turning the vegetables after about 15 minutes.

2 Meanwhile, combine all the marinade ingredients in a shallow dish. Add the lamb, turn to coat, then cover and set aside. Put all the dressing ingredients in a screw-top jar, shake together and set aside.

3 Stir the vegetables once they have roasted for 30 minutes, arrange the lamb on top and pour over the marinade. Return to the oven and continue roasting for a further 30 minutes until the lamb is cooked but still juicy. (You can prepare ahead up to this stage if more convenient and chill for up to 24 hours.)

4 Put the couscous in a heatproof bowl and pour over enough boiling water to cover. Set aside, covered, for about 5 minutes until the water is absorbed and the grains are tender. Fork in the herbs, olives and scallions.

5 Transfer the lamb to a plate and allow to rest for 10 minutes. Stir all the roasted vegetables into the couscous, then thinly slice the lamb and lay it on top of the couscous. Shake the dressing and pour it over the salad. Toss together, then serve warm.

COOK'S TIP

• *If you have time, you can marinate the lamb overnight.*

EACH SERVING

32 g protein • 23.5 g fat of which 6 g saturates • 23.5 g carbohydrate • 4.5 g fibre • 453 Calories

*L*ight meals

Filled, topped, wrapped and sandwiched with scrumptious meat, fish and vegetables, these popular and convenient family favourites contain less fat and salt than most prepared or takeout versions. Pizzas are topped with extra vegetables, sandwiches are packed with salad ingredients and spread with tasty relishes, and burgers are made with lean meat or high-fibre legumes. All make perfect, no-fuss balanced dishes for casual eating—and are the meals children will love the most.

Four seasons pizza

This tasty pizza includes a variety of toppings to suit every taste. It is lower in fat and salt than pre-made pizzas, yet has just as much flavour. Don't be put off by the long ingredients list — it is easy and fun to make and will soon become a favourite. Serve with a big green salad.

Serves 4

Preparation time 30 minutes,
*   plus about 1 hour rising*

Cooking time 35 minutes

PIZZA DOUGH

2¹/₂ cups white bread
or all-purpose flour

7 gram sachet dried yeast

¹/₄ teaspoon salt

2 tablespoons olive oil

²/₃ cup plus 2 tablespoons tepid water

TOPPINGS

150 grams (5 oz) baby leeks, trimmed and sliced

125 grams (¹/₄ lb) mushrooms, sliced

1 tablespoon white wine vinegar

4 large bottled roasted red pepper pieces, drained and thickly sliced

²/₃ cup canned artichoke hearts, drained and quartered

1 garlic clove, finely chopped

²/₃ cup tomato sauce

1 tablespoon tapenade

50 grams (2 oz) prosciutto, thinly sliced

¹/₄ cup pitted black olives, sliced

¹/₂ cup sun-dried tomatoes, chopped

¹/₂ cup grated mozzarella cheese

a few fresh sprigs of oregano

1 Mix together the flour, yeast and salt in a large bowl. Make a well in the centre and stir in the olive oil with enough of the tepid water to make a smooth dough. Turn the dough out onto a lightly floured surface and knead for about 5 minutes until smooth and elastic. Place the dough back in the rinsed-out and lightly oiled bowl, then cover with a damp dish towel or oiled plastic wrap and leave in a warm place for 1 hour or until it has doubled in size.

2 Meanwhile, preheat the oven to 400°F (200°C) and prepare the toppings. Put the leeks in a pot with the mushrooms and vinegar, cover and cook on a high heat for 3–4 minutes, shaking the pot occasionally, until softened. Mix the peppers with the artichokes. Mix the garlic into the tomato sauce.

3 Turn out the risen dough onto the lightly floured surface and punch it down, knead lightly, then roll out or press out with your knuckles to a 30–32 cm round on a lightly greased baking tray.

4 Spread the tomato sauce mixture evenly over the pizza crust, then pile the leeks and mushrooms over one-quarter of the dough and the peppers and artichokes over a second quarter.

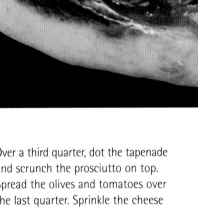

Over a third quarter, dot the tapenade and scrunch the prosciutto on top. Spread the olives and tomatoes over the last quarter. Sprinkle the cheese over the whole pizza.

5 Bake the pizza for about 30 minutes until golden around the edges and lightly browned on top. Scatter some sprigs of oregano over the pizza, cut into slices and serve piping hot.

EACH SERVING

5.5 g protein • 4 g fat of which 1 g saturates • 18 g carbohydrate • 2.5 g fibre • 135 Calories

Pizza slice

Everyone loves pizza and, made as a slice, it can easily be cut into squares and served as casual party food. You can even slice it into bite-sized cubes and serve as finger food.

Serves 6   Preparation time 50 minutes   Cooking time 25 minutes

3½ cups white or multigrain bread mix

1 tablespoon finely chopped fresh rosemary

48 gram can anchovies in oil, drained

¼ cup 1% milk

⅔ cup tomato sauce

200 grams (7 oz) mushrooms, sliced

2½ cans (170 grams each) tuna in water, drained

200 grams (7 oz) cherry tomatoes, quartered

2 tablespoons bottled capers, rinsed

½ cup ricotta cheese

1 tablespoon olive oil

⅓ cup coarsely shredded fresh basil

1 Preheat the oven to 400°F (200°C). In a large bowl, combine the bread mix with the rosemary, then make up the dough and knead following the package instructions. Allow the dough to rest for about 5 minutes.

2 Using a rolling pin, roll out the dough to approximately fit a shallow roasting pan that measures about 27 x 40 cm. Push the dough into the corners to make a neat fit. Cover lightly with a clean dish towel and set aside in a warm place while you prepare the topping.

3 Place the anchovies in a small bowl and cover with the milk. Allow to soak for 5 minutes, then drain and finely chop. (This soaking will remove the excess salt from the anchovies.)

4 Spread the tomato sauce all over the pizza crust, right up to the edges. Scatter the sliced mushrooms over the pizza, then flake over the tuna. Dot the tomato pieces, capers and chopped anchovies all over. Using a teaspoon, add little mounds of ricotta over the top, then drizzle evenly with the olive oil.

5 Bake for 25 minutes or until well risen with a golden crust around the edge. Transfer to a wire rack to cool slightly, then cut into six pieces. Scatter the basil over the slices and serve warm.

VARIATIONS

• If your children do not like the strong flavours of anchovies and capers, replace them with diced red peppers, corn or cubed smoked ham.
• You could add a handful of sunflower seeds, pumpkin seeds or sesame seeds to the dough for a nutty flavour and texture.

EACH SERVING

25 g protein • 9 g fat of which 3 g saturates • 43 g carbohydrate
• 4 g fibre • 364 Calories

Chicken and spinach calzone

Calzone is an Italian pizza pocket that uses pizza dough to wrap up a filling. The delicious filling here is ready-cooked roast chicken mixed with spinach, peppers and creamy ricotta cheese. Serve with a side salad.

Serves 4

Preparation time 30 minutes,
  plus 15 minutes rising

Cooking time 15 minutes

2 cups white bread mix

1²/₃ cups frozen spinach, thawed in a sieve

³/₄ cup ricotta cheese

¹/₂ cup grated Parmesan cheese

4 large bottled roasted red pepper pieces, drained and chopped

6 scallions, finely chopped

2 tablespoons shredded fresh basil

grated nutmeg, to taste

200 grams (7 oz) skinless roast chicken, finely shredded

1 egg, beaten

VARIATION

• For vegetarian calzone, spread each dough round first with one-quarter of the ricotta cheese, then with 2 tablespoons tomato sauce. Top with lightly fried, sliced button mushrooms and sliced, cooked and peeled red peppers. Sprinkle with fresh thyme leaves and a cheese suitable for vegetarians.
Fold, seal and bake as in the main recipe.

1 Make up the dough according to the package instructions. Knead the dough briefly on a lightly floured work surface until smooth, then put into a lightly oiled bowl and cover with a clean dish towel. Leave to rise for about 15 minutes until doubled in size.

2 Meanwhile, prepare the filling. Use your hands to squeeze all excess water from the spinach. Put the spinach in a bowl and mix in the ricotta, Parmesan, peppers, scallions and basil. Season to taste with nutmeg, salt and freshly ground black pepper. Preheat the oven to 425°F (220°C).

3 Punch down the risen dough and cut it into four equal pieces. Roll out each piece on a lightly floured surface to a 20 cm round. Spread one-quarter of the spinach mixture over half of each dough round, taking it to about 2.5 cm from the edge. Pile the chicken on top.

4 Brush the edge of each dough round with beaten egg, then fold over the untopped half to make a half-moon shape. Crimp the edges to seal tightly.

5 Place on a lightly oiled large baking tray. Brush with beaten egg and bake for about 15 minutes until puffed and golden brown. Serve hot.

EACH SERVING

37 g protein • 16 g fat of which 7.5 g saturates • 58.5 g carbohydrate • 9.5 g fibre • 550 Calories

Potato pizza with chicken and arugula

For anyone who enjoys pizza, this rustic version with its wafer-thin sliced potato topping provides a lower-fat alternative. Scattered with pancetta, cooked chicken and peppery arugula leaves, these pizzas are satisfying to eat and quick to prepare using pre-made pizza crusts. Serve with a cherry tomato salad.

Serves 4

Preparation time 30 minutes

Cooking time 25 minutes

500 grams (1 lb) new potatoes, scrubbed

2 tablespoons olive oil

2 red onions, halved and very thinly sliced

75 grams (2²/₃ oz) pancetta, diced

175 grams (6 oz) button mushrooms, sliced

1 tablespoon fresh rosemary

2 pre-made pizza crusts,

6 tablespoons 1% milk

250 grams (½ lb) cooked, skinless chicken breast, shredded

90 grams (3 oz) arugula

2 tablespoons shaved Parmesan

VARIATIONS

• *For a vegetarian version, omit the chicken and pancetta and top the cooked pizzas with arugula, sliced, hard-boiled egg and thin slices of sun-dried tomato. Drizzle each pizza with 2 teaspoons of the oil from the sun-dried tomatoes. Grate an Italian-style hard cheese suitable for vegetarians (see page 9) over the tops.*

• *Flaked drained canned salmon is good with watercress instead of chicken and arugula. Drizzle the can juices from the salmon over the pizzas.*

1 Using a mandolin, a fine slicing disc in a food processor or a very sharp knife, cut the potatoes into wafer-thin slices. Cook in a large pot of lightly salted boiling water for 1–2 minutes until just tender, then drain. Preheat the oven to 425°F (220°C).

2 Heat the oil in a pan and lightly fry the onions with the pancetta for 2–3 minutes until softened, then add the mushrooms and cook for a further 2 minutes. Add the potatoes and rosemary, season with freshly ground black pepper and gently toss, without breaking up the slices.

3 Place the pizza crusts on two lightly greased baking trays, then spread the potato mixture evenly over the tops. Trickle the milk over the topping of both pizzas. Bake for 15 minutes until the potatoes are tender and golden.

4 Remove the pizzas from the oven, cut them into quarters and place two quarters on each plate. Equally divide the chicken among the pieces of pizza, then scatter the arugula and Parmesan shavings over the top. Serve at once.

EACH SERVING

39 g protein • 23.5 g fat of which 5.5 g saturates • 83 g carbohydrate • 9.5 g fibre • 717 Calories

Pita pizzettes

Made mainly from pantry ingredients, these mini pizzas are incredibly quick and easy to prepare. Topped with tasty ham, luscious pineapple and sweet corn kernels, they make a tasty snack and are much lower in salt than most bought pizzas.

Serves 4   Preparation time 15 minutes   Cooking time 15 minutes

4 whole wheat pita breads

¼ cup low-sodium
tomato paste

1 teaspoon olive oil

1 tablespoon chopped fresh oregano
or 1 teaspoon dried oregano

125 grams (¼ lb) lean sliced ham,
cut into thin strips

398 ml can pineapple pieces in
natural juice, drained

1¼ cups frozen corn kernels,
thawed

1¼ cups coarsely grated light
mozzarella cheese

1 Preheat the oven to 375°F (190°C). Place the pita breads on a baking tray. Mix together the tomato paste, olive oil and oregano, season with freshly ground black pepper, then thinly spread over the pitas.

2 Arrange half the strips of ham on top, then scatter with a mixture of pineapple pieces (if these are large, chop them into smaller pieces first) and corn. Top with the remaining ham strips, then sprinkle with mozzarella.

3 Bake the pizzettes for about 15 minutes until the cheese has melted and is beginning to brown. Remove from the oven and allow to cool for a few minutes before serving.

VARIATIONS

• *For tuna pizzettes, spread the pitas with ¼ cup red or green pesto instead of the tomato paste mixture. Drain a 170 gram can of tuna in water and use instead of the ham. Top each pizzette with a few halved, pitted black olives before serving.*
• *To make onion, blue cheese and walnut pizzettes, gently cook 2 thinly sliced red onions in 1 tablespoon olive oil for 7–8 minutes until softened. Mix with ¼ cup tomato paste, a pinch of dried mixed herbs and a pinch of pepper. Spoon over the pitas. Scatter with 150 grams chopped gorgonzola cheese. Bake for 8 minutes, then sprinkle with ⅓ cup chopped walnuts and bake for 3–4 minutes until the nuts are toasted.*

EACH SERVING

23 g protein • 12 g fat of which 5.5 g saturates • 56.5 g carbohydrate
• 9 g fibre • 445 Calories

Ciabatta with feta and vegetables

A feast of colourful vegetables makes a superb topping for a pizza-style ciabatta. The bread soaks up the aromatic roasting juices so that it is deliciously moist with a crunchy crust. If you want to boost your vegetable intake even more, serve it with a leafy herb salad.

Serves **4**   *Preparation time* **30 minutes**   *Cooking time* **35 minutes**

4 tomatoes, diced

¼ cup low-sodium tomato paste

2 garlic cloves, crushed

4 ciabattas, halved horizontally

1 tablespoon finely chopped fresh rosemary

1 teaspoon fennel seeds

¼ cup olive oil

1 eggplant, thinly sliced widthwise

1 red pepper, deseeded and cut into thin strips

1 yellow pepper, deseeded and cut into thin strips

1 tablespoon cider vinegar

1 teaspoon sugar

6 scallions, halved widthwise and cut into strips

pinch of chili flakes (optional)

100 grams (3½ oz) feta cheese, drained and finely crumbled

1 Heat the oven to 465°F (240°C). Mix the tomatoes, tomato paste and half the crushed garlic in a large bowl. Spread over the breads and set aside. In the same bowl, combine the rosemary, fennel seeds, olive oil and remaining garlic.

2 Lay the eggplant slices and pepper strips on a baking tray and brush sparingly all over with some of the herb oil. Bake for 8 minutes until the slices are just beginning to soften. Turn and bake for a further 8 minutes. Remove from the oven and reduce the temperature to 425°F (220°C).

3 Stir the cider vinegar and sugar into the remaining oil. Add the scallions, chili flakes (if using) and some pepper to season. Add the pepper strips and mix well.

4 Top the bread with half the mixed pepper mixture, cover with overlapping eggplant slices, then pile the remaining pepper mixture on top, drizzling over all the herb oil in the bowl. Place the ciabattas on the same baking tray that was used for roasting the vegetables. Top with the feta, pressing it down lightly with a fork, and bake for 10–15 minutes until the feta is golden and the vegetables are browned. Serve two ciabatta halves per portion.

EACH SERVING

18 g protein • 22.5 g fat of which 6 g saturates • 61.5 g carbohydrate • 10.5 g fibre • 543 Calories

Hot Florentine muffins

Toasted muffins, topped with wilted spinach and poached egg, then coated with a creamy yogourt and chive sauce, make a light yet luxurious lunch or supper dish.

Serves **4**

Preparation time *10 minutes*

Cooking time *20 minutes*

1 tablespoon vegetable oil

800 grams (1³/₄ lb) baby spinach leaves

4 eggs

1 teaspoon white wine vinegar

4 whole wheat English muffins, split

8 chives (optional)

YOGOURT AND CHIVE SAUCE

2 egg yolks

1 teaspoon Dijon mustard

¹/₂ cup Greek-style yogourt

8 chives, snipped

COOK'S TIP

• *The yogourt and chive sauce is a lower fat version of traditional hollandaise sauce. You can buy pre-made hollandaise sauce in jars from some supermarkets — but remember that it is high in fat and calories so use only 2 tablespoons per serving.*

1 First make the sauce. Whisk the egg yolks, mustard and yogourt in a heatproof bowl set over a large pot of simmering water (without letting the bowl touch the water) for about 10 minutes until thick, then remove from the heat. Add the chives and season to taste. Cover the bowl to keep the sauce warm.

2 Heat the oil in the pan, add the spinach and stir-fry over a medium heat for 2–3 minutes until wilted. Drain in a sieve, pressing down with the back of a spoon to remove excess moisture. Season to taste, then cover to keep warm.

3 To poach the eggs, fill the pot one-third with water. Add the vinegar and a pinch of salt and heat to simmering. Carefully break in the eggs, one at a time, and cook gently for 2–3 minutes until cooked as you like them, spooning the hot water over the yolks towards the end of the cooking time. Meanwhile, toast the muffins. Using a spatula or slotted spoon, lift the eggs from the water one at a time and drain on paper towel.

4 Divide the spinach among the muffin bases, place a poached egg on top and spoon over the warm sauce. Garnish with whole chives, if you like, sprinkle with pepper and rest the remaining toasted English muffin halves on the side.

EACH SERVING

3 g protein • 17 g fat of which 5 g saturates • 26.5 g carbohydrate • 16 g fibre • 383 Calories

Asparagus and prosciutto bruschetta

Why are the simplest dishes often the best? Here, a few fine ingredients lift this sandwich from the "something on toast" category to a special treat. It makes a delightful, balanced light lunch when fresh asparagus is in season.

Serves 4

Preparation time 5 minutes

Cooking time 15 minutes

200 grams (7 oz) asparagus, trimmed and halved lengthwise

¼ cup olive oil

250 grams (½ lb) cherry tomatoes

1 ciabatta loaf, sliced on the diagonal into 12 pieces

1 garlic clove, halved

50 grams (2 oz) baby arugula

65 grams (2¼ oz) prosciutto, torn into small pieces

¼ cup shaved Parmesan cheese

1 Preheat a cast-iron, ridged grill pan. Brush the asparagus spears with 1 tablespoon of the olive oil and season with freshly ground black pepper, then place in the pan with the cherry tomatoes. Cook for about 8 minutes, turning a few times, until tender and lightly charred. Remove and keep warm (If you don't have a ridged grill pan, cook the vegetables on a rack under a preheated broiler and shorten cooking time.)

2 Place the ciabatta slices on the grill pan and brown lightly on both sides. Rub the cut sides of the garlic over one side of each slice of toast, then arrange the toast on a large serving plate.

3 Divide the arugula among the pieces of toast and top with the asparagus and prosciutto and cherry tomatoes. Drizzle with the remaining oil and scatter the Parmesan shavings over each piece. Serve three pieces per person.

COOK'S TIP

• *Keep the stems of the asparagus spears to flavour a stock, or use in soups or risottos.*

EACH SERVING

13.5 g protein • 19 g fat of which 4 g saturates • 39.5 g carbohydrate • 4 g fibre • 190 Calories

Chicken, avocado and alfalfa club sandwich

This toasted, triple-decker sandwich is packed with creamy, mashed avocado, rich in healthy unsaturated fats. Lean chicken, juicy tomatoes and pretty alfalfa sprouts make up the rest of the tasty filling for this nourishing and satisfying bite.

Serves 2
Preparation time 15 minutes
Cooking time 10 minutes

1½ tablespoons lime juice

1 teaspoon olive oil

½ red onion, very thinly sliced

½ avocado

dash of Tabasco or chili sauce

2 tablespoons light mayonnaise

2 tablespoons chopped cilantro

6 slices whole wheat bread

175 grams (6 oz) cooked, skinless boneless chicken breasts, sliced

2 tomatoes, thinly sliced

¾ cup alfalfa sprouts

1 Whisk together 2 teaspoons of the lime juice, the olive oil and a little pepper in a small bowl. Add the onion slices and toss to coat. Set aside to allow the onion to mellow in flavour while you prepare the remaining ingredients.

2 Roughly mash the avocado with a fork. Add the remaining lime juice and the Tabasco or chili sauce, to taste, and keep mashing until the mixture is fairly smooth. Mix the mayonnaise with the cilantro.

3 Preheat a ridged grill pan over medium heat. Place the bread on the pan and cook for 2–3 minutes on each side until lightly browned.

4 Spread two slices of toast very thinly with some of the mayonnaise, then spread with half the mashed avocado, dividing it equally. Top with the chicken and onion slices. Spread another two slices of toast very thinly with mayonnaise, then place over the chicken filling, mayonnaise-side down. Spread half the remaining mayonnaise thinly over the tops of the sandwiches. Spread with the remaining avocado, then add a layer of sliced tomatoes and the sprouts.

5 Finally, spread the last of the mayonnaise over the last two slices of toast and place on the sandwiches, mayonnaise-side down. Press the sandwiches together, then cut each in half. Serve immediately.

COOK'S TIP
• *Bean sprouts are a source of vitamin C and B vitamins, and are easy to grow yourself. Rinse alfalfa or mung beans and place in a large jar. Half-fill with cold water, then cover with a piece of muslin secured with a rubber band. Leave to soak overnight, then pour off the water through the muslin. Refill the jar with fresh water, then drain and leave the jar on its side in a dark place. Repeat this process twice a day for 2 days until sprouted, then place the jar in a sunny place and continue rinsing for another day or two until the sprouts have grown to the desired size. Rinse well and discard any unsprouted beans before using.*

VARIATION
• *Grated carrot can be used instead of the alfalfa sprouts. Bean sprouts are also a good option — use about 1½ cups.*

EACH SERVING

34.5 g protein • 23 g fat of which 5 g saturates • 44.5 g carbohydrate • 9.5 g fibre • 546 Calories

Sardine and pepper toast

A no-cook recipe is perfect
for a light lunch when time
is short. Remember to
include the sardine bones
in the mixture, as they are
quite soft and mash easily,
adding valuable calcium to
the dish. The raw vegetables
have maximum food value
to keep you going on a busy
working day. Follow with
some juicy fresh fruit.

Serves 4

Preparation time 10 minutes

Cooking time Nil

2 x 105 gram cans sardines in
water, drained

2 celery stalks, finely chopped

1 red pepper, deseeded and
finely chopped

1 red onion, thinly sliced

¼ cup tomato paste

¼ cup lime juice

pinch of celery salt

4 thick slices whole wheat or
multigrain bread

75 grams (2²/₃ oz) watercress leaves

COOK'S TIP

*• When buying watercress,
always buy more than you need
because you will need to cut off
the stems and choose only the
tips of the leaves to use. If your
watercress has wilted, refresh
the picked leaves in a bowl of
cold water, then drain well.*

1 Lightly break up the sardines in a bowl with a fork. Add the chopped celery,
red pepper, onion, tomato paste and lime juice to the sardines. Season lightly
with celery salt and freshly ground black pepper.

2 Lightly toast the bread slices on both sides until golden. Divide the
watercress leaves among the slices and spoon the sardine mixture on top.
Serve immediately.

EACH SERVING

15.5 g protein • 6 g fat of which 1.5 g saturates • 20 g carbohydrate
• 5 g fibre • 208 Calories

Tuna melt

Boosted with vegetable goodness, this tasty treat is ideal for a quick, midweek supper dish. Crisp fennel and red pepper bring terrific texture contrast and a really fresh flavour to tuna and corn toasted on top of focaccia with a sprinkling of cheese.

Serves **4**   *Preparation time* **20 minutes**   *Cooking time* **10 minutes**

1 plain focaccia

1 small fennel bulb, finely diced

1 red pepper, deseeded and finely diced

2 scallions, thinly sliced

284 ml can corn, drained

170 gram can tuna in water, drained

1/3 cup light mayonnaise

1/2 cup finely grated Emmenthal or Gruyère cheese

90 grams (3 oz) watercress or mixed salad leaves

400 grams (14 oz) cherry tomatoes, halved

1/2 English cucumber, diced

1 Preheat the broiler. Slice the focaccia horizontally through the middle into two and place, cut-side down, on the grill tray. Grill for 1–2 minutes until browned, then turn the bread over and set aside on the grill tray. Reduce the heat to medium.

2 Lightly mix the fennel, pepper, scallions, corn and tuna into the mayonnaise. Season to taste with freshly ground black pepper. Divide this mixture among the focaccia halves, spread out and press down gently with a fork to cover the bread completely. Sprinkle with the cheese.

3 Place under the broiler, well away from the heat, and grill for 3–4 minutes until the cheese is melted and bubbling and just beginning to turn golden.

4 Meanwhile, divide the salad leaves among four plates. Cut each piece of toasted focaccia into four and place two pieces on each plate. Arrange the tomatoes and cucumber around the edge and serve at once.

EACH SERVING

24 g protein • 12 g fat of which 4 g saturates • 53.5 g carbohydrate • 7.5 g fibre • 441 Calories

VARIATIONS
* *Canned tuna in water makes an excellent substitute for the sardines.*
* *If you prefer cooked peppers, chargrill them first. Halve and deseed the peppers, then grill them, cut-side down, for about 5 minutes until the skins are blackened. Cool, then peel and chop finely.*

Roast pork and apple baguettes

For a really superb pork sandwich, spread a crusty baguette with spiced apple and shallot sauce and pack it with lean roast pork and fresh watercress.

Serves **4** *Preparation time* **25 minutes** *Cooking time* **20 minutes**

2 teaspoons olive oil

2 shallots, finely chopped

3 apples, peeled, cored and thinly sliced

1 lemon, juiced

7 tablespoons apple juice

1½ tablespoons superfine sugar

pinch of ground allspice

1 baguette

125 grams (¼ lb) lean roast pork, thickly sliced

50 grams (2 oz) watercress leaves

1 Heat the oil in a pot and gently fry the shallots for 5 minutes or until soft and just beginning to colour. Add the apples, lemon juice and apple juice and heat until bubbling. Cover the pan with a lid, reduce the heat to low and cook very gently for 5 minutes.

2 Stir in the sugar and allspice, increase the heat to medium and cook, uncovered, stirring occasionally, for 8–10 minutes until most of the liquid has evaporated and the apple is very tender and just beginning to break down.

3 Using a potato masher, partly mash the apples until they are semi-smooth but retain some of the chunky texture. Set aside until cool.

4 Cut the bread open lengthwise, keeping it still attached along one side like a hinge. With the baguette opened out flat, thickly spread both sides with the apple sauce. Fill with the sliced pork and watercress, then close up and press together. Slice across the loaf into two portions, then cut each portion in half again for serving.

COOK'S TIPS

• *To prepare the applesauce ahead, cook to the end of step 3, then cover and chill in the refrigerator for up to 3 days, or freeze and use within 2 months. The sauce is also good made with pears and freshly squeezed orange instead of apple juice.*
• *For the ultimate impromptu meal, use a good bottled applesauce.*

EACH SERVING

16 g protein • 7.5 g fat of which 1.5 g saturates • 61 g carbohydrate • 5 g fibre • 386 Calories

Toasted turkey and pastrami bagels

With pastrami (cured, smoked meat) and bagels, the inspiration for this thick, filling sandwich can only be Montreal. But unlike that city's favourite snack, this version includes herby, light cream cheese and lean turkey. It is perfect for a tasty lunch-time bite.

Serves 4   Preparation time 20 minutes   Cooking time 5 minutes

4 bagels (plain, poppy seed or sesame), split in half

½ cup light cream cheese

6 small gherkins, rinsed and finely chopped

¼ cup chopped fresh flat-leaf parsley

4 iceberg lettuce leaves

1 large tomato, cut into 4 slices

8 thin slices lean roast turkey breast

4 slices pastrami

1 Preheat the broiler. Put the bagels, cut-side up, on a grill tray and broil until golden brown and toasted.

2 Meanwhile, lightly beat the cream cheese, gherkins and parsley together in a small bowl.

3 Divide the cheese mixture into eight portions and spread over the toasted side of each bagel half.

4 Place a lettuce leaf on the bottom half of each bagel, folded to fit, then top with a thick slice of tomato followed by one-quarter of the turkey and pastrami, loosely folded. Put the tops back on the bagels and press together. Cut in half to serve.

VARIATIONS

• *Try thinly sliced smoked chicken instead of turkey.*
• *For a turkey bagel melt, omit the herby cream cheese, pastrami and gherkins. Split open the bagels, without cutting all the way through, and open flat like a book. Toast the cut side under the grill, then arrange the lettuce, thinly sliced tomatoes and turkey on top. Add 30 grams (1 oz) thinly sliced mozzarella cheese to each bagel, then pop back under the grill until the cheese melts. Serve at once.*

EACH SERVING

27.5 g protein • 8.5 g fat of which 4 g saturates • 55.5 g carbohydrate • 4 g fibre • 420 Calories

Chicken sloppy Joes

As the name suggests, this has a messy appearance — a bolognaise mixture served between whole wheat rolls — but it's a recipe all the family will love, and the filling can be prepared ahead or frozen. Lean ground chicken is used here as a healthy alternative to ground beef, but you could use either.

Serves 4

Preparation time 10 minutes

Cooking time 45 minutes

2 tablespoons vegetable oil

2 celery stalks, finely chopped

1 large onion, finely chopped

1 large carrot, peeled and finely chopped

1 eggplant, finely diced

1 garlic clove, crushed

500 grams (1 lb) lean ground chicken

398 ml can chopped tomatoes

½ cup water

2 teaspoons tomato paste

2 tablespoons chopped fresh basil

4 soft whole wheat bread rolls

VARIATIONS

• *Make this into a more sophisticated dish by spicing it up a little. Add 1 teaspoon chili powder (or to taste) with the vegetables as they are softening in step 1 and/or 1 deseeded and finely chopped red chili with the chicken in step 2.*

• *You can use ground turkey instead of the chicken.*

• *If you prefer the taste of fresh basil to cooked, stir in the basil just before assembling the sloppy Joes.*

1 Heat the oil in a large frying pan over a medium heat. Add the celery, onion, carrot, eggplant and garlic and fry for about 6 minutes, stirring occasionally, until the vegetables are softened.

2 Add the ground chicken to the pan, stirring well to break up the meat and mix with the vegetables. Cook for 5 minutes, stirring occasionally, until there is no trace of pink left in the chicken.

3 Stir in the canned tomatoes with their juice, and the water, tomato paste and basil. Bring the mixture to a boil, then reduce the heat, cover the pan and simmer gently for about 30 minutes, stirring occasionally, until the sauce has reduced and thickened slightly.

4 Just before serving, cut the rolls in half and lightly toast them. Spoon the chicken mixture over the bottom halves of the rolls, then cover with the top halves and serve immediately.

EACH SERVING

34.5 g protein • 22.5 g fat of which 4.5 g saturates • 44 g carbohydrate • 10 g fibre • 538 Calories

Beef and beet coleslaw rolls

A beet and red cabbage coleslaw brings a lively flourish of colour and texture to these hearty rolls, as well as providing a nourishing vegetable accompaniment to the lean roast beef filling. Choose whole wheat rolls for extra fibre.

Serves **4**

Preparation time **10 minutes**

Cooking time **Nil**

1/3 cup light mayonnaise

1 tablespoon whole-grain mustard

4 large whole wheat bread rolls

50 grams (2 oz) watercress or arugula leaves

300 grams (2/3 lb) lean rare roast beef, thinly sliced

200 grams (7 oz) red cabbage, finely shredded

1 small red onion, thinly sliced

150 grams (5 oz) cooked beets, peeled and coarsely grated

1/3 cup low-fat natural yogourt

VARIATION
• *For a horseradish mayonnaise, combine 2 teaspoons horseradish cream sauce, instead of the mustard, with the mayonnaise.*

1 In a large bowl, mix together the mayonnaise and mustard. Split the rolls in half and spread the bottom half of each one with this mixture.

2 Top these bases with the watercress or arugula and divide the slices of roast beef among them.

3 In the same bowl as used for the mayonnaise, make the coleslaw by mixing together the red cabbage, red onion and beets. Add the yogourt and stir together to coat. Pile the coleslaw on top of the beef, season with freshly ground black pepper, then put the tops of the rolls back on. Serve immediately.

EACH SERVING

31 g protein • 9.5 g fat of which 2.6 g saturates • 45.5 g carbohydrate • 8 g fibre • 408 Calories

Pork and apple burgers with chili sauce

Hamburgers are always popular for casual meals, but can be high in saturated fat. This lighter version, made with lean ground pork, apples and scallions is just as flavoursome. Spread with a little sweet chili sauce for a spicy kick.

Serves 4

Preparation time 15 minutes

Cooking time 15 minutes

300 grams (²/₃ lb) lean ground pork

2 small green apples, cored and grated

4 slices whole wheat bread with the crusts removed, made into crumbs

4 scallions, very finely chopped

1 garlic clove, crushed

30 grams (1 oz) fresh ginger, peeled and finely chopped

1 teaspoon dried thyme

pinch of cayenne pepper

8 romaine lettuce leaves, halved

½ English cucumber, thinly sliced

4 soft white bread rolls, split

1 tablespoon sweet chili sauce

COOK'S TIP

• *The pork patties can be shaped up to a day in advance and chilled until required. Remove from the refrigerator 10 minutes before you want to cook them. Raw patties can also be frozen.*

1 Put the pork, apples, breadcrumbs, scallions, garlic, ginger, thyme and cayenne pepper in a large bowl. Mix and squeeze together.

2 Shape the mixture into four balls, then press into flat patties about 10 cm in diameter and 1.5 cm thick. Preheat the broiler and set the shelf to the lowest position.

3 Place the patties on a sheet of foil on the grill tray. Grill until golden brown and cooked through, turning once.

4 Divide the lettuce leaves and cucumber slices among the bun bases. Place the patties on top, then spread with 1 teaspoon of the chili sauce. Cover with the bun tops and serve immediately.

EACH SERVING

25 g protein • 9 g fat of which 2.5 g saturates • 58.5 g carbohydrate • 7 g fibre • 430 Calories

Vegetarian burgers

These protein-packed veggie burgers are made with a delicious high-fibre combo of Brazil nuts and red kidney beans, plus carrots for moistness.

*Serves **4**   Preparation time **25 minutes**   Cooking time **15 minutes***

³/₄ cup Brazil nuts

3 carrots, peeled and cut into chunks

30 grams (1 oz) fresh flat-leaf parsley

2 garlic cloves, peeled

1 lemon, zest pared

2 teaspoons ground coriander

398 ml can red kidney beans, drained and rinsed

4 scallions

2 tablespoons vegetable oil

4 burger buns, split

90 grams (3 oz) baby arugula

½ English cucumber, thinly sliced

1 red onion, thinly sliced

CHUTNEY

2 crisp apples, peeled, quartered and cored

¹/₃ cup dried apricots, chopped

¹/₃ cup mango chutney, chopped if necessary

1 lemon, juiced

1 Preheat the broiler and set the shelf to the lowest position. Cover a baking tray with foil and grease it lightly with oil. Combine the nuts, carrots, parsley, garlic, lemon zest and ground coriander in a food processor and process until finely ground. Add the beans and scallions and briefly pulse the mixture, to chop the onions and crush the beans. Season to taste.

2 Divide the mixture into four and shape each portion into a patty about 10 cm wide and 2 cm thick. Place on the baking tray. (The patties can be prepared ahead, cooked or uncooked, and kept chilled, if more convenient.)

3 Brush the patties with half the oil, then grill for about 5 minutes until well browned and sizzling around the bottom. Turn them over and brush with the remaining oil, then grill for a further 5 minutes. Reduce the heat to medium and turn over once again. (They tend to crack and may spread slightly, so pat them gently to keep them neat.) Grill for a final 5 minutes or until browned. Pat the patties into shape, if necessary, and leave to stand for 2–3 minutes to firm up.

4 Meanwhile, coarsely grate the apples into a bowl. Stir in the apricots, chutney and lemon juice. Toast the cut sides of the burger buns.

5 Put a little arugula and cucumber on the bottom of each bun, add a patty and top with a spoonful of the chutney and a couple of onion rings. Replace the tops of the buns and serve, adding the remaining chutney and salad.

EACH SERVING

17 g protein • 33.5 g fat of which 6 g saturates • 73.5 g carbohydrate • 15.5 g fibre • 687 Calories

VARIATION

• *Using bottled chili sauce is a quick option, but it doesn't take long to make your own. Put 1 thinly sliced red chili in a small pot with 2 teaspoons arrowroot. Slowly stir in ¹/₃ cup lime juice, 2 tablespoons rice vinegar, 1 tablespoon soft brown sugar and 2 teaspoons fish sauce, stirring to blend. Put the pan over a high heat and bring to a boil, stirring until thickened. Remove from the heat and leave to cool.*

Mediterranean beefburgers with red-hot tomato salsa

Sun-dried tomatoes, garlic and herbs create a Mediterranean flavour, and a fresh chili and tomato salsa adds extra zing. Making your own burgers is so worthwhile, as they're much lower in fat than most pre-made burgers, and you can flavour them as you please.

Step 1

Step 3

Step 4

Serves **4**

Preparation time **15 minutes**

Cooking time **10 minutes**

500 grams (1 lb) lean ground beef

¼ cup whole wheat breadcrumbs

2 garlic cloves, crushed

¼ cup sun-dried tomatoes in oil, drained and finely chopped

2 tablespoons chopped cilantro

4 burger buns

50 grams (2 oz) arugula

TOMATO SALSA

250 grams (½ lb) vine-ripened tomatoes, finely diced

1 red pepper, deseeded and finely diced

½ mild green chili pepper, deseeded and finely chopped

1 red chili pepper, deseeded and finely chopped

2 teaspoons balsamic vinegar

1 tablespoon snipped fresh chives

1 tablespoon chopped cilantro

1 Preheat a barbecue or cast-iron grill pan to medium. Place the ground beef, breadcrumbs, garlic, sun-dried tomatoes and cilantro in a large bowl and use your hands to mix the ingredients together thoroughly.

2 Divide the mixture equally into four and shape into patties, about 10 cm across and a similar size to the buns.

3 Brush the grill rack or grill tray lightly with oil and cook the patties for 3–4 minutes on each side, until browned on the outside and cooked through.

4 To make the salsa, mix together all the ingredients in a bowl. Season to taste. You can chop all the salsa ingredients together in the food processor to save time – just use the pulse button to get the right consistency.

5 Split the buns in half and pop onto the barbecue rack or grill pan to toast lightly. Place a few arugula leaves on each base, top with a patty and add a spoonful of salsa, then replace the tops. Serve immediately.

EACH SERVING

34 g protein • 12 g fat of which 4 g saturates • 42 g carbohydrate • 5.5 g fibre • 428 Calories

• Make the patties in advance. Cover with plastic
wrap and refrigerate for up to 2 days, or freeze
for up to 1 month. Thaw before cooking. The
salsa can be made the day before and stored
in the refrigerator, covered with plastic wrap.

Honeyed five-spice chicken pockets

Five-spice powder — a fragrant mix of cinnamon, cloves, fennel seeds, star anise and Sichuan peppercorns — is used a great deal in Chinese cooking, and here it adds an Asian flavour to appetizing pita bread sandwiches.

Serves 4

*Preparation time 10 minutes, plus
  at least 30 minutes marinating*

Cooking time 25 minutes

¼ cup lemon juice

2 tablespoons honey

½ teaspoon five-spice powder

3 skinless chicken breasts

4 large whole wheat pita breads

3 romaine lettuce leaves, shredded

16 cherry tomatoes, halved

1 large carrot, peeled and coarsely grated

LEMON AND HERB YOGOURT DRESSING

½ cup low-fat plain yogourt

½ lemon, zest grated and juiced to yield 2 teaspoons juice

2 tablespoons chopped fresh flat-leaf parsley

VARIATION
• *Grilled chicken breasts also make a great sandwich filling. Lightly toast two slices of multigrain bread for each sandwich. Cover a slice of toast with mixed salad greens and sliced cucumber tossed with the lemon and herb dressing. Add the chicken slices, then top with second slice of toast.*

1 Put the lemon juice, honey and five-spice powder in a shallow dish large enough to hold the chicken breasts in a single layer, and mix together until well blended. Make three deep slashes in each chicken breast, then put into the dish. Rub the marinade all over the chicken, and well into the slashes. Cover with plastic wrap and marinate in the refrigerator for at least 30 minutes.

2 To make the dressing, blend together the yogourt, lemon zest and juice and the parsley and season to taste. Cover and chill until required.

3 Remove the chicken from the refrigerator to bring to room temperature. Preheat the grill to medium and line the grill tray with foil. Set the shelf on the lowest position. Put the chicken breasts on the tray and cook for about 20 minutes, basting occasionally with the marinade and turning halfway through cooking. Thinly slice the chicken on the diagonal and set aside to cool.

4 Sprinkle the pita breads with a little water and warm under the grill for 2–3 minutes. Meanwhile, toss the lettuce, tomatoes and carrot with the dressing. Slice open one side of each pita bread to make a pocket. Divide the chicken and salad among the pitas and serve immediately.

EACH SERVING

33.5 g protein • 8.5 g fat of which 2.5 g saturates • 66.5 g carbohydrate
• 8.5 grams fibre • 499 Calories

Falafel pitas

Falafel are spicy chickpea cakes. They are a popular street food all over the Middle East. Served in pita bread pockets with a colourful crunchy salad, they are deliciously healthy as well as fun to eat.

Serves 4

*Preparation time 20 minutes,
    plus 30 minutes chilling*

Cooking time 10 minutes

2 x 398 ml cans chickpeas, drained and rinsed

2 garlic cloves, crushed

1 teaspoon ground cumin

1 teaspoon ground coriander

1 green chili pepper, deseeded and finely chopped

2 tablespoons chopped cilantro

1 small egg, beaten

2 tablespoons all-purpose flour

2 tablespoons canola oil

4 whole wheat pita breads

½ lemon, juiced

⅓ cup hummus

SALAD

100 grams (3½ oz) red cabbage, finely shredded

1 carrot, peeled and coarsely grated

⅓ English cucumber, cut into matchsticks

1 small red onion, thinly sliced

COOK'S TIP
• If you'd like to make your own hummus, follow the recipe on page 78.

1 To make the falafel, put the chickpeas in a blender or food processor and process until smooth. Add the garlic, cumin and ground coriander and process again until well mixed. Add the chili pepper, cilantro, egg and 1 tablespoon of the flour and process again briefly. Season to taste. Transfer to a bowl and chill for about 30 minutes to firm the mixture.

2 Meanwhile, to prepare the salad, put the cabbage, carrot, cucumber and onion in a bowl and mix together.

3 Lightly flour your hands with the remaining flour and shape the chickpea mixture into eight patties. Heat the oil in a frying pan and fry the patties, in batches if necessary, for about 3 minutes on each side until crisp and golden. Drain well on paper towel.

4 Meanwhile, warm the pita breads in a toaster or under the grill and stir the lemon juice into the hummus to thin it slightly. Cut a slit lengthwise in the side of each bread to form a pocket. Spread 1 tablespoon of hummus inside each pocket, then stuff in two falafel with some salad. Serve immediately.

EACH SERVING

21 g protein • 17.5 g fat of which 3 g saturates • 67 g carbohydrate • 19 grams fibre • 547 Calories

Greek lamb koftas

Pan-fried lamb meatballs make a delicious filling for warm pita bread pockets, packed with a crisp cucumber and leafy salad. Serve with cherry tomatoes.

Serves 6

Preparation time 40 minutes

Cooking time 15 minutes

350 grams (12 oz) extra lean ground lamb

1 egg

2 large garlic cloves, crushed

1 tablespoon chopped fresh oregano or 1 teaspoon dried oregano

1 tablespoon chopped fresh thyme or 1/2 teaspoon dried thyme

1 large onion, finely chopped

1 3/4 cups fresh whole wheat breadcrumbs

1 tablespoon olive oil

1/2 cup chopped fresh herbs, such as basil, flat-leaf parsley and mint

6 scallions, thinly sliced

50 grams (2 oz) arugula

6 large pita breads

1 lemon, cut into six wedges

1/2 English cucumber, thinly sliced

1/3 cup low-fat plain yogourt

COOK'S TIP
• *The kofta can be prepared a day or two in advance and refrigerated or frozen until you are ready to cook them.*

EACH SERVING

23.5 g protein • 10.5 g fat of which 3 g saturates • 51 g carbohydrate • 5 grams fibre • 405 Calories

1 To make the kofta, put the lamb in a large bowl and break it up with a wooden spoon. Add the egg, garlic, oregano, thyme and onion and mix well. Add the breadcrumbs and use your hands to mix well.

2 Have a large board or plate ready, then roll the lamb mixture into 24 even walnut-sized balls. Flatten the balls slightly on the palm of your hand to make small patties, about 5 cm across and about 1 cm thick.

3 Heat the oil in a large frying pan. Add the koftas, nudging them up to each other — they should just about fit, as they shrink as they begin to cook. Cook over a high heat for 2 minutes until browned underneath, then turn them over and cook for a further 2 minutes. Reduce the heat to medium, turn the patties again and cook for about 8 minutes, shaking the pan occasionally, and turning the patties once more, until cooked through.

4 Meanwhile, mix the chopped fresh herbs with the scallions and arugula. Warm the pita breads in a toaster, turning them once.

5 Slit the pita breads open and place four koftas in each. Add some cucumber slices and herb salad and squeeze over a little lemon juice. Drizzle with yogourt and eat at once.

Cream cheese and smoked trout wraps

A delicious, moist filling of herby soft cheese and flaked, smoked fish is rolled up inside tortillas with crisp bean sprouts and salad leaves.

Serves 4   Preparation time 25 minutes   Cooking time 5 minutes

½ English cucumber, cut into matchsticks

8 soft flour tortillas

¾ cup reduced-fat cream cheese

⅓ cup low-fat plain yogourt

2 tablespoons snipped fresh chives

2 tablespoons chopped fresh dill

125 grams (¼ lb) skinless smoked trout, flaked

2 cups bean sprouts

125 grams (¼ lb) mixed baby leaf and herb salad

1 Preheat the oven to 400°F (200°C). Put the cucumber sticks in a bowl and sprinkle with a little salt. Mix well, then leave for about 10 minutes. (This draws out some of the moisture so that the filling in the wraps will remain crisp.)

2 Wrap the tortillas in foil and warm in the oven for 5 minutes, or according to the package instructions. Put the cream cheese, yogourt, chives and dill into a small bowl and mix together. Stir in the flaked trout and season to taste.

3 Separate the tortillas and spread out on two large boards (alternatively, you can prepare four tortillas at a time). Spread each tortilla with one-eighth of the trout mixture.

4 Rinse the cucumber in a sieve, then tip onto paper towel and pat dry. Divide among the tortillas, arranging them lengthwise so the tortillas will be easier to roll up. Scatter over the bean sprouts and salad leaves.

5 Roll up the tortillas tightly to enclose the filling. Cut each rolled tortilla in half on the diagonal and serve four pieces per person.

VARIATIONS

* *Smoked salmon or shredded smoked chicken breast would make equally delicious alternatives to the smoked trout used here.*
* *Wraps are also delicious filled with taramasalata. Spread the warm tortillas with 200 grams (7 oz) light taramasalata. Grind over a little black pepper, then scatter with ½ finely diced English cucumber and ½ deseeded and finely sliced yellow pepper. Sprinkle with the leaves of 2 shredded baby romaine lettuces before rolling up.*

VARIATIONS

* *Try ground pork with sage, or ground chicken or turkey with tarragon.*
* *Instead of filling pita breads, roll up the kofta and salad in wraps. Spread the yogourt over the wraps first.*
* *The cooked kofta could also be tossed with 2 x 398 ml cans of chickpeas, 200 grams (7 oz) halved cherry tomatoes and the herb salad, then topped with cucumber raita.*

EACH SERVING

18.5 g protein • 13 g fat of which 6.5 g saturates • 25 g carbohydrate • 3 grams fibre • 296 Calories

Spicy chicken fajitas

Satisfyingly spicy and quick to prepare, chicken and papaya fajitas make an easy, healthy meal. Sweetly fragrant papaya is rich in beta-carotene and its gorgeous colour enhances any dish.

Serves 4 (Makes 8)
Preparation time 10 minutes
Cooking time 10 minutes

2 large skinless chicken breasts

1½ tablespoons Cajun spice mixture

few drops of Tabasco, to taste

8 soft flour tortillas

1 papaya

¼ cup olive oil

juice of 1 lime

125 grams (¼ lb) mixed baby leaf salad or other delicate mixed salad greens

VARIATIONS

• *Slices of fresh mango would be good as an alternative to papaya.*
• *Cajun seasoning is a New Orleans-style blend of herbs and spices including chili powder, but you could use any similar spicy seasoning.*

1 Cut each chicken breast lengthwise into about eight long strips. Sprinkle the spice mixture over a plate, add the chicken strips and toss to coat. Sprinkle lightly with a little Tabasco, then set aside for 5 minutes.

2 Meanwhile, warm the tortillas, following the package instructions. Cut the papaya in half lengthwise and scoop out the seeds, then cut each half into eight slices and peel.

3 Heat 2 tablespoons of the oil in a large frying pan. Add the coated chicken strips and stir-fry for 6 minutes over a medium heat. Remove from the heat, sprinkle with half the lime juice and toss, scraping the residue from the pan.

4 Divide the salad leaves among the warm tortillas. Sprinkle over the rest of the oil and lime juice, then top with the chicken strips and slices of papaya. Season to taste, then roll up loosely and serve at once, allowing two per person.

EACH SERVING

48 g protein • 29 g fat of which 6 g saturates • 28.5 g carbohydrate • 4 grams fibre • 575 Calories

Mexican bean burritos

A fabulous vegetarian bite that's deliciously healthy as well as fun to eat. The bean and vegetable mixture has a great spicy kick, and is combined with crunchy salad, grated cheese and creamy yogourt in tortilla wraps.

Serves 4 (Makes 8)
Preparation time 15 minutes
Cooking time 10 minutes

8 soft flour tortillas

1 tablespoon canola oil

1 onion, chopped

2 garlic cloves, crushed

1 small green pepper, deseeded and chopped

1 small red pepper, deseeded and chopped

1 red chili pepper, deseeded and finely chopped (optional)

½ teaspoon ground cumin

398 ml can red kidney beans, drained and rinsed

1 cup frozen corn kernels

1 large tomato, chopped

¼ cup no-salt-added tomato sauce

1 tablespoon chili sauce

2 tablespoons water

2 tablespoons chopped cilantro

½ iceberg lettuce, shredded

½ cup grated mature cheddar cheese

½ cup low-fat plain yogourt

VARIATION
• *For a spicier version, include the seeds of the fresh chili pepper or add some chopped jalapeño peppers that you can buy in a jar at supermarkets.*

1 Warm the tortillas following the package instructions. Meanwhile, make the filling. Heat the oil in a large frying pan, add the onion, garlic and peppers and cook over a medium heat, stirring, for 3 minutes until they begin to soften. Add the red chili pepper (if using) and the ground cumin and stir for 1 minute.

2 Put the red kidney beans onto a plate and lightly crush with a fork, then add to the frying pan together with the corn and chopped tomato. Stir in the tomato and chili sauces and the water and continue to cook gently for about 4 minutes. Stir in the cilantro.

3 Serve the hot bean mixture, lettuce, cheese and yogourt in separate bowls for everyone to help themselves. To assemble a burrito, place some lettuce in the middle of a tortilla, spoon some of the bean mixture on top, add some grated cheese and top with a dollop of yogourt. Roll up and eat immediately.

EACH SERVING

16.5 g protein • 13.5 g fat of which 4 g saturates • 50 g carbohydrate
• 10 grams fibre • 410 Calories

Zucchini and onion eggah

The French have omelettes, the Spanish tortillas, the Italians frittatas and Arabic nations have eggahs. Eggahs are good served straight from the pan or left to cool as a light lunch or supper with a colourful salad.

Serves 4

Preparation time 10 minutes

Cooking time 25 minutes

⅓ cup olive oil

2 onions, very thinly sliced

2 garlic cloves, finely chopped

4 large eggs

⅓ cup 1% milk

⅓ cup chopped fresh flat-leaf parsley or cilantro

2 tablespoons chopped fresh dill (optional)

1 large zucchini, halved lengthwise, then thinly sliced

chili sauce or harissa (optional)

COOK'S TIPS

• *This can be made up to 2 days in advance and stored in the refrigerator until about 15 minutes before serving.*
• *This could serve two for a more substantial meal.*

VARIATION

• *For a chickpea and onion eggah, replace the zucchini with 2 x 398 ml cans of chickpeas, drained, omit step 3 and use just 2 tablespoons oil.*

1 Heat 1 tablespoon of the oil in a large, non-stick frying pan with a flameproof handle over a medium heat. Add the onions and stir for 3 minutes, then add the garlic and continue frying for a further 2–3 minutes, stirring occasionally, until the onion is soft and golden brown.

2 Meanwhile, beat the eggs and milk together in a large bowl with the herbs. When the onions are golden, stir them into the egg mixture.

3 Heat another 2 tablespoons of the oil in the pan. Add the zucchini and gently fry for about 5 minutes, stirring frequently, until tender and lightly browned. Add the zucchini to the egg mixture.

4 Add the remaining oil to the pan and swirl it around to coat the edge. Pour in the eggs and zucchini, using a spatula to spread them out. Leave the eggah to cook for about 8 minutes, shaking the pan occasionally, until the egg mixture is almost set and only a small amount of unset mixture remains on the surface. Meanwhile, preheat the grill to high and position the grill shelf about 10 cm from the heat.

5 Place the pan under the grill and grill the eggah for 2–3 minutes until the surface is just set. Run the spatula around the edge and invert onto a large platter. Serve immediately or set aside and leave to cool. Serve cut into wedges, sprinkled with chili sauce or harissa, if you like.

EACH SERVING

10 g protein • 24.5 g fat of which 4.5 g saturates • 5 g carbohydrate • 2 grams fibre • 283 Calories

Spanish tortilla

Colourful and packed with flavours, this thick, flat omelette, called a tortilla in Spanish, tastes good served at any temperature. The classic recipe contains only potatoes, onions and eggs, but this version has extra vegetables and tasty lean ham added. Serve with a green salad.

Serves 4

Preparation time 15 minutes

Cooking time 30 minutes

400 grams (14 oz) new potatoes, scrubbed and thinly sliced

1 cup frozen peas

¼ cup canola oil

1 large onion, halved and thinly sliced

2 large garlic cloves, crushed

6 large eggs

⅓ cup chopped fresh flat-leaf parsley

175 grams (6 oz) lean cooked ham, about 5 mm thick, chopped

6 cherry tomatoes, quartered

VARIATION

• *Extra or alternative vegetables can be added for variety and to suit your own preference. Why not try corn kernels, finely diced red or green peppers or thinly sliced zucchini?*

1 Bring a large pot of lightly salted water to a boil. Add the potatoes and peas and return to a boil. Reduce the heat and simmer for 3 minutes or until the potatoes are just beginning to soften. Drain and set aside.

2 Heat 2 tablespoons of the oil in a frying pan with a flameproof handle. When the oil is hot, reduce the heat to medium, add the onion and cook for 2 minutes. Add the garlic and cook for a further 3 minutes until the onion is soft, but not brown. Add the potatoes and peas and continue frying, stirring, for 5 minutes or until the potatoes are tender. Remove the pan from the heat.

3 In a large bowl, lightly beat the eggs with the parsley and a little black pepper, then stir in the ham, the potato, onion and pea mixture and the tomatoes.

4 Place the frying pan back over a medium heat, add the remaining oil and swirl it around. When the oil is hot, pour in the egg mixture, spreading it out evenly. Cook the tortilla for 5–7 minutes on a low heat, shaking the pan frequently, until the base is set. Use a spatula to loosen and lift the edges of the tortilla, allowing the uncooked egg mixture to run underneath. Meanwhile, preheat the grill to medium.

5 Place the pan under the grill and cook the tortilla for 5 minutes until it is golden and set. Pierce the top with a knife to make sure it is cooked through. Slide the tortilla onto a board and cool for 2 minutes. Serve cut into wedges.

EACH SERVING

24.5 g protein • 25.5 g fat of which 5.5 g saturates • 17 g carbohydrate • 5.5 grams fibre • 406 Calories

Broccoli and salmon frittata

A really fantastic midweek dish, this is so easy. And if you use frozen broccoli florets it is a great standby meal. Serve it at the table straight from the pan, with a fresh tomato salad and crusty bread.

Serves 4

Preparation time 10 minutes

Cooking time 15 minutes

2 cups broccoli florets

6 eggs

¼ cup snipped fresh chives

1 tablespoon canola oil

2 teaspoons unsalted butter

415 gram can red salmon, drained and flaked

1 cup canned or frozen corn kernels, thawed if necessary

2 tablespoons grated Parmesan cheese

1 Blanch the broccoli in a pot of lightly salted, boiling water for 4 minutes or until almost tender. Drain well and set aside.

2 Beat the eggs lightly with the chives and season with freshly ground black pepper. Heat the oil and butter in a large, heavy-based frying pan with a flameproof handle, then pour in the egg mixture. Scatter the broccoli, flaked salmon and corn over the egg, stirring lightly to distribute evenly.

3 Using a spatula, pull the sides of the egg mixture in slightly to allow the uncooked egg to set, and cook for 3–4 minutes until the underside is golden and the top almost set.

4 Meanwhile, heat the grill to high. Sprinkle the Parmesan over the top of the frittata, then place it under the grill. Cook for 2–3 minutes until the top is bubbling and golden. Serve cut into quarters.

EACH SERVING

34.5 g protein • 24.5 g fat of which 8 g saturates • 8 g carbohydrate • 3 grams fibre • 398 Calories

Watercress, cheddar and tomato omelette

Watercress teams well with eggs and is highly nutritious, providing iron and beta-carotene. The cheddar cheese supplies plenty of taste without too much fat. Serve with crusty French bread for a well-balanced meal.

Serves 1

Preparation time 10 minutes

Cooking time 5 minutes

2 eggs

1 tablespoon cold water

2 teaspoons unsalted butter

2 ripe roma tomatoes, peeled and chopped

¼ cup grated reduced-fat cheddar cheese

30 grams (1 oz) watercress leaves, roughly chopped

COOK'S TIP

• Roma tomatoes are a good variety to use here as they are firm-fleshed and less watery than regular tomatoes.

1 Using a fork, whisk the eggs with the water and freshly ground black pepper in a bowl until frothy.

2 Heat the butter in an omelette pan or non-stick frying pan over a medium heat until foaming. Tilt the pan to coat the bottom with the butter, then pour in the beaten egg mixture. Cook for about 1 minute, stirring gently with a spatula and pulling the cooked egg in from the edges so that the unset egg runs onto the hot pan and starts cooking.

3 When the egg is lightly set, stop stirring and scatter the chopped tomatoes into the pan. Cook for a further 30 seconds or until the egg is just set and golden underneath. Remove from the heat.

4 Sprinkle the cheese and watercress over the omelette, then slide the omelette onto a warmed plate, folding it over in half as it slides from the pan. Serve immediately.

EACH SERVING

27 g protein • 21 g fat of which 10 g saturates • 7 g carbohydrate • 5 grams fibre • 335 Calories

Shrimp and vegetable foo yong

This Chinese-style dish starts with a stir-fry of colourful vegetables and shrimp
that is then layered with omelette underneath and omelette ribbons over the top.

Serves 4

Preparation time 15 minutes

Cooking time 15 minutes

8 eggs

1 teaspoon sesame oil

¼ cup chopped cilantro (optional)

2 teaspoons cornstarch

1 tablespoon salt-reduced
soy sauce

2 tablespoons dry or medium sherry

2 tablespoons canola oil

2¼ cup broccoli florets, thinly
sliced

1 orange or red pepper, deseeded
and thinly sliced

50 grams (2 oz) fresh ginger,
peeled and cut into thin strips

2 garlic cloves, chopped

4 scallions, sliced

350 grams (12 oz) peeled raw
shrimp, thawed and drained if
frozen

1½ cups bean sprouts

VARIATIONS
• *Frozen stir-fry vegetable mixes
are ideal for making foo yong in
a hurry.*
• *Omit the shrimp for a
vegetarian version.*

1 Beat the eggs with the sesame oil and cilantro, if using, then set aside. Mix
the cornstarch to a smooth paste with the soy sauce and sherry; set aside.

2 Heat half the canola oil in a large frying pan or wok. Add the broccoli,
pepper, ginger, garlic and scallions, and stir-fry for 5 minutes or until the
broccoli looks bright green and is just tender. Pour in the cornstarch mixture and
stir for 1 minute.

3 Add the shrimp and cook for 2 minutes, then add the bean sprouts and cook
for a further 1 minute or until the shrimp are pink. Transfer to a large bowl,
including all the juices, and keep warm. Wipe the pan with a piece of paper towel.

4 Add the remaining canola oil to the pan and heat it for a few seconds. Pour
in just over half the egg mixture and swirl the pan to spread it out evenly.
Stir once or twice, then let the egg set for about 3 minutes. Loosen the omelette
with a spatula and transfer it to a serving dish.

5 Add the remaining egg mixture to the pan and cook for 1–2 minutes until
just set. Turn out onto a board and cut into ribbons. Spoon the vegetables
on top of the whole omelette, then scatter with the omelette ribbons and serve.

EACH SERVING

38 g protein • 22.5 g fat of which 5 g saturates • 7 g carbohydrate
• 6 grams fibre • 402 Calories

Spiced pea and corn pancakes

It's always a treat to have pancakes. These high-fibre, oaty mini ones are mildly spicy and packed with juicy corn and peas. Serve with a simple salad for a nutritious casual meal.

Serves 4 (Makes 12)
Preparation time 25 minutes
Cooking time 20 minutes

½ cup all-purpose flour

¼ cup whole wheat flour

1½ teaspoons baking powder

¼ cup rolled oats

2 teaspoons curry paste, or to taste

½ cup plus 2 tablespoons 1% milk

2 eggs, lightly beaten

1 cup canned or frozen corn kernels, thawed if necessary

½ red pepper, deseeded and diced

1⅓ cups frozen peas, thawed

2 tablespoons canola oil

1 Sift the plain and whole wheat flours and baking powder into a bowl, adding any bran left in the sieve. Stir in the oats.

2 Blend the curry paste with 2 tablespoons of the milk, then stir this into the remaining milk.

3 Make a well in the middle of the dry ingredients and add the eggs and milk. Gradually beat in the flour and oats to make a smooth batter. (Alternatively, the batter can be made in a food processor: put the eggs, milk and curry paste in a food processor or blender, add the flours and process to a smooth paste. Add the oats and process for a few more seconds.) Leave the batter to stand for 5 minutes to thicken.

4 Meanwhile, tip the corn kernels, diced pepper and peas onto a plate lined with several sheets of paper towel, to soak up any excess moisture. Add the vegetables to the batter, then lightly season and stir together well.

5 Heat a large, heavy-based frying pan, preferably non-stick, over a medium heat, then brush with a little of the oil. Using a large spoonful of batter per pancake, cook them in batches for 2–3 minutes until dark golden. Turn the pancakes over using a spatula, then cook the other side for 2–3 minutes. Remove from the pan and keep warm in a low oven while you cook the remaining batter. You should get 12 pancakes in total. Serve hot.

EACH SERVING

12.5 g protein • 14.5 g fat of which 2.5 g saturates • 35.5 g carbohydrate • 6 grams fibre • 334 Calories

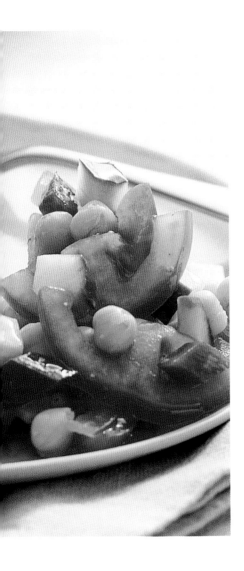

Cheesy chicken and vegetable pancakes

If you have some cooked chicken left over from a roast, why not use it to make this quick filling for savoury pancakes?

Serves **4** *Preparation time* **25 minutes** *Cooking time* **1 hour**

PANCAKES

¾ cup all-purpose flour

1 egg, beaten

1¼ cups 1% milk

2 tablespoons canola oil

FILLING

1 cup frozen peas

1⅔ cups frozen broccoli florets

1 tablespoon butter

1 small onion, finely chopped

¼ cup all-purpose flour

1¼ cups 1% milk

250 grams (½ lb) skinless roast chicken meat, cut into thin strips

2 teaspoons chopped fresh tarragon or 1 teaspoon dried tarragon

2 tablespoons finely grated aged cheddar or Parmesan cheese

1 Preheat the oven to 375°F (190°C). For batter, sift the flour into a bowl, add the egg and a pinch of salt, then gradually whisk in the milk to form a smooth batter. (This can be done in a blender or food processor.) Transfer to a jug.

2 Heat a frying pan, preferably non-stick, and brush lightly with a little oil. Pour one-eighth of the batter into the pan and quickly swirl to coat the bottom. Cook for 1–2 minutes until set, then flip over and cook the other side. Remove and place on paper towel. Repeat to make eight pancakes, greasing the pan with oil as necessary. Stack the pancakes, interleaved with paper towel or baking paper. (The pancakes can be frozen.)

3 To make the filling, cook the peas and broccoli in a pot of boiling water, or in the microwave, following the package instructions. Drain, then roughly chop the broccoli. Meanwhile, melt the butter in a pot, add the onion and cook gently for 3–4 minutes until softened. Add the flour and cook, stirring, for 1 minute, then gradually stir in the milk. Bring to a boil, still stirring, then simmer for 2–3 minutes. Stir in the chicken, peas, broccoli and tarragon and season.

4 Spoon some filling onto the centre of each pancake, spreading it out a little, then roll up to enclose the filling. Arrange the filled pancakes, in a single layer, in a lightly greased, shallow oblong ovenproof dish, such as a lasagna dish, then sprinkle evenly with the cheese. Bake for 25 minutes or until golden.

COOK'S TIP
• *The batter can be made a day in advance and kept in the refrigerator.*

EACH SERVING

32 g protein • 24 g fat of which 8 g saturates • 37 g carbohydrate • 5 grams fibre • 501 Calories

COOK'S TIPS
• *These can be made in advance, then gently warmed in a medium oven before serving.*
• *For vegetarians, pick a curry paste that does not contain shrimp paste.*

VARIATION
• *To make chili and cilantro pancakes, omit the curry paste and peas and use a 398 ml can of corn, drained, 1 deseeded and finely chopped red chili pepper and ¼ cup chopped cilantro.*

Baked spinach and ham pancakes

You can cook the pancakes well in advance. Assemble the whole dish, then bake just before serving. The pancakes are made with half whole wheat flour and half all-purpose flour to be light yet higher in fibre than regular pancakes.

Serves 4

Preparation time 15 minutes

Cooking time 45 minutes

PANCAKES

⅓ cup all-purpose flour

⅓ cup whole wheat flour

1 egg

1 cup 1% milk

2 tablespoons canola oil

FILLING

1 tablespoon olive oil

6 scallions, sliced

2 cups mushrooms, sliced

6½ cups spinach

150 grams (5 oz) cooked smoked ham, diced

½ teaspoon grated nutmeg

1 cup reduced-fat ricotta cheese

¼ cup grated Parmesan cheese

1 Preheat the oven to 400°F (200°C). To make the pancakes, sift both flours into a bowl, adding any bran left in the sieve to the bowl. Add the egg and a pinch of salt, then gradually whisk in the milk to form a smooth batter. (This can be done in a blender or food processor.) Transfer to a jug.

2 Heat a frying pan to very hot and brush lightly with some of the oil. Pour a little pancake batter into the pan and quickly swirl around to coat the base evenly. When the batter is set and the underside is lightly browned, turn the pancake and cook the other side until golden. Remove and place on paper towel. Repeat with the remaining batter to make eight pancakes. Stack them, interleaved with paper towel or baking paper. (The pancakes can be frozen.)

3 To make the filling, heat the oil in the frying pan and fry the scallions and mushrooms for 2–3 minutes to soften. On a high heat, add the spinach leaves, stirring until the leaves wilt and all the excess liquid has evaporated. Remove from the heat and stir in the ham. Add the nutmeg and season to taste.

4 Lay the pancakes out flat and spoon a little ricotta onto each. Top with one-eighth of the mushroom and spinach mixture, then roll up.

5 Place the pancakes, seam-sides down, in a lightly oiled, shallow ovenproof dish. Sprinkle with Parmesan and bake for 15 minutes until thoroughly heated and lightly browned. Serve hot.

EACH SERVING

26 g protein • 27 g fat of which 8.5 g saturates • 23.5 g carbohydrate • 7.5 grams fibre • 451 Calories

COOK'S TIPS

• *Make sure you dry the spinach as much as possible after washing, or the pancake filling will be too watery.*

• *The pancake batter can be made up to a day ahead and kept, covered, in the refrigerator.*

VARIATION

• *For a vegetarian version, omit the ham, add 50 grams chopped walnuts or toasted pine nuts to the filling and use Italian-style hard cheese in place of Parmesan.*

Tuna and corn pots

This is modern-day comfort food, combining an interesting fusion of tuna and mixed vegetables in sauce with a crisp topping of bread cubes, tangy feta and diced tomatoes.

Serves 4

Preparation time 15 minutes

Cooking time 25 minutes

250 grams (½ lb) thin green beans, cut into 2.5 cm lengths (or frozen cut green beans)

2 tablespoons cornstarch

1 can (170 grams) tuna in water

1¼ cups 1% milk

1⅓ cups frozen corn kernels, thawed

4 scallions, thinly sliced

4 tomatoes, diced

100 grams (3½ oz) feta cheese, drained and finely diced or crumbled

1 tablespoon olive oil

4 thick slices whole wheat bread with crusts on, diced

1 Preheat the oven to 425°F (220°C). Place the beans in a pot and cover with boiling water, then bring back to a boil and cook for 3 minutes. Drain and set aside.

2 Mix the cornstarch with the water from the tuna in the same pot. Stir with a whisk until smooth, then stir in the milk. Bring to a boil, whisking vigorously until the sauce is thickened and smooth. Remove the pan from the heat.

3 Use a spoon to stir the corn into the sauce, then stir in the scallions, beans and tuna. Season to taste. Divide this mixture among four individual ovenproof soufflé or gratin dishes, each about 300 ml capacity. Alternatively, turn the mixture into a 1.5 litre ovenproof dish.

4 Mix the tomatoes, feta cheese and olive oil together in a bowl. Stir in the diced bread until thoroughly combined. Pile this mixture on top of the tuna sauce, pressing it on gently with your fingers so that it will stay in place without squashing the topping.

5 Bake the tuna and corn pots for 15 minutes or until the bread is browned and crisp, the cheese has softened and the tomatoes are lightly cooked. Underneath, the tuna mixture should be bubbling and piping hot. Serve at once.

EACH SERVING

25 g protein • 15 g fat of which 6 g saturates • 40 g carbohydrate • 8 grams fibre • 411 Calories

Cauliflower and Stilton soufflé

A soufflé is always bound to impress. Here's a classic combo that adds vegetable value to a light and fluffy soufflé. Serve straight from the oven, with whole wheat bread and a tomato salad.

Serves **4** *Preparation time* **15 minutes** *Cooking time* **50 minutes**

1 teaspoon unsalted butter

2 tablespoons grated Parmesan cheese

1½ tablespoons fine dry breadcrumbs

1 small cauliflower

1¼ cups 1% milk

¼ cup cornstarch

1 bay leaf

4 eggs, separated

90 grams (3 oz) white Stilton cheese or strongly flavoured cheese, finely crumbled

1 tablespoon whole-grain mustard

2 tablespoons snipped fresh chives

1 Preheat the oven to 375°F (190°C) and put a baking tray in the oven to heat. Lightly grease a large soufflé dish (about 1.75 litres) with the butter. Mix together the Parmesan and breadcrumbs and sprinkle half of this mixture over the bottom and side of the dish, turning the dish to coat evenly. Set aside.

2 Cut the cauliflower into small florets and cook in a steamer over boiling water for 8–10 minutes until very tender. Tip onto a plate and leave to cool for a few minutes, then purée with 100 ml of the milk in a food processor or blender to a smooth consistency.

3 Mix the cornstarch with a little of the remaining milk to make a smooth paste. Heat the rest of the milk until almost boiling, then pour onto the cornstarch mixture, stirring constantly. Return to the pan, add the bay leaf and stir over a medium heat until the sauce is thickened and smooth.

4 Pour the sauce into a large bowl and remove the bay leaf. Beat in the egg yolks, one at a time. Add the Stilton and stir until melted, then stir in the cauliflower purée, mustard and chives. Season to taste.

5 Whisk the egg whites in a large, clean bowl, until stiff peaks form. Whisk one-third of the whites into the sauce mixture to lighten it, then gently fold in the rest of the whites.

6 Spoon the mixture into the prepared soufflé dish and sprinkle the top with the remaining breadcrumb mixture. Set the dish on the hot baking tray and bake for 35 minutes or until well risen and golden brown. Serve at once.

COOK'S TIP
• *For an extra cheesy taste, grate some cheddar or Parmesan cheese over the top of each pot before cooking them.*

EACH SERVING

18 g protein • 15.5 g fat of which 8 g saturates • 16 g carbohydrate • 2 grams fibre • 278 Calories

COOK'S TIP
• You will know the egg whites are stiff enough when you can turn the bowl upside down without them falling out.

Spinach and goat's cheese soufflé

This is a light, cheesy soufflé topping with a tasty base of baby spinach leaves.
Serve for a summer lunch with crusty bread and a green salad.

Step 2

Step 3

Step 4

Serves 4

Preparation time 15 minutes

Cooking time 45 minutes

2 tablespoons fine dry breadcrumbs

1 tablespoon unsalted butter

2 tablespoons all-purpose flour

1 cup 1% milk, warm

grated nutmeg, to taste

500 grams (1 lb) baby spinach leaves, rinsed

4 eggs, separated

60 grams (2 oz) soft rindless goat's cheese, crumbled

¼ cup grated Parmesan cheese

1 teaspoon Dijon mustard

1 Preheat the oven to 400°F (200°C) and put a baking tray in the oven to heat. Lightly oil the inside of a medium soufflé dish (about 1.25 litres). Sprinkle with the breadcrumbs, then tilt the dish and tap around the edge to distribute evenly.

2 Melt the butter in a pot over a medium heat. Sprinkle in the flour, then cook for 1 minute, stirring all the time. Slowly add the milk, whisking constantly, until the sauce comes to a boil and thickens. Simmer for 2 minutes, stirring occasionally, then season with nutmeg and salt and pepper to taste. Meanwhile, gently steam the spinach leaves with just the water clinging to their leaves until dark green. Squeeze out all excess water and season to taste.

3 Remove the sauce from the heat and cool slightly, then beat in the egg yolks, one at a time. Stir in the spinach leaves. Add the goat's cheese, half the Parmesan and the mustard and beat well to mix. Return the pan to the heat and reheat gently, just until the cheese has melted to make a thick, smooth sauce. Set aside to cool.

4 Whisk the egg whites in a large, clean bowl until stiff peaks form. Whisk one-third of the egg whites into the soufflé mixture to lighten, then use a large metal spoon to fold in the remaining whites.

5 Spoon the cheese mixture into the soufflé dish and sprinkle with the remaining Parmesan. Place on the preheated baking tray and bake for 30–40 minutes until well risen and golden. Serve at once.

EACH SERVING

18 g protein • 16 g fat of which 8 g saturates • 12 g carbohydrate • 8.5 grams fibre • 278 Calories

Flamenco eggs

This spectacular Spanish-style egg and vegetable dish looks wonderful and is incredibly easy to cook for a light lunch or supper. Serve with crusty bread.

Serves 4

Preparation time 10 minutes

Cooking time 40 minutes

350 grams (12 oz) potatoes, peeled and cut into small dice

1 tablespoon olive oil

1 red onion, thinly sliced

1 garlic clove, crushed

1 red pepper, deseeded and thinly sliced

1 green pepper, deseeded and thinly sliced

1 yellow pepper, deseeded and thinly sliced

2 zucchini, sliced

6 tomatoes, cut into chunks

2 tablespoons chopped fresh oregano or 2 teaspoons dried oregano

4 large eggs

COOK'S TIP

• *Using three different colours of peppers is very colourful, but if you prefer, you could choose just one variety.*

1 Parboil the potatoes in a pot of lightly salted boiling water for 5 minutes. Drain and set aside.

2 Heat the oil in a large, deep frying pan and fry the onion and garlic over a medium heat for 2–3 minutes to soften. Add the peppers and zucchini and fry, stirring occasionally, for a further 10 minutes.

3 Add the potatoes and tomatoes and continue cooking, stirring occasionally, for 6–8 minutes or until all the vegetables are tender.

4 Stir in the oregano and season to taste. Make four hollows in the vegetable mixture and break an egg into each hollow. Cover the pan, with a lid or a baking tray, and cook for 8–10 minutes or until the egg whites are set. Serve immediately while piping hot.

EACH SERVING

14 g protein • 11 g fat of which 2.5 g saturates • 20.5 g carbohydrate • 6.5 grams fibre • 247 Calories

Pasta, asparagus and pea frittata

Little soup pasta shapes make a great filling for this Italian-style flat omelette with tender sliced asparagus and frozen peas. It's delicious served hot, warm or cold, with a simple salad for a light meal. Add some garlic bread for a more hearty meal.

Serves 4   Preparation time 15 minutes   Cooking time 20 minutes

250 grams (½ lb) asparagus, trimmed

1¼ cups frozen peas

150 grams (5 oz) soup pasta, such as small bows or shells

8 eggs

6 scallions, thinly sliced

2 tablespoons chopped fresh mint

2 tablespoons olive oil

½ cup grated cheddar cheese

1 Half-fill a large frying pan with water and bring to a boil. Add the asparagus and cook for 4–5 minutes until the spears are just tender. Lift them out with tongs or a slotted spoon, transfer to a board and leave until they are cool enough to handle.

2 Bring the water in the pan back to a boil. Add the peas and pasta, bring back to a boil again and cook for 5 minutes or until tender.

3 Meanwhile, beat the eggs in a large bowl. Cut the tips off the asparagus and set them aside. Slice the asparagus stalks and add to the eggs together with the scallions and mint. Drain the pasta and peas and immediately stir them into the egg mixture.

4 Preheat the grill to high. Dry the frying pan, then heat the oil over a medium heat. Pour in the egg mixture, making sure all the ingredients are evenly distributed. Reduce the heat slightly and cook for about 5 minutes until the omelette is two-thirds set, but still moist on top, and browned underneath.

5 Sprinkle the cheese over the frittata and place under the grill. Cook for about 5 minutes to brown the top. Cut into four large wedges and serve garnished with the reserved asparagus tips.

VARIATIONS

• *For a non-vegetarian version, fry about 150 grams chopped back bacon with the onion in step 2. Or, for a spicier flavour, add skinned diced chorizo.*
• *Smoked salmon pieces can also be added at the start of step 4.*

COOK'S TIP

• *The trick for a perfect frittata is to cook over a medium to low heat and allow the mixture to set slowly without stirring. Stirring once the egg has begun to set will break the mixture apart. Too high a heat will burn the base before the egg is set sufficiently to finish under the grill.*

EACH SERVING

25 g protein • 24.5 g fat of which 7 g saturates • 28 g carbohydrate
• 6.5 grams fibre • 444 Calories

Rice, pasta and grains

Healthy and versatile, grain-based dishes make great comfort food and are perfect for both easy family meals and entertaining. Rice and other grains like barley and buckwheat help to boost your regular intake of slowly-digested carbohydrates, and they are wonderfully useful pantry ingredients. Enjoy rice-, pasta- and grain-based classics from around the world. Choose from simple pasta meals that are perfect for weeknight suppers; creamy risottos that will warm up the coldest evening; and impressive paellas for entertaining.

Pumpkin and corn risotto

A vibrant, golden yellow vegetarian risotto that looks good, tastes wonderful and is packed with healthy beta-carotene and fibre. The mozzarella added right at the end melts into creamy goodness. Serve with a crisp green leaf salad.

Step 2

Step 3

Step 4

Serves **4**

Preparation time **15 minutes**

Cooking time **30 minutes**

2 tablespoons olive oil

1 onion, finely chopped

1 garlic clove, crushed

1 cup risotto rice

500 grams (1 lb) pumpkin or
1 small butternut squash, peeled,
deseeded and cut into 1 cm pieces

2 large fresh sage leaves,
finely chopped

pinch of saffron threads

3⅓ cup plus 2 tablespoons diluted
salt-reduced or homemade
vegetable stock (page 29), hot

¾ cup frozen corn kernels

125 grams (¼ lb) mozzarella
cheese, diced

⅓ cup pumpkin seeds

COOK'S TIP

*• The secret of a good risotto
lies in using the right rice —
arborio, carnaroli or vialone
nano — and a well-flavoured
stock that should be added to
the risotto gradually.*

1 Heat the oil in a large, heavy-based pot over a medium heat. Stir in the onion and garlic and cook gently for 4–5 minutes until softened but not browned, stirring occasionally.

2 Stir in the rice, pumpkin and sage leaves and cook for 2 minutes longer. Stir the saffron into the hot stock, then pour about one-quarter of the stock into the pan and stir well until it has almost all been absorbed, stirring frequently.

3 Continue adding the stock, only a ladleful at a time, making sure each is almost completely absorbed before adding the next, and stirring frequently to produce a creamy texture.

4 With the last addition of stock, add the corn and stir well. Once all the stock has been absorbed and the rice is tender (this will take about 20 minutes), stir in the mozzarella cheese.

5 Season to taste, then cover the pot and allow to stand for about 5 minutes. Sprinkle the risotto with the pumpkin seeds and serve at once.

EACH SERVING

20.5 g protein • 22 g fat of which 6 g saturates • 62.5 g carbohydrate
• 4 g fibre • 420 Calories

VARIATIONS

• In summer you can replace the pumpkin with zucchini. Cut into small pieces and add to the risotto with the corn in step 4 as it does not need a long cooking time.

• For a greener version of this risotto, omit the saffron, sage and pumpkin and add 150 grams (5 oz) chopped spinach leaves and 2 tablespoons chopped fresh basil leaves with the corn in step 4.

Spring vegetable risotto

Risotto is comfort food at its best, and you can easily change the basic recipe to suit the season by adding almost any fresh ingredients you have at hand.

Serves *4*

Preparation time *15 minutes*

Cooking time *30 minutes*

4 cups diluted salt-reduced or homemade vegetable stock (page 29)

1 bunch asparagus, trimmed

100 grams (3½ oz) baby carrots, halved lengthwise

200 grams (7 oz) fresh young peas, shelled

500 grams (1 lb) baby fava beans, shelled

2 tablespoons olive oil

2 baby leeks, trimmed and thinly sliced

1½ cups risotto rice

1 tablespoon pesto

2 tablespoons pine nuts, toasted

VARIATION
• *When fresh peas and fava beans are not in season, use frozen peas and fava beans.*

1 Bring the stock to a boil in a large pot, then reduce the heat, add the asparagus, carrots, peas and fava beans and simmer for 4–5 minutes until the vegetables are tender. Remove the vegetables with a slotted spoon and set aside. Keep the stock simmering over a gentle heat.

2 Meanwhile, heat the oil in a large, heavy-based frying pan and add the leeks. Stir-fry for 2 minutes until they are bright green, then stir in the rice.

3 Add 2–3 tablespoons of the hot stock and cook gently, stirring until the liquid is absorbed. Continue adding the stock, only a ladleful at a time, making sure each is almost completely absorbed before adding the next, and stirring frequently to produce a creamy texture.

4 Once all the stock has been absorbed and the rice is tender (this will take about 20 minutes), stir in the pesto and season to taste. Gently stir in the asparagus, carrots, peas and beans and cook for a few more minutes until the vegetables are heated through. Serve in heated soup plates and scatter the pine nuts over the top.

EACH SERVING

21 g protein • 16 g fat of which 2.5 g saturates • 78 g carbohydrate • 12 g fibre • 392 Calories

Mushroom risotto

This risotto makes the most of both fresh and dried mushrooms. The fresh add texture and a deliciously subtle flavour, while the dried mushrooms come to life with a rich, earthy flavour once they have been rehydrated.

Serves 4   Preparation time 15 minutes   Cooking time 30 minutes

30 grams (1 oz) dried porcini mushrooms

2 cups boiling water

¼ cup olive oil

1 large onion, finely chopped

2 large garlic cloves, crushed

2 cups risotto rice

⅓ cup dry white wine or vermouth

250 grams (½ lb) large flat mushrooms, stalks trimmed and caps sliced

4 cups diluted salt-reduced or homemade vegetable stock (page 29), hot

2 tablespoons butter

¼ cup grated Parmesan cheese

2 tablespoons chopped fresh flat-leaf parsley

1 Soak the dried mushrooms in the boiling water. Meanwhile, heat the oil in a deep frying pan over a medium heat. Add the onion and cook for 3 minutes, then add the garlic and stir for a further 2 minutes until the onion is softened.

2 Add the rice to the pan, stir for about 1 minute, then add the wine or vermouth and cook briskly, stirring, until almost all of it has evaporated.

3 Strain the dried mushrooms, reserving the soaking liquid. Stir the fresh mushrooms into the rice, then start adding the stock, only a ladleful at a time, making sure each is almost completely absorbed before adding the next, and stirring frequently to produce a creamy texture. When all the stock has been absorbed, gradually add the mushroom soaking liquid and continue cooking until the rice is tender.

4 Stir in the soaked porcini mushrooms and the butter, cover and remove from the heat. Stand for 5 minutes, season to taste, then serve sprinkled with Parmesan cheese and parsley.

EACH SERVING

13.5 g protein • 22 g fat of which 6.5 g saturates • 85 g carbohydrate • 3.5 g fibre • 383 Calories

COOK'S TIPS

• *There are many varieties of pre-made pesto on the market. Those that contain Parmesan cheese are not suitable for strict vegetarians.*

Chicken and zucchini risotto

The salty tang of pancetta creates a flavourful base for this risotto, offsetting the milder flavours of chicken and zucchini. This dish is a great way to make the most of a bountiful crop of summer zucchini.

*Serves **4**   Preparation time **15 minutes**   Cooking time **30 minutes***

2 tablespoons olive oil

50 grams (2 oz) pancetta, diced

4 small skinless boneless chicken breasts, cut into small cubes

2 leeks, trimmed and sliced

2 garlic cloves, crushed

2 zucchini, halved lengthwise, then cut into half-moon shapes

1½ cups risotto rice

½ cup dry white wine

3¾ cups diluted salt-reduced or homemade chicken stock (page 28), hot

1¼ cups frozen peas

1 Heat the oil in a large, heavy-based frying pan over a medium heat. Add the pancetta and stir for 2 minutes until it is sizzling and starting to colour.

2 Add the chicken pieces and stir around for 2 minutes. Stir in the leeks, garlic and zucchini and fry, stirring frequently, for 3–5 minutes until they soften.

3 Stir in the rice, then pour in the wine. Increase the heat and simmer, stirring until almost all the wine has evaporated.

4 Reduce the heat to medium and start adding the stock, a ladleful at a time, stirring frequently, making sure each is almost completely absorbed before adding the next, and stirring frequently to produce a creamy texture.

5 When there are just two ladles of stock left, stir in the peas. Continue adding the stock, stirring until the risotto is moist and creamy.

VARIATION
• Sliced green beans or snow peas would be good as alternatives to peas.

EACH SERVING

70 g protein • 28 g fat of which 6.5 g saturates • 67 g carbohydrate • 6 g fibre • 665 Calories

COOK'S TIPS
• *Some companies are now producing packaged biryani spice mixes, which you can use instead of the spices in this recipe.*
• *A good accompaniment to the biryani is a simple tomato salad. Chop 2 tomatoes and a few sprigs of cilantro and mix together.*

Mixed vegetable biryani

Here is a vegetarian one-pot meal of golden saffron-scented basmati rice combined with spiced vegetables. Serve with a cooling banana mint raita (page 27) or a simple cucumber and mint salad to make a feast.

Serves **6**   *Preparation time* **20 minutes**   *Cooking time* **50 minutes**

¼ cup canola oil

1 onion, thinly sliced

⅓ cup raisins

1 cinnamon stick, broken in half

8 black peppercorns

6 cloves

6 green cardamom pods, crushed and pods discarded

1 tablespoon coriander seeds, lightly crushed

2 teaspoons ground cumin

½ teaspoon cayenne pepper

4 garlic cloves, crushed

200 grams (7 oz) new potatoes, scrubbed and cubed

1 carrot, peeled and sliced

150 grams (5 oz) thin green beans, trimmed and chopped

1 zucchini, sliced

1 cup frozen peas

¾ cup Greek-style yogourt

2⅔ cups water

1½ cups basmati rice, rinsed

pinch of saffron threads

1 tablespoon flaked almonds, lightly toasted

10 sprigs of cilantro

3 hard-boiled eggs, quartered

1 Heat 1 tablespoon of the oil in a large flameproof casserole dish or deep frying pan. Add the onion and fry over a medium heat, stirring occasionally, for 12–15 minutes until golden. Remove from the dish and set aside. Add the raisins to the dish and stir around for 30 seconds, then remove and set aside with the onion.

2 Add the remaining oil to the dish and heat, then add the cinnamon, peppercorns, cloves, cardamom and coriander seeds and stir around for 1 minute. Reduce the heat to low. Add the ground cumin, cayenne and garlic and stir for a further 30–60 seconds until you can smell the aroma of the spices.

3 Stir in all the vegetables, then gradually add the yogourt, still

over a low heat. Add ⅓ cup of the water, cover the pan tightly and leave the vegetables to simmer gently for 12 minutes.

4 Meanwhile, put the rice in a pot with the saffron threads, the rest of the water and a pinch of salt, stir and bring to a boil. Reduce the heat to low, cover the pan tightly with a lid and leave to simmer for about 10 minutes until the liquid has been absorbed and the rice is just starting to become tender.

5 Spoon the cooked rice on top of the vegetables. Re-cover the dish tightly and cook gently for a further 10–15 minutes until both the rice and vegetables are tender. Alternatively, layer the vegetable curry and rice in a casserole dish, cover tightly and bake at 350°F (180°C) for 20–30 minutes.

6 Scatter the reserved onion and raisins over the top of the biryani together with the almonds, cilantro and wedges of egg. Serve immediately.

EACH SERVING

13 g protein • 16.5 g fat of which 3.5 g saturates • 58 g carbohydrate • 6 g fibre • 326 Calories

Shrimp and spinach biryani

A fragrantly spiced pilaf-style dish that doesn't take much more effort than ordering takeout, yet is much healthier as it is lower in fat. Serve with a refreshing raita (page 27) to complete the meal.

Serves **4**

Preparation time **15 minutes**

Cooking time **25 minutes**

398 ml can chopped tomatoes

2 tablespoons canola oil

1 large onion, halved and thinly sliced

1 red chili pepper, deseeded and thinly sliced

15 grams (½ oz) fresh ginger, peeled and finely chopped

1 tablespoon ground cumin

1 tablespoon ground coriander

1 teaspoon ground turmeric

½ teaspoon ground nutmeg

1 cup basmati rice, rinsed

pinch of sugar

6⅔ cups baby spinach leaves, roughly torn

250 grams (½ lb) peeled raw shrimp, thawed if frozen

VARIATIONS

• *Replace some or all of the spinach with thinly sliced mushrooms, adding them to the casserole dish with the rice.*
• *Sliced red or green peppers would also work well in this dish. Add them with the onion.*
• *Serve any leftovers cold the next day as a rice salad.*

1 Drain the tomatoes in a sieve over a heatproof measuring cup, then set aside. Bring a kettle of water to a boil.

2 Heat the oil in a large flameproof casserole dish over a medium heat. Add the onion, chili and ginger and stir for 3 minutes. Stir in the cumin, coriander, turmeric and nutmeg and continue stirring until the onion is softened.

3 Add the rice and drained tomatoes to the casserole dish and stir to mix with the spices. Add enough boiling water to the reserved tomato juice to make up to 2 cups. Stir this liquid into the rice with the sugar and a pinch of salt, then bring to a boil.

4 Reduce the heat to low, cover tightly and leave the rice to cook without lifting the lid for 10–12 minutes until all the liquid has been absorbed, the rice grains are tender and tiny holes appear on the surface.

5 Stir in the spinach, as much as you can at a time, adding more as each addition wilts. When all the spinach has been added, lay the shrimp on top, re-cover the casserole dish and turn down the heat to very low. Cook for 2 minutes, then turn off the heat and leave to stand for 1 minute, without lifting the lid, by which time the spinach will have wilted further and the shrimp will have cooked through. Gently fork together to combine the rice, spinach and shrimp. Serve immediately.

EACH SERVING

20 g protein • 11.5 g fat of which 1 g saturates • 47 g carbohydrate • 5.5 g fibre • 260 Calories

Salmon and pea pilaf

Canned salmon is very versatile and super healthy, being rich in omega-3 fatty acids. Combined with rice and peas, and subtly flavoured with cardamom, this is a terrific easy-to-make main dish.

Serves **4**

Preparation time **15 minutes**

Cooking time **40 minutes**

3/4 cup wild rice, rinsed

1 bay leaf

6 green cardamom pods, crushed and pods discarded

4 cups diluted salt-reduced or homemade vegetable stock (page 29), hot

418 gram can pink salmon in spring water

1 cup basmati rice, rinsed

2 teaspoons cumin seeds

1 3/4 cups frozen peas, thawed

4 scallions, thinly sliced

1 lemon, zest grated

2 tablespoons chopped cilantro

8 lemon wedges

VARIATION

• *For a vegetarian pilaf, omit the salmon. Add a cinnamon stick with the stock. Add a 398 ml can mixed beans or chickpeas, drained and rinsed, with the peas and fork 250 grams (1/2 lb) shredded spinach through the rice, 5 minutes before the end of cooking. Add chopped fresh mint instead of the cilantro.*

1 Place the wild rice in a large pot with the bay leaf, cardamom seeds and vegetable stock. Bring to a boil, reduce the heat and cover the pan, then simmer for 15 minutes.

2 Meanwhile, drain the salmon and reserve the liquid from the can. Remove and discard the skin and bones and flake the fish, then set it aside. Add the basmati rice and reserved salmon liquid to the wild rice with a pinch of salt. Bring back to a boil and stir once, then reduce the heat and cover the pan. Cook gently for 15 minutes.

3 Roast the cumin seeds in a small, heavy-based frying pan for 2–3 minutes over a medium heat, shaking the pan until they give off their aroma. Tip the seeds out of the pan onto a small plate as soon as they smell aromatic.

4 Add the peas and cumin seeds to the rice, fork them lightly into the grains, re-cover the pan and cook for a further 5 minutes. Add the salmon, leaving it on top of the rice without forking it in, cover and leave to cook gently for 5 minutes until the rice is tender and all the cooking liquid has been absorbed.

5 Finally, add the scallions, lemon zest and cilantro and fork through. Check the seasoning and discard the bay leaf before serving. Add some lemon wedges to squeeze over the top as desired.

EACH SERVING

31.5 g protein • 8 g fat of which 2 g saturates • 78 g carbohydrate • 6 g fibre • 326 Calories

VARIATIONS
• For a salmon kedgeree, use salmon fillets and replace the chives with chopped fresh dill.
• For vegetarians, omit the fish and pan-fry 200 grams (7 oz) sliced, assorted mushrooms with the shallots and spices. Add 1 diced avocado just before serving.

Smoked cod kedgeree

A subtly spiced rice dish, this is based on a classic kedgeree recipe but with extra vegetables to add vitamins. Serve with a side salad.

Step 2

Step 3

Step 4

Serves **4**

Preparation time **10 minutes**

Cooking time **35 minutes**

275 grams (9 oz) smoked cod fillet

1 bay leaf

2 cups diluted salt-reduced or homemade vegetable stock (page 29), hot

1 tablespoon canola oil

2 shallots, finely chopped

½ teaspoon ground cumin

½ teaspoon ground coriander

1 teaspoon mild curry powder

1½ cups basmati rice, rinsed

small strip of lemon zest and 1 tablespoon lemon juice

1 cup shelled fresh or frozen peas

4 tomatoes, peeled and chopped

2 tablespoons snipped fresh chives

2 eggs, hard-boiled and quartered

1 Put the smoked cod in a deep frying pan. Add the bay leaf, then pour over the stock. Heat to simmering point, then reduce the heat, half-cover the pan with a lid and poach for 6–8 minutes until the flesh flakes easily when tested with the tip of a knife. (If you prefer, the fish can be cooked in a microwave.) Lift the fish out of the cooking liquid and set aside. Make up the volume of the cooking liquid/stock to 2 cups with water and reserve with the bay leaf.

2 Rinse out the pan, then add the oil and heat over a medium heat for a few seconds. Add the shallots and cook for 4–5 minutes until softened, then stir in the spices, followed by the rice. Stir for a few seconds to coat with the oil and spices, then add the reserved cooking liquid and bay leaf and the strip of lemon zest. Bring to a boil.

3 Reduce the heat to a gentle simmer, cover and cook for 10 minutes. Add the peas, cover again and cook for a further 5 minutes or until the rice is tender and nearly all the stock has been absorbed.

4 Meanwhile, flake the fish, removing any skin and bones. Reduce the heat under the pan to very low, then gently stir the fish into the rice together with the tomatoes, lemon juice and chives.

5 Season to taste, bearing in mind that smoked cod is quite salty, then transfer the kedgeree to a warm serving dish and garnish with the egg quarters.

EACH SERVING

25 g protein • 9 g fat of which 1.5 g saturates • 29 g carbohydrate • 5 g fibre • 310 Calories

Mexican arroz rojo

Flavoured with a small amount of spicy sausage and chili flakes, this is a traditional taste of Mexico. Guacamole (page 27) and tortillas complete the meal.

Serves **4**

Preparation time **15 minutes**

Cooking time **50 minutes**

2 tablespoons canola oil

75 grams (2½ oz) chorizo sausage, skinned and chopped

1 onion, finely chopped

2 garlic cloves, crushed

1 cup long-grain brown rice, rinsed

2 x 398 ml cans chopped tomatoes

2 teaspoons tomato paste

¾ cup frozen corn kernels

¾ cup frozen peas

1 bay leaf

¾ cup plus 1 tablespoon water or salt-reduced or homemade vegetable stock (page 29)

½ teaspoon chili flakes

½ teaspoon sugar

8 sprigs of cilantro

4 lime wedges

4 flour tortillas

1 Heat the oil in a large flameproof casserole dish or pot with a tight-fitting lid over a medium–high heat. Add the chorizo and stir for 2 minutes. Add the onion and garlic and continue cooking for 3–5 minutes, stirring, until they are soft.

2 Add the rice to the dish and stir for 1 minute, then stir in the tomatoes with their juice, the tomato paste, corn, peas, bay leaf, stock, chili flakes and sugar.

3 Slowly bring to a boil, stirring occasionally, then reduce the heat to low, cover the pan tightly with a lid and leave to simmer for 30–40 minutes until the rice is tender and all the liquid has been absorbed. Add a little more stock if the mixture becomes too dry before the rice is cooked. Season to taste.

4 Remove the dish from the heat and leave to stand for 5 minutes, with the pan covered. Heat the flour tortillas under a hot grill until warm. Serve the rice with cilantro sprigs, lime wedges and the tortillas.

EACH SERVING

20.5 g protein • 18 g fat of which 3.5 g saturates • 141 g carbohydrate • 11.5 g fibre • 503 Calories

Caribbean coconut rice and peas

This recipe is based on a traditional Caribbean favourite that is often made with red kidney beans, which are called peas in Jamaica — hence the name of the dish. Red pepper has been added for extra vegetable content and a small amount of lean bacon lifts the flavour.

Serves **4**   *Preparation time* **15 minutes**   *Cooking time* **30 minutes**

1 tablespoon canola oil

3 slices back bacon, trimmed and diced

1 large onion, finely chopped

1 large red pepper, deseeded and thinly sliced

2 garlic cloves, finely chopped

1 red or green chili pepper, deseeded and finely chopped

1¼ cups long-grain rice, rinsed

2 cups boiling water

398 ml can reduced-fat coconut milk

398 ml can red kidney beans, drained and rinsed

2 sprigs of fresh thyme

2 tomatoes, diced

Tabasco (optional), to serve

1 Heat the oil in a large pot or deep frying pan, add the bacon and cook over a gentle heat for 2 minutes until lightly browned. Add the onion and cook, stirring, for 3 minutes or until softened. Reduce the heat and stir in the pepper, garlic and chili pepper and cook for 1 minute.

2 Stir in the rice, then pour in the boiling water and coconut milk and add a pinch of salt. Bring to a boil, then reduce the heat. Add the drained beans and thyme, then cover and simmer for 10 minutes.

3 Add the diced tomatoes to the pan and continue to cook gently for a further 10 minutes until the rice is just tender. (The mixture should still be a little sloppy.) Remove the sprigs of thyme and serve with Tabasco to sprinkle over the top, if you like.

VARIATIONS
• *Instead of using bacon, just cook the onion in the oil, then add some cooked meat, such as shredded chicken or pork, to the finished dish before serving.*
• *For a vegetarian meal, simply leave out the bacon.*

EACH SERVING

25 g protein • 10.5 g fat of which 3 g saturates • 75 g carbohydrate • 7 g fibre • 372 Calories

VARIATION
• *In Mexico, this popular "red rice" dish is made with fresh, bright red, juicy tomatoes. When you have well-flavoured fresh tomatoes, use 600 grams (1¹/₃ lbs), deseeded and chopped, in place of the canned tomatoes and increase the amount of water or stock to 2¹/₂ cups.*

Spicy rice with chickpeas

This lightly curried rice dish makes a simple yet satisfying vegetarian meal, with the chickpeas providing valuable protein. Serve with a yogourt raita (page 27) and mango chutney. A fresh, green, baby spinach leaf salad would also make a good accompaniment to this meal.

Serves **4**

Preparation time **15 minutes**

Cooking time **35 minutes**

1 tablespoon canola oil

1 onion, sliced

¼ cup medium curry paste

1 cup basmati rice, rinsed

2 cups water

1 orange sweet potato, peeled and chopped into small chunks

4 tomatoes, chopped

¼ cup sultanas

398 ml can chickpeas, drained and rinsed

¼ cup chopped cilantro

⅓ cup unsalted cashew nuts, roughly chopped

COOK'S TIPS

• *Choose a curry paste without any shrimp paste to make this suitable for vegetarians.*
• *The rice needs to be rinsed thoroughly, in a sieve under cold running water, before cooking. This removes excess starch so the rice will be light and fluffy when cooked.*

VARIATION

• *If you like, you could add a small amount of diced firm tofu at the end of cooking, or for a non-vegetarian version, some diced, cooked chicken.*

1 Heat the oil in a large pot and fry the onion over a medium heat for about 8 minutes, stirring until pale golden. Add the curry paste and stir-fry for about 1 minute.

2 Stir in the rice, then add the water, sweet potato, tomatoes and sultanas. Bring to a boil, then reduce the heat to a simmer. Cover the pan and leave on a low heat for 20–25 minutes, stirring occasionally, until the rice is just tender and the water has been absorbed. Add a little more water if the mixture becomes too dry before the rice is cooked.

3 Stir in the chickpeas and gently heat through. Stir in the cilantro, season to taste and scatter with the cashew nuts before serving.

EACH SERVING

12 g protein • 17.5 g fat of which 2.5 g saturates • 42 g carbohydrate • 11 g fibre • 394 Calories

Jambalaya

The spicy tomato flavour and aroma of this one-pot rice dish make it really appealing. Tender chunks of fish, juicy shrimp and plenty of vegetables all combine to make a well-balanced, complete meal.

Serves **4**

Preparation time **30 minutes**

Cooking time **40 minutes**

¼ cup olive oil

1 large red onion, finely chopped

2 garlic cloves, finely chopped

½ head of celery, finely diced and leaves reserved for garnish

1 red pepper, deseeded and chopped

½ teaspoon chili powder, or to taste

1 teaspoon ground cumin

1¼ cups long-grain rice

2 x 398 ml cans chopped tomatoes

1 tablespoon chopped fresh thyme or 1 teaspoon dried thyme

300 g (10½ oz) skinned firm white fish fillet, cut into four pieces

8 peeled raw shrimp

2 tablespoons chopped fresh flat-leaf parsley

4 lemon wedges

1 Put the oil in a large, deep frying pan and heat gently. Add the onion, garlic, celery, red pepper, chili and cumin. Cook, stirring often, for 10–12 minutes until softened. Add the rice and cook, stirring, for 2 minutes.

2 Drain the tomatoes in a sieve over a heatproof measuring cup or bowl, then set aside. Bring a kettle of water to a boil. Add the tomatoes to the rice, sprinkle the thyme over the top, stir well and reduce the heat a little.

3 Make up the tomato juice to 4 cups with boiling water, pour into the pan and stir well. Bring to a boil, then reduce the heat, cover the pan with the lid slightly ajar, and simmer gently for 10 minutes.

4 Season the rice to taste, then place the pieces of fish on top. Continue cooking, partly covered as before, for 5 minutes. Stir the rice carefully and turn the fish over, then add the shrimp. Partly cover the pan again and cook for a further 5 minutes or until the shrimp have turned pink, the fish pieces are cooked, and the rice is tender. The dish should be moist, not dry.

5 Remove from the heat, cover tightly and leave for 5 minutes. Scatter the celery leaves and parsley over the top and serve with lemon wedges to squeeze over.

EACH SERVING

27 g protein • 16 g fat of which 2 g saturates • 64 g carbohydrate • 8 g fibre • 378 Calories

Seafood paella

An ideal dish for entertaining, this colourful and exotic dish is made with a mixture of white fish and seafood, plus red pepper, asparagus, tomatoes and artichokes. Serve with a green salad.

Serves **4**

Preparation time **25 minutes**

Cooking time **35 minutes**

4 cups diluted homemade fish or chicken stock (page 29)

2 cups water

1 small onion, halved

large pinch of saffron threads

¼ cup olive oil

2 large garlic cloves, crushed

1 red pepper, deseeded and chopped

2¼ cups paella or risotto rice

⅔ cup dry white wine

350 g (12 oz) firm white fish, skinned and cut into chunks

250 grams (½ lb) peeled raw shrimp, thawed if frozen

125 grams (¼ lb) squid, cleaned and sliced

150 grams (5 oz) asparagus, trimmed and sliced

2 large tomatoes, peeled, deseeded and chopped

12 pitted olives, sliced

2 tablespoons chopped fresh parsley

1 tablespoon lemon juice

398 ml can artichoke hearts, drained, rinsed and halved

8 small lemon wedges

2 tablespoons chopped fresh parsley, extra

1 Pour the stock and water into a very large pot with the onion and saffron. Bring to a boil, then cover and reduce the heat. Simmer gently for 10 minutes, then strain into a large jug.

2 Heat the oil in the pot or a paella pan and add the garlic and red pepper. Cook gently for 2–3 minutes, then add the rice. Cook for 5 minutes, stirring often, until the rice looks transparent.

3 Add the wine, stir, then allow it to bubble up and evaporate. Ladle about one-third of the reserved stock into the rice. When it has all been absorbed, add a further third, then cook gently until it has been absorbed.

4 Add the remaining ingredients (except the lemon wedges and extra chopped parsley) to the pan, along with the rest of the stock. Cook gently, stirring occasionally, for about 10 minutes until all the seafood is cooked and the rice and vegetables are tender, adding extra stock or hot water, if needed.

5 Season to taste and tip into a serving dish if not cooked in a paella pan. Garnish with lemon wedges and extra chopped parsley.

EACH SERVING

44 g protein • 3 g fat of which 0.5 g saturates • 38 g carbohydrate • 4.5 g fibre • 397 Calories

Chicken and chorizo paella

A little spicy chorizo goes a long way and adds a fabulous flavour to this colourful dish. Brown rice has a wonderful nutty texture and it is more nutritious than white rice.

Serves **4**   *Preparation time* **25 minutes**   *Cooking time* **45 minutes**

90 grams (3 oz) chorizo sausage, skinned and diced

1 tablespoon olive oil

350 grams (12 oz) skinless boneless chicken breasts, cubed

1 large onion, chopped

2 celery stalks, diced

2 garlic cloves, crushed

1 red pepper, deseeded and diced

1 green pepper, deseeded and diced

1 yellow pepper, deseeded and diced

1¼ cups brown rice

4 tomatoes, finely diced

2 bay leaves

2 sprigs of fresh thyme

3 cups boiling water

1 cup frozen peas

1 cup frozen corn kernels

¼ cup chopped fresh flat-leaf parsley, chopped

1 Dry-fry the chorizo in a large, heavy-based pot or flameproof casserole dish over a medium heat for about 2 minutes, stirring continuously. Add the oil and chicken and increase the heat slightly, then cook for about 5 minutes until coloured all over, stirring occasionally. Remove the chicken and chorizo from the pan using a slotted spoon and set aside.

2 Add the onion, celery, garlic and peppers to the oil remaining in the pan. Cook, stirring frequently, for 5 minutes until the vegetables are softened slightly. Stir in the rice, tomatoes, bay leaves and thyme, then replace the chicken and chorizo and pour in the water. Bring back to a boil, stirring occasionally. Reduce the heat to low, cover and cook gently for 25 minutes.

3 Add the peas and corn, forking them lightly into the rice mixture. Re-cover and continue to simmer for a further 5 minutes until the rice is tender and all the liquid has been absorbed. Discard the bay leaves and thyme stalks and season to taste, then fork through the parsley and serve.

VARIATION
• *For vegetarians, omit the chorizo and chicken and cook the vegetables in 2 tablespoons oil. Season with paprika and nutmeg when adding the rice. Add 2 x 398 ml cans of chickpeas, drained and rinsed, with the peas.*

EACH SERVING

36 g protein • 15.5 g fat of which 4 g saturates • 74 g carbohydrate • 10 g fibre • 456 Calories

Vegetarian paella

A wonderfully rich and satisfying dish, this vegetarian version of a classic is a great way to introduce your family to tofu, which is a good source of protein, vitamins and minerals. Serve hot with a tomato salad.

Serves **4** *Preparation time* **30 minutes** *Cooking time* **1¼ hours**

2 tablespoons olive oil

2 shallots, chopped

2 garlic cloves, crushed

1 eggplant, diced

1 red pepper, deseeded and diced

1 cup long-grain brown rice

4 cups diluted homemade vegetable stock (page 29), hot

2 zucchini, diced

175 grams (6 oz) brown mushrooms, quartered

250 grams (½ lb) firm tofu, diced

¼ cup chopped fresh tarragon (optional)

1 Heat the oil in a paella pan or other large, heavy-based pan and fry the shallots and garlic gently for 4–5 minutes to soften. Add the eggplant and fry over a medium heat, stirring occasionally, until beginning to brown.

2 Add the pepper pieces and stir for a further 2–3 minutes, then stir the rice into the pan, turning to coat evenly. Add about half the stock and bring to a boil, stirring.

3 Partially cover the pan and cook on a low heat, stirring occasionally, for 25–30 minutes, until the rice is beginning to swell. Add a little more stock to moisten, then stir in the zucchini and mushrooms. Continue to cook, uncovered, for 20–30 minutes, adding more stock as necessary, until the rice is tender and the stock is absorbed. (You might not need all the stock as there will be some variation in absorption depending on the diameter of the pan used and the degree of heat.)

4 Stir lightly and test the rice by tasting a grain – the grains should be tender with just a slight firmness in the centre. Stir in the tofu and tarragon, if using, then warm through and season to taste. Serve hot.

EACH SERVING

13.5 g protein • 13 g fat of which 2 g saturates • 49 g carbohydrate • 6 g fibre • 266 Calories

Indonesian fried rice

Flavoured with garlic, ginger and chili, this tempting dish with thin and tender strips of lean beef and juicy shrimp is a variation on the classic "Nasi goreng." It's perfect for a relaxed lunch because much of the dish can be prepared ahead.

Serves *4*

Preparation time 25 minutes, plus
    at least 30 minutes marinating

Cooking time 10 minutes

2 teaspoons sesame oil

2 teaspoons sherry vinegar

2 tablespoons soy sauce

250 grams (½ lb) tenderloin or
round steak, cut across the grain
into thin strips

1⅔ cups long-grain white rice

2 eggs

3 scallions, sliced on
the diagonal

2 tablespoons chopped cilantro

2½ tablespoons canola oil

150 grams (5 oz) peeled raw
shrimp

2 garlic cloves, crushed

1 green chili pepper, deseeded
and thinly sliced

15 grams (½ oz) fresh ginger,
peeled and finely chopped

2 carrots, peeled and
coarsely grated

¾ cup frozen peas, thawed

splash of chili sauce (optional)

1 Whisk together the sesame oil, vinegar and 1 tablespoon of the soy sauce in a bowl, add the beef and toss to coat in the marinade. Cover and chill for at least 30 minutes or overnight if you have time.

2 Meanwhile, cook the rice in lightly salted boiling water for 12 minutes, or according to the package instructions, until almost tender, then drain and rinse with boiling water. Spread out on a tray and leave to cool. (You will get the best results if you cool the rice overnight.)

3 Lightly beat the eggs in a small bowl or jug, then stir in the scallions and cilantro and season with freshly ground black pepper. Heat 2 teaspoons of the oil in a non-stick omelette pan or frying pan and pour in the beaten egg mixture. Cook the eggs for a few seconds, then use a fork to stir gently for about a minute until the base begins to set. Stop stirring and cook for a further 2 minutes until lightly set. Roll up the omelette, slide it onto a plate and cover with foil to keep warm.

4 Heat 1 tablespoon of the remaining oil in a wok or large, deep frying pan until hot. Add the beef with the marinade and stir-fry on a high heat for about 1 minute until well browned. Remove with a slotted spoon leaving all the juices behind. Set aside.

5 Add the remaining oil to the pan. Add the shrimp, garlic, chili pepper and ginger and stir-fry for 2 minutes until the shrimp have just turned pink, then add the carrots, peas and rice and toss on the heat for a further minute. Finally, add the cooked beef, sprinkle with the remaining soy sauce and stir-fry for a final 1–2 minutes until everything is heated through.

6 Spoon the rice mixture into a warmed serving bowl. Cut the omelette into thin strips and scatter over the rice. For those who like an extra spicy kick, serve with chili sauce.

EACH SERVING

37 g protein • 23 g fat of which 5 g saturates • 75.5 g carbohydrate
• 5 g fibre • 469 Calories

COOK'S TIPS

• *To prepare ahead, marinate the beef and cook the rice up to 8 hours ahead. You could also make the omelette. Cover and keep everything in the refrigerator until ready to use. Make sure that the rice is reheated thoroughly.*
• *This is an ideal way to use up leftover rice and many types can be used, including brown rice and basmati.*

Yakitori domburi

Domburi is a Japanese dish, the name of which originally referred to the bowl in which it was cooked, and Yakitori domburi is traditionally a one-pot meal of chicken and rice. The addition of bok choy will increase your daily vegetable count.

Serves 4

Preparation time 15 minutes, plus
at least 4 hours marinating

Cooking time 25 minutes

4 small skinless boneless chicken breasts

2 tablespoons salt-reduced soy sauce

1/3 cup mirin

2 tablespoons water

2 teaspoons grated fresh ginger

1 garlic clove, chopped

2 cups short-grain white rice

4 cups water, extra

1 tablespoon canola oil

2 tablespoons sugar

1 bunch baby bok choy

2 scallions, thinly sliced

COOK'S TIP
• *If you can find only large chicken breasts, buy two and cut them in half lengthwise.*

1 In a glass bowl, combine the chicken breasts, soy sauce, mirin, water, ginger and garlic. Cover and marinate in the refrigerator for at least 4 hours.

2 Wash the rice under several changes of water until it almost runs clear. Drain, add to a pot and pour in 3 cups of the extra water. Cover with a lid and bring to a boil, then reduce the heat to a simmer and cook for 12–14 minutes or until all the water has been absorbed. Remove from the heat and allow the rice to sit covered for 10 minutes.

3 Meanwhile, remove the chicken from the marinade, reserving the marinade. Heat a frying pan over a medium heat, add the oil and cook the chicken breasts for about 5 minutes on each side or until the chicken is cooked. Remove from the heat and slice the chicken into 1 cm thick slices, keeping warm.

4 In the same pan, add the reserved marinade, adding the remaining water and the sugar. Bring to a boil, then allow it to simmer for 1–2 minutes. Skim off any scum with a metal spoon. Add the bok choy and cook until it starts to wilt, about 1 minute. Just before serving, add the scallions.

5 To serve, divide the rice into some deep bowls, top with the bok choy and sliced chicken, and gently spoon over the sauce. Enjoy while hot.

EACH SERVING

38.5 g protein • 15 g fat of which 3.5 g saturates • 38.5 g carbohydrate • 1.5 g fibre • 467 Calories

Lemon barley pilaf with chicken

Barley is a much underrated and seldom-used grain, which is a great shame since it has a pleasing flavour and texture as well as being a good source of fibre. Here it is cooked with a medley of vegetables in a lemon and thyme stock. The addition of cooked chicken turns the dish into a great main course.

Serves **4**

Preparation time **15 minutes**

Cooking time **40 minutes**

1 tablespoon olive oil

1 onion, finely chopped

2 carrots, peeled and diced

2 celery stalks, diced

1 garlic clove, crushed

1¼ cups pearl barley

2½ cups diluted salt-reduced or homemade chicken stock (page 28), hot

1 tablespoon chopped fresh thyme or 1 teaspoon dried thyme

1 lemon, zest grated and juiced

1 cup frozen peas

400 grams (14 oz) skinned roasted chicken breast, shredded

50 grams (2 oz) arugula

VARIATION

• *This pilaf is also delicious eaten at room temperature as a salad. Allow the pilaf to cool before adding the chicken and arugula.*

1 Heat the oil in a large, heavy-based pot over a medium heat. Stir in the onion, carrots, celery and garlic, then cook gently for about 10 minutes, stirring occasionally, until softened but not browned.

2 Stir in the barley and cook for 1 minute longer. Pour in the stock and bring to a boil. Add the thyme and lemon zest. Reduce the heat to very low, cover and simmer, stirring occasionally, for 20 minutes or until the barley is almost soft.

3 Add the peas, re-cover and simmer for a further 4–5 minutes until the barley is soft but not mushy and all the stock is absorbed. Stir in the lemon juice and season to taste.

4 Add the chicken pieces and arugula to the pot and lightly toss together. Serve at once.

EACH SERVING

37 g protein • 14 g fat of which 3 g saturates • 54 g carbohydrate • 12 g fibre • 517 Calories

Fusilli with summer pesto

Whole wheat pasta is a good source of complex carbohydrate and has a low GI value. Tossed with steamed summer vegetables and a fresh herb pesto, this makes a tempting and satisfying meal.

Serves **4**

Preparation time **20 minutes**

Cooking time **15 minutes**

3 zucchini, sliced

8 scallions, sliced

1½ cups shelled fresh peas

1¼ cups shelled fresh baby fava beans

350 grams (12 oz) whole wheat fusilli

PESTO

15 grams (½ oz) fresh flat-leaf parsley

15 grams (½ oz) cilantro

15 grams (½ oz) fresh mint

¼ cup pine nuts

1 large garlic clove, peeled

3 tablespoons extra virgin olive oil

½ cup grated Parmesan cheese

1 To make the pesto, remove any large stalks from the herbs, then put the leaves in a small blender or food processor with the pine nuts, garlic and a little of the oil. Blend until well mixed. Gradually add the remaining oil to form a fairly smooth paste. Add the Parmesan and freshly ground black pepper to taste and process briefly to mix. Set the pesto aside.

2 Bring a large pot of lightly salted water to a boil. Spread out the zucchini, scallions, peas and fava beans in a steamer basket that will sit snuggly over the pot.

3 Add the pasta to the pot of boiling water and bring the water back to a boil, then reduce the heat slightly and set the steamer basket on top of the pan. Boil the pasta and steam the vegetables for 11–13 minutes until both are cooked and just tender.

4 Drain the pasta and turn it into a large serving bowl. Add all the pesto and stir it thoroughly through the pasta, then add the steamed vegetables and toss gently until well mixed. Serve immediately or allow to cool and serve as a salad.

EACH SERVING

23.5 g protein • 27 g fat of which 5 g saturates • 54 g carbohydrate • 18 g fibre • 566 Calories

Pasta carbonara with leeks

A fabulously quick egg and pancetta pasta favourite with added vegetables for extra nutrition. It's surprising how little pancetta and Parmesan cheese you need to achieve a really deep, rich flavour.

Serves **4** *Preparation time* **10 minutes** *Cooking time* **15 minutes**

2 leeks, trimmed and sliced

90 grams (3 oz) smoked pancetta

300 grams (10½ oz) fettuccine

1 cup frozen peas

4 eggs, lightly beaten

¼ cup light sour cream

2 tablespoons chopped fresh flat-leaf parsley

½ cup grated Parmesan cheese

1 Put a large pot of lightly salted water on to boil. Add the leeks and cook gently for 3 minutes until just tender. Remove the leeks to a plate using a slotted spoon. Preheat a grill to medium.

2 Place the pancetta on the rack of the grill and cook for 2 minutes until beginning to become crisp (or use a ridged grill pan on the stove). Remove and break into rough pieces.

3 Bring the water back to a boil and if necessary, top up with a little more boiling water from the kettle. Drop the pasta into the water and cook for 6 minutes, or according to the package instructions. Add the peas to the water for the last 3 minutes of the cooking time and bring back to a boil. Stir occasionally to make sure that no pasta is sticking to the base of the pan.

4 Lightly whisk the eggs with the sour cream and freshly ground black pepper to season. Drain the pasta and peas and immediately return them to the hot pan. Stir in the egg mixture, which will cook in the heat of the pasta. Then quickly add the pancetta, leeks and parsley and lightly toss everything together.

5 Sprinkle the Parmesan over the top and season to taste with more pepper. Serve immediately.

VARIATION

• *You can replace the pancetta with 90 grams (3 oz) smoked salmon or smoked lean ham, cut into strips. Neither needs cooking. Just toss into the cooked pasta at step 4.*

EACH SERVING

26.5 g protein • 16 g fat of which 7.5 g saturates • 49 g carbohydrate • 7.5 g fibre • 462 Calories

VARIATIONS

• *If you prefer, you can replace the fava beans with thin green beans that have been halved.*
• *For a more traditional pesto, use fresh basil leaves rather than cilantro and mint.*
• *Flaked almonds work well as an alternative to pine nuts in the pesto.*

Linguine with crab

This dish bursts with the colour and flavour of fresh herbs, zesty lemon and piquant chili that enhance the sweet crabmeat and pasta. It's an all-round star because it's so easy to make in the time that it takes to cook the pasta.

Serves 4

Preparation time 15 minutes

Cooking time 10 minutes

250 grams (½ lb) cherry tomatoes

1 tablespoon olive oil

350 grams (12 oz) linguine

1 red chili pepper, deseeded and finely chopped

½ English cucumber, diced

1 lemon, zest grated

30 grams (1 oz) fresh chives, snipped

30 grams (1 oz) fresh herb fennel or fennel leaves, chopped, or 15 grams (½ oz) fresh dill, chopped

200 grams (7 oz) fresh crabmeat

2 cups baby arugula

4 lemon wedges

VARIATIONS

• *Add smoked salmon pieces or cooked, peeled shrimp instead of the crabmeat.*
• *If fresh crab is unavailable, substitute 2 x 170 g cans of white crabmeat, drained.*
• *Add another red chili pepper for an extra kick. If you like things really hot, leave the seeds in the chili pepper(s).*

1 Preheat the broiler. Cut the tomatoes in half, then place them, cut-sides up, on a heatproof dish. Sprinkle generously with freshly ground black pepper and trickle the oil over them. Broil the tomatoes until browned on top but still firm. Turn off the heat and leave them under the grill to keep warm while you prepare the rest of the meal.

2 Meanwhile, cook the linguine in a large pot of lightly salted boiling water for 10 minutes or according to the package instructions, until tender but still firm.

3 Put the chili pepper, cucumber, lemon zest, chives and fennel or dill in a large serving bowl and mix together thoroughly. Add the crabmeat and mix together lightly so the crabmeat doesn't break up too much.

4 Drain the cooked pasta, add it to the crab mixture and toss together. Add the tomatoes and their juices together with the arugula and mix lightly, taking care not to break up the tomatoes. Serve at once, with lemon wedges to squeeze over the top.

EACH SERVING

16 g protein • 6 g fat of which 1 g saturates • 53 g carbohydrate • 6 g fibre • 346 Calories

Sardine, tomato and olive pasta

Brilliant for a midweek meal, this punchy pasta dish uses heart-healthy oily fish with a mixture of popular deli foods — salami, olives and sun-dried tomatoes — for speed and convenience.

Serves **4** *Preparation time* **20 minutes** *Cooking time* **15 minutes**

300 grams (10½ oz) whole wheat fusilli

2 x 105 g cans sardines in oil, drained

1 teaspoon extra virgin olive oil or oil from the tomatoes

8 thin slices salami, cut into thin strips

398 ml can artichoke hearts, drained and quartered

8 sun-dried tomatoes, drained and chopped

1 tablespoon bottled capers, rinsed

12 pitted black olives, rinsed

1 teaspoon red wine or sherry vinegar

12 large fresh basil leaves, roughly torn

1 Cook the pasta in a large pot of boiling water for 11–13 minutes, or according to the package instructions, until tender.

2 Meanwhile, split each sardine in half lengthwise and remove the skins, if preferred. A few minutes before the pasta is cooked, heat the oil in a large, non-stick frying pan, add the salami strips and cook over a medium heat for a minute, until the fat from the salami starts to run. Stir in the artichokes, tomatoes, capers and olives, then sprinkle the vinegar over the top.

3 Carefully place the sardine halves on top, then cover with a lid. Turn the heat to the lowest setting, so that the sardines warm through in the steam.

4 Drain the pasta, reserving a few spoons of the cooking water, then add to the sardine mixture. Carefully toss together for 1–2 minutes until everything is piping hot. If the mixture seems dry, add a little of the pasta cooking water. Gently stir in the basil leaves, then serve right away.

EACH SERVING

22 g protein • 14.5 g fat of which 4 g saturates • 46 g carbohydrate • 12.5 g fibre • 414 Calories

Tomato, shrimp and pepper pasta

Rice and corn pasta is great for those with a wheat intolerance. It cooks and tastes just like wheat pasta and comes in a variety of shapes. This is a flavour-packed dish and simply needs a crunchy green salad to complete the meal.

Serves **4**   *Preparation time* **10 minutes**   *Cooking time* **15 minutes**

250 grams (½ lb) rice and corn fusilli

2 large red peppers, deseeded and cut into wide strips

1 tablespoon olive oil

16 raw shrimp

½ cup (125 ml) tomato sauce

2 tablespoons vermouth or dry sherry

2 tablespoons chopped cilantro

1 Bring a large pot of lightly salted water to a boil. Add the pasta and cook for 8–10 minutes, or according to the package instructions, until tender.

2 Meanwhile, preheat a cast-iron, ridged grill pan. Add the pepper strips and cook for about 3 minutes on each side until lightly charred. Remove from the heat and transfer to a bowl. Pour the oil over the pepper and toss to coat. Cover and reserve.

3 Reheat the grill pan and cook the shrimp briefly for about 1 minute on each side until pink and cooked through. Add to the peppers.

4 Drain the pasta in a colander. Pour the tomato sauce and the vermouth or sherry into the pan and place over a low heat for 1 minute to warm through.

5 Return the pasta to the pan with the peppers, shrimp and the chopped cilantro. Season to taste. Toss well to combine and serve at once.

VARIATIONS

• *You could use scallops or sliced squid in place of the shrimp, cooking them in the same way until just cooked through.*
• *Use wheat pasta if you prefer and cook according to the package instructions until tender.*

EACH SERVING

22 g protein • 6 g fat of which 0.5 g saturates • 117 g carbohydrate • 5.5 g fibre • 593 Calories

Warm tuna, pasta and parsley salad

This is a simple and delicious pasta dish that is just as good served hot as it is cold. It makes a great lunch for friends because you can make it a day in advance, so you can relax and enjoy the company.

Serves 4–6
Preparation time 15 minutes
Cooking time 20 minutes

250 grams (½ lb) cherry tomatoes

1 large red onion, cut into wedges

2 garlic cloves, sliced

¼ cup pine nuts

1 tablespoon olive oil

300 grams (10½ oz) penne or other pasta shapes

2½ cans (170 grams each) tuna in water, drained

199 ml can corn kernels, drained and rinsed

½ cup chopped fresh flat-leaf parsley

DRESSING

1 lemon, juiced

⅓ cup extra virgin olive oil

2 teaspoons whole-grain mustard

1 tablespoon bottled capers, rinsed and roughly chopped

1 Preheat the oven to 350°F (180°C). Line a baking tray with baking parchment and lay out the cherry tomatoes, onion, garlic and pine nuts. Drizzle everything with the oil, season to taste and gently toss together. Roast for 15–20 minutes or until the tomatoes are softened and the pine nuts are lightly browned. Remove from the oven and set aside.

2 Meanwhile, cook the pasta in a large pot of boiling water according to the package instructions until tender.

3 To make the dressing, combine the lemon juice, extra virgin olive oil, mustard and capers in a small bowl and mix together thoroughly.

4 Once the pasta is cooked, strain in a colander, then return to the pot. Add the roasted tomato mixture, tuna, corn, parsley and dressing to the pasta and mix gently, without breaking up the tomatoes too much.

COOK'S TIP
• *The pasta can be served right away if you prefer it warm, or can be made in advance and the flavours allowed to develop — they will improve over time. Allow it to come to room temperature, or warm up slightly in the microwave to remove the chill.*

EACH SERVING (6)

21 g protein • 19.5 g fat of which 2.5 g saturates • 34 g carbohydrate • 4.5 g fibre • 404 Calories

VARIATIONS
• *You could use Roma tomatoes instead of cherry tomatoes. Cut into quarters before roasting.*
• *For a more leafy salad, add 100 grams arugula or baby spinach leaves to the salad when you add the parsley.*

Stir-fries and pan-fries

Delicious, healthy stir-fries and pan-fries are the ideal fast food. The ingredients are prepared in advance and cooked briefly over a high heat, in a wok or a deep-sided frying pan. Quick-cooking retains many of the ingredients' nutritional benefits, and only a little oil is needed. From tasty family meals to quick after-work dishes and impressive dinner-party delights, these are great tastes from around the world you are certain to enjoy.

Lamb with zucchini and ginger

The addition of thick french fries and a generous amount of green vegetables turns
a lean lamb stir-fry into a simple but delicious meal, served straight from the wok.

Serves 4
Preparation time 15 minutes
Cooking time 25 minutes

2 teaspoons sesame oil

1 tablespoon lemon juice

30 grams (1 oz) fresh ginger,
peeled and finely chopped

¼ cup chopped fresh mint

350 grams (12 oz) lean lamb, cut
into thin slices

700 grams (1½ lb) large waxy
new potatoes, scrubbed

¼ cup canola oil

2 zucchini, sliced on the diagonal

6 scallions, sliced on the diagonal

1 cup shelled fresh or frozen peas,
thawed if necessary

1 tablespoon salt-reduced
soy sauce

⅓ cup diluted salt-reduced or
homemade beef or vegetable stock
(pages 28–29)

2 teaspoons honey

COOK'S TIP
• *If time permits, marinate the
lamb for 2–3 hours to intensify
the flavour.*

1 Whisk together the sesame oil, lemon juice, half the ginger and 1 tablespoon of the chopped mint in a shallow dish. Add the lamb and stir well, then cover and leave to marinate while you prepare the remaining ingredients.

2 Put the potatoes in a large pot and pour over enough boiling water to cover them. Bring back to a boil, half-cover the pan with a lid and simmer for 12 minutes or until almost tender when pierced with the tip of a sharp knife. Drain and leave until they are cool enough to handle. Cut across into slices slightly thicker than 5 mm, then cut the slices into thick french fries. Put them in a bowl, drizzle with 1 tablespoon of the canola oil and gently toss to coat. (This will stop the potatoes from sticking together when stir-fried.)

3 Heat 1 tablespoon of the remaining oil in a wok or large frying pan. When the oil is hot, add the lamb and stir-fry over a high heat for 1 minute or until just browned, but still fairly rare. Quickly remove and set aside.

4 Add the remaining oil to the wok and, when hot, add the sliced zucchini. Stir-fry for 1 minute, then add the french fries. Cook for 3–4 minutes, stirring all the time, until lightly browned, taking care not to break up the potatoes. Add the scallions and cook for 1 more minute, stirring.

5 Reduce the heat to medium and add the peas, soy sauce, stock, honey and remaining ginger. Return the lamb with any juices. Stir-fry for 2–3 minutes or until the liquid is bubbling and everything is tender and hot. Season to taste, scatter the remaining chopped mint over the top, then serve.

VARIATIONS
• *For a pork and pear stir-fry, use 350 grams lean pork. Instead of zucchini, quarter and slice 2 firm but ripe pears, preferably red-skinned; add them after the potatoes, at the same time as the scallions.*
• *For a vegetarian stir-fry, replace the lamb with 350 grams firm tofu (preferably smoked), cut into bite-sized cubes. Marinate the tofu in a mixture of 2 teaspoons sesame oil, 1 tablespoon salt-reduced soy sauce, 1 tablespoon mirin or sherry, 1 crushed garlic clove and 1 tablespoon finely chopped fresh ginger.*

EACH SERVING

28 g protein • 22 g fat of which 4.5 g saturates • 32 g carbohydrate
• 7.5 g fibre • 451 Calories

Stir-fried greens with bacon and chestnuts

Stir-frying is a great method of cooking that retains many of the vitamins and minerals that may be lost during boiling. This is a great way to cook Brussels sprouts and cabbage, sure to tempt even the most reluctant eaters of greens. Serve with bread.

Serves 4

Preparation time 20 minutes

Cooking time 30 minutes

30 fresh chestnuts

1½ tablespoons canola oil

3 slices back bacon, cut into thin strips

2 teaspoons sesame oil

2 leeks, trimmed and thinly sliced

250 grams (½ lb) Brussels sprouts, sliced

½ Savoy cabbage, shredded

1 tablespoon salt-reduced soy sauce

¼ cup squeezed orange juice

1 To prepare the chestnuts, score a cross in the base of each chestnut with a small, sharp knife. Cook in a pot of boiling water for 7 minutes, remove using a slotted spoon, then, when cool enough to handle, peel off the shell and inner skin. Return the chestnuts to the pot of boiling water and simmer for 10–12 minutes until tender. Remove from the pot; drain.

2 Heat the oil in a wok or large, deep frying pan, then fry the bacon for about 2 minutes until lightly browned. Remove from the pan with a slotted spoon and set aside, leaving any fat and juices behind in the wok.

3 Pour the sesame oil into the wok and heat for a few seconds until fragrant, then add the leeks

and fry gently for 30 seconds until just softened. Add the Brussels sprouts and cabbage and stir-fry for 4–5 minutes until almost tender but still slightly crisp.

4 Return the bacon to the wok together with the chestnuts, then stir in the soy sauce and orange juice. Cook for a further 2 minutes to heat everything through and to allow the greens to finish cooking. Season to taste with freshly ground black pepper. (There is no need to add salt as there is plenty in the dish already from the bacon and soy sauce.) Serve right away while piping hot.

EACH SERVING

12.5 g protein • 14.5 g fat of which 5 g saturates • 21 g carbohydrate • 9 g fibre • 276 Calories

Spicy pork and baby corn stir-fry

Tender pork is perfect in a stir-fry, particularly when combined with fresh baby corn and a subtle curry flavour. The addition of Hokkien noodles makes a completely satisfying meal.

Serves 4   Preparation time 20 minutes   Cooking time 20 minutes

2 tablespoons canola oil

350 grams (12 oz) lean boneless pork, cut into thin strips

1 teaspoon ground turmeric

1 tablespoon ground coriander

50 grams (2 oz) fresh ginger, peeled and cut into thin strips

2 garlic cloves, crushed

2 green peppers, deseeded and cut into thin strips

398 ml can baby corn, drained, halved lengthwise

6 scallions, sliced on the diagonal

1/3 cup dry or medium dry sherry

1/3 cup diluted salt-reduced or homemade chicken or vegetable stock (pages 28–29)

2 tablespoons salt-reduced soy sauce

4 cups bean sprouts

300 grams (10 oz) Hokkien noodles

1/3 cup roughly chopped cilantro

1 Heat 1 tablespoon of the oil in a wok or large frying pan. Add the pork and stir-fry for 5 minutes over a high heat. Reduce the heat, sprinkle in the turmeric and ground coriander and continue to stir-fry for 2 minutes. Transfer the meat to a plate and set aside.

2 Pour the remaining oil into the wok and add the ginger, garlic, peppers, corn and scallions. Stir-fry for 5 minutes, then return the meat to the wok with any juices on the plate. Stir-fry the meat and vegetables together so they are well mixed.

3 Pour in the sherry, stock and soy sauce, then reduce the heat and simmer for 5 minutes. Add the bean sprouts and noodles, cook for 2 more minutes, then sprinkle with the cilantro. Stir and serve immediately.

VARIATIONS

• *Good-quality curry powder or a curry paste can be used instead of turmeric and coriander. Add 2–3 teaspoons to the meat in step 1.*
• *Chicken or lamb may be used instead of the pork.*
• *A can of sliced bamboo shoots, drained, would make a handy alternative to baby corn.*

EACH SERVING

27 g protein • 13 g fat of which 2 g saturates • 26 g carbohydrate • 5 g fibre • 359 Calories

VARIATIONS

• *For a vegetarian dish, replace the bacon with 250 grams cubed firm tofu, adding it with the chestnuts in step 4 and without frying it first.*
• *Add some fava beans to this dish for added flavour. Add 1 cup frozen fava beans, thawed, with the Brussels sprouts and cabbage in step 3.*

Stir-fried beef with vegetables

A stir-fry is a tasty way to combine meat and vegetables in the one dish. The trick with stir-fries is to have everything ready to go before you start cooking as once you fire up the wok there can be no stopping. Serve with steamed rice or noodles.

Serves 4

Preparation time 15 minutes, plus 15 minutes marinating

Cooking time 10 minutes

450 grams (1 lb) round steak, thinly sliced

2¹/₂ tablespoons oyster sauce

3 teaspoons salt-reduced soy sauce

¹/₂ teaspoon sugar

2 tablespoons cornstarch

2 garlic cloves, chopped

2 tablespoons canola oil

1 small onion, cut into wedges

1 small carrot, peeled and sliced

1 red pepper, deseeded and sliced

100 grams (3¹/₂ oz) broccoli florets

5 baby corn, halved lengthwise

1 bunch asparagus, trimmed and cut on the diagonal into 5 cm lengths

¹/₂ cup water

1 Put the beef in a bowl with the oyster and soy sauces, sugar, cornstarch and garlic. Mix together and allow to marinate for at least 15 minutes.

2 Heat a well-seasoned wok or large, non-stick frying pan over a high heat. Add 1 tablespoon of the oil, then add all of the meat and stir-fry for about 3 minutes until the meat is cooked and browned. Remove and keep warm.

3 Clean the wok out by wiping with paper towel. Heat over a medium heat and add the remaining oil. Add the onion, carrot, pepper and broccoli and cook for 1 minute, tossing frequently. Add the corn, asparagus and water and return the meat to the wok and cook for a further minute, or until the sauce has thickened. The vegetables should be slightly softened but still retain their crispness. Serve immediately.

EACH SERVING

28.5 g protein • 15.5 g fat of which 4 g saturates • 13 g carbohydrate • 3 g fibre • 311 Calories

Chicken, snow pea and corn stir-fry

This crunchy, refreshing stir-fry is just what you need for a midweek meal — it can be on the table in under 30 minutes from when you walk through the door. The corn provides carbohydrate, so you don't even need to cook rice or noodles.

Serves **4**   *Preparation time* **10 minutes**   *Cooking time* **10 minutes**

1 tablespoon oyster sauce

¼ cup diluted salt-reduced or homemade chicken or vegetable stock (pages 28–29)

¼ cup canola oil

1 tablespoon black mustard seeds

8 scallions, thinly sliced

3 large garlic cloves, crushed

400 grams (14 oz) skinless boneless chicken breasts, cut into thin strips

200 grams (7 oz) snow peas

284 ml can corn kernels, drained and rinsed

1 tablespoon sesame seeds

2 tablespoons chopped cilantro

1 Mix the oyster sauce and stock together in a small bowl, then set aside.

2 Heat a wok or large frying pan over a high heat, add 1 tablespoon of the canola oil and heat until it is very hot. Add the mustard seeds and stir-fry them for 10–15 seconds until they crackle and "jump."

3 Immediately add the remaining oil, scallions and garlic and stir-fry for 1 minute. Add the chicken and continue stir-frying for a further 2 minutes.

4 Add the snow peas to the wok and stir in the reserved oyster sauce mixture. Continue stir-frying over a high heat for about 3 minutes until the chicken is cooked through and the snow peas are just tender to the bite.

5 Add the corn and stir around for 2 minutes or until warmed through. Sprinkle with sesame seeds and snip cilantro leaves over the top just before serving.

VARIATIONS

• *Vary the vegetables as much as you like. Try small broccoli florets, thickly sliced flat mushrooms or sliced red or green peppers.*
• *Supermarkets sell a variety of bottled, ready-to-use, stir-fry sauces, which are useful to have in the cupboard. If you use one, omit the oyster sauce and stock.*

EACH SERVING

24.5 g protein • 26 g fat of which 5 g saturates • 14 g carbohydrate • 4 g fibre • 396 Calories

COOK'S TIPS
• *To make it easier to slice the meat thinly, put it in the freezer for 30 minutes before slicing it.*
• *Before you begin stir-frying, the wok or pan must be very hot. You can tell it is ready to use when a smoky haze appears over the surface.*

Chicken satay stir-fry

This Indonesian-style stir-fry combines colourful crunchy vegetables and tender chicken strips. Serve with toasted white or whole wheat pita bread.

Serves 4

Preparation time 20 minutes

Cooking time 15 minutes

¼ cup smooth peanut butter

⅓ cup reduced-fat coconut milk

2 tablespoons diluted salt-reduced or homemade chicken stock (page 28)

1 lemon, zest finely grated

1 tablespoon canola oil

2 garlic cloves, crushed

1 red chili pepper, deseeded and finely chopped

350 grams (12 oz) skinless boneless chicken breasts, cut into thin strips

1 tablespoon five-spice powder

1 red pepper, deseeded and sliced

2 carrots, peeled and cut into julienne strips

175 g (6 oz) button mushrooms, sliced

2 tablespoons chopped cilantro

COOK'S TIP

• *You can spice things up a little by leaving the seeds in the chili pepper – chili peppers contain most of their heat in the seeds and membrane.*

1 In a small bowl, whisk together the peanut butter, coconut milk, stock and lemon zest until blended, then set aside.

2 Heat the oil in a wok or large frying pan over a high heat. Add the garlic and chili pepper and stir-fry for 30 seconds to release the flavours.

3 Add the chicken and five-spice powder and stir-fry for 3–4 minutes until the chicken has coloured all over. Add the red pepper, carrots and mushrooms and stir-fry for 2–3 minutes until slightly softened.

4 Pour the peanut butter mixture into the wok and stir-fry for a further 2–3 minutes until the chicken is cooked through and tender. Remove from the heat, stir in the chopped cilantro and serve immediately.

EACH SERVING

28.5 g protein • 20.5 g fat of which 4 g saturates • 8.5 g carbohydrate • 5.5 g fibre • 342 Calories

Stir-fried chicken livers with mushrooms

The delicate flavour and creamy texture of chicken livers work well with mushrooms and sherry, while broccoli adds further vitamins and minerals. The stir-fry is served on toasted ciabatta to soak up the juices.

Serves **4**   *Preparation time* **15 minutes**   *Cooking time* **10 minutes**

400 grams (14 oz) chicken livers, thawed if frozen

200 grams (7 oz) small brown mushrooms, sliced

200 grams (7 oz) broccoli

2 tablespoons olive oil

1 red onion, finely chopped

2 garlic cloves, finely chopped

1/3 cup dry sherry

1 tablespoon currant jelly

1 ciabatta, cut into 8 thick slices

1 Tip the chicken livers into a colander and rinse gently under cold running water. Drain thoroughly, then pat them dry with paper towel. Using kitchen scissors, trim off any stringy white pieces and any discoloured edges. Season to taste and set aside.

2 Wipe the mushrooms with a damp cloth to remove any grit but do not wash. Trim the broccoli to remove any coarse or woody stems.

3 Gently heat the oil in a wok or large, non-stick frying pan. Add the onion and cook, stirring frequently, until it is soft and translucent. Add the livers and gently stir-fry over a medium heat for 2 minutes until they are lightly coloured. Preheat the grill to medium.

4 Add the mushrooms and broccoli and stir-fry for 2 minutes. Add the garlic, sherry and currant jelly. Stir well, then cover the wok and leave to simmer gently for 3 minutes until the broccoli is just tender when pierced with the tip of a sharp knife and the livers are slightly pink inside.

5 Meanwhile, toast the ciabatta. Check the stir-fry for seasoning, then arrange the ciabatta on individual plates, two slices per serving, and spoon the livers and vegetables over the top. Serve immediately.

VARIATION
• *Replace the broccoli with coloured peppers — one each green, red and yellow, deseeded and thinly sliced.*

EACH SERVING

31.5 g protein • 16 g fat of which 3 g saturates • 59 g carbohydrate • 6.5 g fibre • 270 Calories

VARIATION
• *Turkey breasts could be used in place of chicken, 2 small zucchini rather than carrots and a drained can of sliced bamboo shoots as an alternative to the button mushrooms.*

VARIATIONS
• If bok choy is not available, substitute shredded napa cabbage or young spring greens.
• To make a vegetarian version of this dish, replace the duck with firm tofu.

Sweet and sour duck

Kumquats are a small citrus fruit, like an orange, but the whole fruit is edible, adding a great tangy flavour to this easy stir-fry dish. Kumquats are believed to symbolize good fortune in the Far East. If you prefer, you may omit them.

Step 1

Step 2

Step 4

Serves 4

Preparation time 25 minutes

Cooking time 15 minutes

2 tablespoons salt-reduced soy sauce

2 tablespoons rice vinegar

1/3 cup plum sauce

2 tablespoons tomato paste

2 tablespoons canola oil

8 scallions, sliced

30 grams (1 oz) fresh ginger, peeled and cut into strips

4 duck breasts, skinned and thinly sliced

2 red peppers, deseeded and thinly sliced

8 kumquats, thinly sliced (optional)

250 grams (1/2 lb) bok choy, sliced lengthwise

440 gram package Hokkien noodles

1 Mix together the soy sauce, vinegar, plum sauce and tomato paste in a jug or small bowl and set aside.

2 Heat the oil in a wok or large frying pan and stir-fry the scallions and ginger over a fairly high heat for about 30 seconds. Add the duck and stir-fry over a high heat for about 2 minutes until lightly cooked.

3 Add the peppers to the wok and continue to stir-fry for 4–6 minutes until the peppers and duck are just tender and the juices have evaporated. Add the kumquats (if using) and cook for a further 1 minute.

4 Stir the sauce mixture, then pour it into the wok, tossing everything together to coat with the sauce and heat through. Add the bok choy and stir-fry for about 1 minute or until wilted.

5 Finally, add the noodles to the wok and stir-fry for 2–3 minutes until thoroughly heated. Serve immediately.

EACH SERVING

42.5 g protein • 25 g fat of which 5.5 g saturates • 46 g carbohydrate • 3 g fibre • 583 Calories

Lemon chicken with broccoli

A family favourite that mixes succulent strips of chicken with a zesty, hot and sour sauce. The inclusion of whole cashews adds a satisfying crunch.

Serves **4**   *Preparation time* **15 minutes**   *Cooking time* **20 minutes**

250 grams (½ lb) dried noodles

2 large lemons, zest grated and juiced

1½ tablespoons cornstarch

½ cup diluted salt-reduced or homemade chicken or vegetable stock (pages 28–29)

1 tablespoon salt-reduced soy sauce

2 teaspoons superfine sugar

½ teaspoon chili pepper flakes,

½ cup unsalted cashews

2½ tablespoons canola oil

2 small onions, finely chopped

2 garlic cloves, crushed

500 grams (1 lb) skinless boneless chicken breasts, cut into thin strips

250 grams (½ lb) broccoli, cut into small florets

30 grams (1 oz) fresh ginger, peeled and finely chopped

⅓ cup chopped cilantro

1 Bring a large pot of lightly salted water to a boil. Add the noodles and boil for about 6 minutes, or according to the package instructions, until soft.

2 Meanwhile, make up the lemon juice to ½ cup with water, if necessary, then blend with the cornstarch in a bowl or jug until smooth. Stir in the stock, soy sauce and sugar, then add the lemon zest and chili pepper flakes. Set aside.

3 Heat a wok or large frying pan over a high heat. Add the cashews and stir for about 1 minute until browned in places. Tip them out and set aside.

4 Return the wok to the heat and add the oil, swirling it around to coat the sides. Add the onions and garlic and stir-fry for 3 minutes or until tender. Add the chicken pieces and stir-fry for 2–3 minutes until the chicken is cooked through and beginning to brown.

5 Pour in the reserved lemon-flavoured sauce and add the broccoli florets and ginger. Bring to a boil, then cover and simmer for 4–5 minutes until the broccoli florets are tender but still crisp.

6 Drain the noodles well, then add them to the wok. Use two large forks to mix them in with the other ingredients. Scatter the cilantro and cashews over the top, then serve.

EACH SERVING

38.5 g protein • 30 g fat of which 5.5 g saturates • 53 g carbohydrate • 6 g fibre • 649 Calories

Teriyaki chicken with vegetables

You can prepare the chicken ahead of time — this will not only increase the flavour, but it means that all you have to do before serving is briefly cook it with vitamin-rich vegetables. If you like, serve with steamed rice.

Serves 4 *Preparation time* *10 minutes, plus at least 1 hour marinating*
Cooking time *15 minutes*

500 grams (1 lb) skinless boneless chicken breasts, cut into strips

150 grams (5 oz) shiitake mushrooms, halved

1 teaspoon grated fresh ginger

200 grams (7 oz) snow peas

2¾ cups bean sprouts

199 ml can bamboo shoots, drained

1 cup frozen peas

TERIYAKI MARINADE

2 garlic cloves, crushed

2 tablespoons dry sherry

1 tablespoon salt-reduced soy sauce

1 tablespoon sesame oil

2 teaspoons canola oil

1 teaspoon rice vinegar

½ teaspoon superfine sugar

1 Combine all the marinade ingredients in a large bowl. Add the chicken strips and gently toss to coat well. Cover and leave to marinate in the refrigerator for about 1 hour or up to 4 hours.

2 Heat a wok or large, non-stick frying pan over a medium heat until quite hot. Tip in the chicken with the marinade. Cook for about 4 minutes, stirring occasionally. Remove from the heat. Transfer the chicken to a dish using a slotted spoon, leaving the liquid in the pan. Cover the chicken to keep warm.

3 Return the wok to the heat and add the mushrooms with the grated ginger. Cook for about 2 minutes, stirring frequently.

4 Add the snow peas and stir-fry for 1 minute, then add the bean sprouts and stir-fry for a further 1 minute. Stir in the bamboo shoots and peas, cover the wok and cook gently for 2 minutes. Return the chicken to the pan and reheat for 1–2 minutes, if necessary, then serve.

EACH SERVING

34 g protein • 14.5 g fat of which 3 g saturates • 13 g carbohydrate • 6.5 g fibre • 336 Calories

Seafood and vegetable stir-fry

Enjoy the bounty of the sea with this fresh and colourful stir-fry. By cooking the seafood only briefly, the flavour is maximized.

Serves 4

Preparation time 25 minutes

Cooking time 10 minutes

350 grams (12 oz) raw jumbo shrimp

500 grams (1 lb) cod or sole

2 squid (500 grams/1 lb in total)

2 tablespoons canola oil

1 cm piece fresh ginger, peeled and julienned

2 garlic cloves, chopped

70 grams (2½ oz) broccoli florets

1 carrot, peeled and julienned

2 scallions, roughly sliced

SAUCE

1 cup water or salt-reduced or homemade chicken stock (page 28)

2 tablespoons oyster sauce

2 teaspoons salt-reduced soy sauce

2 teaspoons sugar

1 tablespoon cornstarch

1 To prepare the seafood, peel and devein the shrimp. Cut the fish into 3 cm chunks. Gently grasp the squid body with one hand; with the other, pull the tentacles and the quill from inside the body. Wash the insides and remove the flaps and skin by pulling off. Cut the squid in half, then gently score the inside of the flesh in a crisscross pattern (without cutting through), then slice into bite-sized pieces. To use the tentacles, cut into shorter lengths.

2 Combine all the sauce ingredients in a jar, ensuring that the cornstarch is well blended.

3 Heat a wok or non-stick frying pan over a high heat. Add 1½ tablespoons of the oil and cook the fish for 1 minute, tossing frequently. Add the shrimp and squid and cook for 1–2 minutes or until the shrimp are almost cooked. Transfer to a plate to keep warm.

4 Heat the remaining oil in the wok, then toss the ginger and garlic for 30 seconds. Cook the broccoli and carrot for 1 minute, until they begin to soften but still retain their crispness. Return the seafood to the wok, add the scallions and the sauce. Cook for 1 minute or until the sauce thickens and the seafood is perfectly cooked.

EACH SERVING

64 g protein • 14 g fat of which 2.5 g saturates • 9.5 g carbohydrate • 1.5 g fibre • 428 Calories

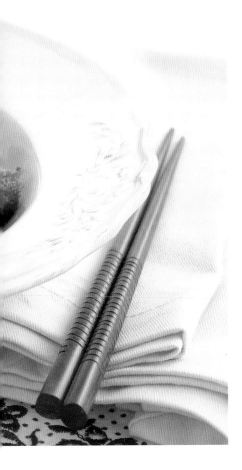

Fish with bok choy

Firm, meaty white fish fillets are perfect for stir-frying as they keep their shape well and don't break up easily. Serve the fish on a bed of tender vegetables and top with salty prosciutto, all cooked in the same wok. Some crusty bread rolls would complete the meal nicely.

Serves 4   Preparation time 15 minutes   Cooking time 15 minutes

2 tablespoons canola oil

4 firm white fish steaks, cut into 5 cm chunks

4 slices prosciutto, torn into pieces

2 garlic cloves, crushed

2.5 cm piece fresh ginger, peeled and finely shredded

1 red chili pepper, deseeded and finely diced

6 scallions, sliced on the diagonal

200 grams (7 oz) snow peas, halved on the diagonal

1¾ cups shelled young fava beans

200 grams (7 oz) small bok choy, sliced lengthwise

1 tablespoon salt-reduced soy sauce

1 Heat 1 tablespoon of the oil in a wok or large frying pan until very hot, then add the fish pieces. Stir-fry for about 5 minutes until lightly browned all over and cooked through. Remove from the wok and keep warm.

2 Add the prosciutto to the wok and stir-fry over a fairly high heat for 1–2 minutes until golden and crisp. Remove and keep warm.

3 Add the remaining oil to the wok and stir-fry the garlic, ginger and chili pepper for about 30 seconds, without browning. Add the scallions, snow peas and beans and stir-fry for 3–4 minutes. Stir in the bok choy and stir-fry for about 2 minutes until the leaves are wilted.

4 Pile the vegetables onto warmed serving plates, place the fish pieces on top and add a few crisp pieces of prosciutto. Drizzle with the soy sauce and serve immediately.

VARIATIONS

• *A vegetarian version could be made with chunks of firm tofu. Lightly fry it in half the oil, then continue from step 3 as in the recipe. Pile the tofu on top of the vegetables and drizzle with soy sauce to serve.*
• *If bok choy is not available, you can use roughly shredded napa cabbage.*

EACH SERVING

41.5 g protein • 12 g fat of which 2 g saturates • 9.5 g carbohydrate • 6 g fibre • 326 Calories

COOK'S TIPS

• *This meal is relatively high in sodium, so enjoy it as an occasional treat.*
• *If you prefer, you can leave the tails on the shrimp — they look quite attractive with the tails intact. Provide a bowl for the discarded tails.*
• *Some fish markets sell ready-cleaned squid, or will clean it for you if you ask them.*

Peppered fish with lemon and basil

This is a fantastically healthy meal with a real peppery kick balanced by sweet basil and peppers. Serve with ciabatta or focaccia.

Serves 4

Preparation time 10 minutes

Cooking time 10 minutes

2 tablespoons canola oil

1 onion, finely chopped

2 red peppers, deseeded and thinly sliced

2 yellow peppers, deseeded and thinly sliced

175 g (6 oz) sugar snap peas

500 grams (1 lb) white fish steak, skinned and cut into 4 cm chunks

1 lemon, zest grated and juiced

2 teaspoons mixed peppercorns, coarsely crushed

1¼ cups frozen peas, thawed

1¼ cups bean sprouts

15 grams (½ oz) fresh basil, finely shredded

1 Heat a wok or large frying pan over a high heat and add 1 tablespoon of the oil. Add the onion and stir-fry for 1 minute. Stir in the peppers and sugar snap peas and continue stir-frying for 3–5 minutes until the vegetables are tender but still crisp. Transfer the vegetables to a plate using a slotted spoon and keep them in a warm place.

2 Add the remaining oil to the wok and heat, then add the fish and stir-fry over a gentle heat for about 4 minutes, carefully turning the chunks so as not to break them up, until the fish is cooked through and flakes easily when tested with the point of a knife.

3 Add the lemon zest, lemon juice and crushed peppercorns to the wok. Return the stir-fried vegetables to the wok together with the peas and bean sprouts. Heat through, stirring, for 2–3 minutes. Scatter the basil over the top and serve at once.

COOK'S TIP

• *A mortar and pestle is ideal for crushing the peppercorns, but if you don't have one, put them in the corner of a strong plastic bag and press down with the end of a rolling pin or the back of a wooden spoon. Alternatively, some spice manufacturers sell mixed peppercorns in a pepper grinder, which makes the job very easy — look in the spice aisle of your local supermarket.*

VARIATIONS

• *If you prefer, you can use strips of chicken breast instead of the fish. Cook until lightly browned.*
• *You can be as adventurous as you like with the choice of vegetables. Try broccoli or halved beans instead of the sugar snap peas, or fava beans instead of the frozen peas.*

EACH SERVING

32.5 g protein • 10.5 g fat of which 1.5 g saturates • 13.5 g carbohydrate • 7 g fibre • 295 Calories

Pad Thai noodles with shrimp

Typical Thai flavours, including chili pepper, lime and coconut, combine in this aromatic stir-fry of shrimp, noodles and Asian vegetables. By using a curry paste, the preparation time is reduced.

Serves 4 Preparation time 20 minutes Cooking time 10 minutes

1 tablespoon lime juice

2 tablespoons soy sauce

1 tablespoon fish sauce

250 grams (½ lb) shelled raw shrimp, thawed if frozen

250 grams (½ lb) medium dried rice noodles

¼ cup canola oil

1 tablespoon Thai green curry paste, or more to taste

1 teaspoon sesame oil

6 baby corn, halved lengthwise

2¾ cups bean sprouts

200 grams (7 oz) bok choy, finely shredded

199 ml can water chestnuts, drained

1 cup coconut milk

1 lime, cut into wedges

1 Mix together the lime juice, soy sauce and fish sauce in a bowl. Add the shrimp and toss together, then set aside to marinate for a few minutes.

2 Meanwhile, put the noodles in a large heatproof bowl. Pour over boiling water to cover, add 1 teaspoon of the canola oil and stir gently. Soak for 4 minutes, then drain thoroughly.

3 Lift the shrimp out of the marinade and pat dry with paper towel. Stir the curry paste into the marinade and set aside. Heat a wok or heavy-based frying pan until very hot, then add 1 teaspoon of the canola oil and the sesame oil and swirl to coat the pan. Add the shrimp and stir-fry for about 2 minutes until they have turned pink. Remove with a slotted spoon, leaving any remaining oil behind.

4 Add the rest of the oil to the pan. Toss in the corn and stir-fry for about 30 seconds. Add the bean sprouts and bok choy and stir-fry for a minute, then add the curry paste mixture. Cook for a few seconds, stirring all the time, then add the water chestnuts and drained noodles. Continue to stir-fry for a further 1 minute.

5 Return the shrimp to the wok and pour in the coconut milk. Toss everything together over a high heat until bubbling. Serve immediately, with lime wedges to squeeze over.

EACH SERVING

23.5 g protein • 19.5 g fat of which 3 g saturates • 53.5 g carbohydrate • 5 g fibre • 500 Calories

Tofu noodles

Popular in Northern Japan, soba noodles are made from buckwheat flour, which gives them a slightly nutty flavour. In this quick and simple dish, the thin brown noodles are delicious stir-fried with protein-rich tofu and crunchy water chestnuts.

Serves **4** *Preparation time* **15 minutes** *Cooking time* **10 minutes**

2 tablespoons salt-reduced soy sauce

2 tablespoons dry sherry

2 teaspoons sesame oil

2 garlic cloves, crushed

½ teaspoon chili pepper flakes

pinch of superfine sugar

250 grams (½ lb) firm tofu, cubed

250 grams (½ lb) soba noodles

1 tablespoon canola oil

250 grams (½ lb) bok choy, finely shredded

199 ml can water chestnuts, drained

2 tablespoons sesame seeds, toasted

1 Put the soy sauce, sherry, sesame oil, garlic, chili pepper flakes and sugar in a bowl. Whisk together with a fork, add the tofu cubes and toss to coat in the mixture. Cover and set aside. (Leave to marinate if convenient.)

2 Bring a large pot of water to a boil, add the noodles and boil for 5 minutes until softened. Tip into a colander and drain well.

3 While the noodles are cooking, heat a wok or large, deep frying pan until hot, then add the oil. Drain the tofu, reserving the marinade, and stir-fry in the hot oil for about 30 seconds. Add the bok choy and water chestnuts and cook for a further minute, stirring all the time.

4 Tip in the cooked noodles and reserved marinade. Cook for a further 1–2 minutes or until heated through and the bok choy has wilted. Serve sprinkled with sesame seeds.

EACH SERVING

16.5 g protein • 15 g fat of which 2 g saturates • 32 g carbohydrate • 4 g fibre • 336 Calories

COOK'S TIP
• Don't use any of the Swiss chard stems for this recipe — only the leaves are needed.

VARIATION
• If Swiss chard is not available, you can make this dish using fresh spinach leaves, washed and torn into large pieces. Cook the spinach in the same way as for the Swiss chard. For the best results, make sure to dry the leaves before cooking with them.

Spaghetti with scallops, asparagus and Swiss chard

This is a sophisticated dish, combining pasta with a stir-fry of creamy white scallops and vibrant green vegetables. The scallops are low in fat and rich in vitamin B_{12} and many minerals. By cooking the vegetables briefly in very little liquid they retain all their nutrients.

Step 1

Step 2

Step 3

Serves 4

Preparation time 10 minutes

Cooking time 15 minutes

300 grams (10 oz) spaghetti

1 tablespoon olive oil

350 grams (12 oz) scallops, quartered if large

200 grams (7 oz) asparagus, trimmed and cut into 3 cm lengths

½ teaspoon grated fresh ginger

½ lemon, zest grated and juiced

250 grams (½ lb) Swiss chard leaves, coarsely shredded

⅓ cup water

1 Cook the spaghetti in a large pot of lightly salted boiling water for 10–12 minutes, or according to the package instructions, until tender. When ready, drain in a colander.

2 While the pasta is cooking, heat the oil in a wok or large frying pan over a high heat. Add the scallops in a single layer and cook, turning occasionally, for about 3 minutes or until lightly golden and almost cooked through. Transfer the scallops to a plate, using a slotted spoon, and keep warm.

3 Add the asparagus to the wok with the ginger and lemon zest. Cook, stirring frequently, for about 4 minutes until starting to soften.

4 Add the Swiss chard leaves to the wok and lightly toss to mix well. Pour in the water, cover the wok and cook for about 5 minutes until the Swiss chard is wilted and the asparagus is tender.

5 Return the scallops to the wok with the lemon juice and season to taste. Add the spaghetti to the wok and gently toss to mix with the scallops and asparagus. Serve at once.

EACH SERVING

19 g protein • 8 g fat of which 1.5 g saturates • 44.5 g carbohydrate • 6 g fibre • 338 Calories

Steak with puttanesca sauce

This is a really quick recipe for dressing up lean round steak. A gutsy tomato sauce, boosted with anchovies and capers, is made in the same pan, and all that's needed is some crusty French bread and a side salad for a deliciously easy meal.

Serves 4

Preparation time 10 minutes

Cooking time 15 minutes

30 grams (1 oz) anchovy fillets, drained

2 tablespoons 1% milk

2 tablespoons olive oil

1 red onion, roughly chopped

2 garlic cloves, crushed

1 red chili pepper, deseeded and finely chopped

350 grams (12 oz) cherry tomatoes, halved

2 tablespoons bottled capers, rinsed

1 teaspoon dried oregano

4 lean round steaks

1 Lay the anchovies flat in a small dish, spoon over the milk and leave to soak while you begin preparing the sauce. (This soaking will remove a lot of the saltiness from the anchovies to give a mellower flavour.)

2 Heat 1 tablespoon of the oil in a large, heavy-based, ridged frying pan, add the onion and cook gently for 3–4 minutes until soft.

3 Stir in the garlic and chili pepper, then add the tomatoes, capers and oregano. Drain off and discard the milk from the anchovies, roughly chop the anchovies and add to the sauce. Stir around and cook gently for 5 minutes or until the tomatoes are lightly cooked. Tip the sauce out into a bowl and set aside while cooking the steaks.

4 Rinse out the pan and reheat. Brush the steaks lightly on both sides with the remaining oil and season with some freshly ground black pepper. Place the steaks in the hot pan and cook over a medium-high heat for 2–3 minutes on each side for rare or 4–6 minutes on each side for medium.

5 Pour the sauce over the steaks in the pan and heat through, then serve immediately.

EACH SERVING

28 g protein • 15.5 g fat of which 4 g saturates • 5 g carbohydrate • 2.5 g fibre • 275 Calories

VARIATIONS
• This sauce is equally
good served with pan-
fried skinless chicken
breasts or chunky white
fish steaks.
• For a vegetarian option,
leave out the anchovies
and serve the puttanesca
sauce with pasta or
cheesy potato cakes.

Beef stroganoff

Combined with mushrooms, a small amount of meat goes a long way. Cooked in a creamy sauce made with light sour cream, then tossed with tagliatelle, this makes a luxurious dish, with much less fat than the original version.

Serves **4** *Preparation time* **20 minutes** *Cooking time* **15 minutes**

350 grams (12 oz) tagliatelle

2 tablespoons canola oil

350 grams (12 oz) lean beef, cut into thin strips

1 onion, halved and thinly sliced

1 large garlic clove, finely chopped

300 grams (10 oz) brown mushrooms, thickly sliced

2 tablespoons dry sherry

⅓ cup diluted salt-reduced or homemade beef or vegetable stock (pages 28–29)

1 teaspoon cornstarch

½ cup light sour cream

2 teaspoons fresh thyme

pinch of grated nutmeg

1 teaspoon ground paprika

pinch of cayenne pepper

1 Cook the tagliatelle in a large pot of boiling water for 10–12 minutes, or according to the package instructions, until tender.

2 Meanwhile, heat 1 tablespoon of the oil in a large frying pan over a high heat. Add the beef and stir-fry for 1–2 minutes until browned all over. Remove from the pan and set aside.

3 Add the remaining 1 tablespoon oil to the pan, then reduce the heat to medium. Add the onion and fry for about 4 minutes, stirring frequently until beginning to soften, then stir in the garlic and mushrooms and continue cooking for a further 3–4 minutes until tender. Stir in the sherry and cook for a few seconds, then add the stock.

4 Blend the cornstarch with 2 teaspoons cold water in a small bowl or jug. Stir in the sour cream, thyme, nutmeg, paprika and cayenne pepper, then stir this mixture into the pan and cook until it starts to bubble. Return the beef to the pan and cook for a few more seconds to heat through. Season to taste.

5 Tip the tagliatelle into a colander over the sink and drain thoroughly. Add to the stroganoff mixture and gently toss together, then serve right away.

VARIATION
• Rather than beef, use pork tenderloin or boneless skinless chicken breasts.

EACH SERVING

31 g protein • 21 g fat of which 7 g saturates • 55 g carbohydrate • 6.5 g fibre • 555 Calories

Lamb with feta and mint

This Greek-style dish is simple to cook but wonderfully flavoured. It combines lamb fillets with colourful vegetables, feta and fresh mint – perfect for entertaining.

Serves 4

Preparation time 15 minutes

Cooking time 25 minutes

4 lamb fillets, trimmed of all excess fat

¼ cup olive oil

300 grams (10 oz) new potatoes, scrubbed and thinly sliced

1 large zucchini, sliced

1 red onion, sliced

2 red peppers, deseeded and sliced

8 garlic cloves, peeled

⅓ cup (80 ml) red wine vinegar

70 grams (2½ oz) feta cheese, drained

30 grams (1 oz) fresh mint, finely shredded

VARIATION

• *Pork and fennel is a popular flavour combination in Greece. Replace the lamb fillets with 4 well-trimmed pork loin chops and the zucchini with 2 thinly sliced fennel bulbs. Use a white onion instead of the red and add 1 teaspoon fennel seeds to the vegetables in step 4.*

1 Heat a large frying pan with a tight-fitting lid over a medium heat. Brush the lamb fillets on one side with a little of the oil. Add the fillets to the pan, oiled-side down, and fry for 3–4 minutes until nicely browned. Lightly brush the lamb fillets with a little more oil, then flip them over and continue frying for a further 1 minute. Transfer the lamb fillets to a plate and set aside.

2 Add 1 tablespoon of the oil to the pan and heat. Add the potatoes and fry, turning occasionally, for 5 minutes or until golden and they start to soften.

3 Add another 1 tablespoon of oil to the pan. Add the zucchini, onion, peppers and garlic and continue frying, stirring occasionally, for 5 minutes or until all the vegetables are tender.

4 Meanwhile, mix the remaining oil with the vinegar in a small jug or bowl. Return the lamb fillets to the pan, placing them on top of the vegetables, and pour in the oil and vinegar mixture. Crumble the feta cheese over the top. Reduce the heat to low, cover the pan with a lid and cook for about 5 minutes for medium-rare or 7 minutes for medium.

5 Uncover the pan and scatter the mint over the top. Season with freshly ground black pepper to taste. Serve at once, straight from the pan, with a drizzling of the pan juices.

EACH SERVING

30.5 g protein • 25 g fat of which 8.5 g saturates • 15 g carbohydrate • 5 g fibre • 420 Calories

Blackened chicken

The spiced coating on the chicken breasts cooks to a delicious crunchy crust, keeping the inside flesh really juicy. It's served on a simple avocado, bean and tomato salad, but add some rustic bread to complete the meal.

Serves 4
Preparation time 15 minutes
Cooking time 20 minutes

2 teaspoons coriander seeds

2 teaspoons cumin seeds

2 teaspoons black peppercorns

2 garlic cloves, crushed

2 teaspoons dried oregano

1 tablespoon paprika

2 tablespoons olive oil

3 skinless boneless chicken breasts

4 lime wedges

SALAD

1 avocado

4 tomatoes, sliced

398 ml can pinto beans, drained and rinsed

1 tablespoon lime juice

1 tablespoon olive oil

2 tablespoons chopped fresh flat-leaf parsley

VARIATION
• *The spice mix is also very good with pork — try it rubbed over lean pork chops, and chargrill in the same way as for the chicken.*

1 Place the coriander and cumin seeds, peppercorns and garlic in a mortar and crush with a pestle until roughly ground. Add the oregano, paprika and oil and crush to a paste.

2 Use a sharp knife to cut 3–4 deep slashes across each chicken breast. Spread the spice mix over the chicken, rubbing deep into the cuts.

3 Heat a heavy-based frying pan until very hot and add the chicken breasts. Reduce the heat to medium and fry the chicken for 15–20 minutes, turning occasionally, until it is slightly charred on the outside and thoroughly cooked inside. (It can be served warm or cooled and then chilled, to serve later.)

4 Meanwhile, or shortly before serving, make the salad. Peel and slice the avocado, then put in a bowl with the tomatoes and beans. Drizzle with the lime juice and olive oil, add the parsley and season lightly.

5 Heap the salad onto a serving plate. Cut the chicken, on the diagonal, into neat slices and arrange on top of the salad. Garnish with lime wedges to squeeze over the chicken.

EACH SERVING

32 g protein • 35 g fat of which 7 g saturates • 16.5 g carbohydrate • 5 g fibre • 526 Calories

Chicken with lentils and chorizo

Chicken and spicy chorizo sausage combine well with vegetables and lentils, which are naturally low in fat and a good source of fibre, to create this hearty and flavourful pan-fry. Serve with a green salad to round out the meal.

Serves 4   Preparation time 20 minutes   Cooking time 40 minutes

125 grams (4 oz) chorizo sausage, skinned and thinly sliced

1 red onion, finely chopped

1 garlic clove, crushed

1 celery stalk, finely chopped

300 grams (10 oz) skinless boneless chicken breasts, thinly sliced

1 red pepper, deseeded and sliced

1¼ cups French green lentils

1 cup dry white wine

1 cup diluted salt-reduced or homemade chicken stock (page 28), hot

2 tablespoons chopped fresh flat-leaf parsley

1 Heat a non-stick frying pan over a medium heat, add the chorizo sausage, red onion, garlic and celery and cook for about 5 minutes until the onion is beginning to soften.

2 Add the chicken pieces and red pepper to the pan and cook for about 4 minutes until the chicken is coloured all over.

3 Stir in the lentils, wine and stock. Bring to a boil, then reduce the heat, cover and cook gently for about 30 minutes until the lentils are tender, stirring occasionally. Season to taste and serve sprinkled with chopped parsley.

COOK'S TIP

• *French green lentils are tiny, grey-green lentils. They have a distinctive flavour and hold their shape and colour when cooked. But if they are not available, you can use any other green or brown lentils.*

EACH SERVING

29.5 g protein • 10 g fat of which 4 g saturates • 16.5 g carbohydrate • 5 g fibre • 322 Calories

Tuna steaks with salsa rossa

Heart-healthy tuna has a unique flavour and a firm texture. Here, it is briefly pan-fried, then gently cooked in a red pepper and tomato sauce. Delicious with ciabatta.

Serves **4**   *Preparation time* **20 minutes**   *Cooking time* **20 minutes**

2 tablespoons olive oil

2 teaspoons red wine vinegar

4 tuna steaks (about 2 cm thick)

2 red peppers, halved lengthwise and deseeded

350 grams (12 oz) vine-ripened tomatoes, peeled and diced

1 small red onion, finely chopped

1 red chili pepper, deseeded and finely chopped

1 large garlic clove, finely chopped

pinch of ground cinnamon

pinch of sugar

150 grams (5 oz) thin green beans, halved

1 tablespoon water

1/3 cup pitted black olives, halved

1 tablespoon chopped fresh mint

12 fresh basil leaves, roughly torn

1 Preheat the broiler. Whisk together 1 tablespoon of the oil and 1 teaspoon of the vinegar. Brush over the tuna steaks and lightly season with pepper. Set aside to marinate while you prepare the vegetables.

2 Put the peppers, skin-side up, on a grill tray and broil for 5 minutes or until the skins are blackened and blistered. Put them in a plastic bag and leave until cool enough to handle, then, working over a bowl to catch the juice, peel them. Cut into dice and add to the juice in the bowl. Add the tomatoes.

3 Heat a heavy, non-stick frying pan, add the tuna steaks and cook over a medium–high heat for 1 minute on each side until lightly browned but still very rare in the middle. Remove from the pan and set aside.

4 Heat the remaining oil in the pan and gently cook the onion for 5 minutes until soft. Add the chili pepper, garlic, cinnamon and sugar and stir for a few seconds, then tip in the peppers, tomatoes, green beans, remaining vinegar and water. Bring to a boil, then cover and simmer for 3 minutes. Stir in the olives and place the tuna steaks on top of the salsa. Cover and cook for 3–4 minutes until the tuna is cooked to your liking and the beans are just tender.

5 Transfer the tuna to warmed plates. Stir the mint into the salsa and bubble for a few seconds, then stir in half the basil. Spoon the salsa over and around the tuna, scatter over the remaining basil and serve.

EACH SERVING

38 g protein • 17.5 g fat of which 4.5 g saturates • 5.5 g carbohydrate • 3 g fibre • 339 Calories

Spicy cod with chickpeas and spinach

Succulent chunks of creamy cod, gently cooked in an aromatic, slightly spicy sauce with a colourful mix of vegetables and chickpeas, makes a satisfying, nutrient-rich meal. If you like, serve with French bread.

Serves 4

Preparation time 20 minutes

Cooking time 20 minutes

2 tablespoons olive oil

1 onion, finely chopped

1 green chili pepper, deseeded and finely chopped

2 carrots, peeled and diced

2 celery stalks, diced

40 grams (1½ oz) fresh ginger, peeled and finely chopped

2 garlic cloves, crushed

6 green cardamom pods, crushed and pods discarded

1 teaspoon ground turmeric

2 cups diluted salt-reduced or homemade fish or vegetable stock (pages 28–29), hot

398 ml can chickpeas, drained and rinsed

500 grams (1 lb) tomatoes, peeled and quartered

1 cup frozen peas

600 grams (21 oz) skinless thick cod steak, cut into chunks

250 grams (½ lb) baby spinach leaves

1 Heat the oil in a large, deep frying pan. Add the onion, chili pepper, carrots, celery, ginger, garlic and cardamom seeds. Stir well, then cover the pan and cook over a medium heat for 5 minutes or until the onions are slightly softened.

2 Stir in the turmeric, then pour in the stock and bring to a boil. Reduce the heat, cover and simmer for 10 minutes or until the vegetables are tender.

3 Add the chickpeas, followed by the tomatoes, peas and fish. Mix in gently, taking care not to break up the fish. Bring back to a simmer. When the stock is bubbling gently, pile the spinach on top – there's no need to stir it in – and cover the pan. Cook for 5 minutes or until the chunks of fish are white and firm, and the spinach has just wilted.

4 Use a fork to combine the spinach gently with the fish and vegetables. Ladle the mixture into shallow bowls and serve at once.

VARIATIONS

• *Other white fish or salmon steak can be used instead of the cod. With salmon, try using white kidney beans in place of the chickpeas.*
• *For a vegetarian meal, replace the fish with either 8 halved, hard-boiled eggs (add at the end of cooking and heat through gently), or a 398 ml can each of red kidney and pinto beans, drained and rinsed (add with the chickpeas). Use vegetable stock for either option.*

EACH SERVING

38.5 g protein • 12 g fat of which 1.5 g saturates • 23.5 g carbohydrate • 12.5 g fibre • 380 Calories

Vegetable hash

Traditionally, a hash was the perfect way to use up leftovers from a roast dinner. Here, a glorious mix of colourful vegetables with crumbly cheddar cheese makes a complete vegetarian dish. Accompany with a good fruity relish or chutney.

Serves 2

Preparation time 15 minutes

Cooking time 15 minutes

1 tablespoon olive oil

500 grams (1 lb) cooked potatoes, cubed

200 grams (7 oz) Savoy cabbage, shredded

200 g (7 oz) carrots, peeled and thinly sliced

7 tablespoons water

5 scallions, sliced

50 grams (1¾ oz) crumbly cheddar cheese

2 tablespoons chopped fresh flat-leaf parsley

COOK'S TIP

• Savoy cabbage is easy to recognize because of its wrinkled leaves and loose head. If you can't find it, use another type of cabbage.

1 Heat the oil in a large, non-stick frying pan over a medium heat. Add the potatoes and fry, stirring occasionally, for about 3 minutes or until lightly browned all over.

2 Add the cabbage and carrots and stir gently to mix with the potatoes. Continue to fry, stirring occasionally, for about 2 minutes until the vegetables start to soften.

3 Pour in the water and cover the pan. Allow the vegetables to steam for about 3 minutes. Stir in the scallions and cook, covered, for about 6 minutes longer. Season to taste.

4 Crumble the cheese over the vegetable hash and sprinkle with the chopped parsley. Serve immediately.

EACH SERVING

17.5 g protein • 18 g fat of which 6.5 g saturates • 43.5 g carbohydrate • 16.5 g fibre • 440 Calories

Spiced fish with couscous

As this recipe shows, it is easy to make your own spice mix. And the best thing about it is that you can vary the ingredients to suit yourself, so it can be as mild or hot as you like.

Serves 4 Preparation time 15 minutes, plus 15 minutes marinating
Cooking time 15 minutes

2 teaspoons grated lemon zest

1 1/2 teaspoons ground cumin

1 1/2 teaspoons ground coriander

1/2 teaspoon freshly ground black pepper

2 teaspoons paprika

1/2 teaspoon sea salt flakes

1 tablespoon olive oil

4 x 180 grams (6 1/2 oz) fish steaks, such as snapper or cod

4 lemon wedges

COUSCOUS

1 1/2 cups instant couscous

2 cups boiling water

40 grams (1 1/2 oz) butter, melted

1/4 cup slivered almonds, toasted

3 tablespoons reserved spice mix

1/3 cup currants or sultanas

1/3 cup chopped fresh coriander

398 ml can chickpeas, drained and rinsed

1 Combine the lemon zest, cumin, coriander, pepper, paprika and salt in a small bowl, mixing well. Set aside 3 tablespoons of the spice mix for the couscous. With the remaining, gently rub the spice onto both sides of the fish and allow them to sit for 15 minutes.

2 Meanwhile, prepare the couscous. In a large bowl, combine the couscous and water. Allow this to sit for 5 minutes or until all the liquid has been absorbed, then gently fluff with a fork. Add the remaining ingredients and combine well. Set aside, covered, while the fish is cooking.

3 Heat a non-stick frying pan over a medium heat, add the oil and cook the fish for 2–3 minutes on each side or until the fish flakes easily when tested with a fork.

4 To serve, place a mound of couscous onto each plate and top with a fish steak. Serve with a lemon wedge to squeeze over the fish.

COOK'S TIP
• *This is a mildly spiced dish. If you like, you can substitute 1 teaspoon of the mild paprika for some chili powder for a hotter dish.*

EACH SERVING

48 g protein • 23 g fat of which 7.5 g saturates • 36 g carbohydrate • 7.5 g fibre • 552 Calories

VARIATIONS
• *For a non-vegetarian hash, add 175 grams diced, cooked ham with the scallions.*
• *Shredded Brussels sprouts make a good tasty alternative to cabbage.*
• *For added colour and flavour, replace half the potatoes with squash.*

From the grill

Grilling is a fast and healthy method of cooking, since only a light basting of oil or a marinade is needed to keep food moist. It's ideal for tender foods because it seals in their tasty juices. From spicy, exotic options to vegetarian treats, you can enjoy the healthy mouth-watering flavours of grilled food all year-round. Get the kids involved making kebabs, using all kinds of fish, meat, poultry and vegetables — they will love helping and the whole family will enjoy the results.

Jerk pork with grilled pineapple and corn

A spicy Jamaican paste, made with fiery chili peppers, fragrant allspice and thyme, flavours and tenderizes the pork in this dish. They are served with wedges of juicy pineapple and corn, all cooked under the grill. Serve with toasted French bread.

Step 1

Step 3

Step 4

Serves **4**

Preparation time 20 minutes,
* plus at least 1 hour marinating*

Cooking time 25 minutes

4 pork loin steaks, trimmed
of all excess fat

4 fresh ears of corn

1 tablespoon unsalted butter,
softened

1 ripe pineapple

2 tablespoons honey

JERK SEASONING

2 habañero chili peppers, deseeded
and roughly chopped

10 allspice berries, crushed,
or ½ teaspoon ground allspice

pinch of grated nutmeg

1 teaspoon chopped fresh thyme

2 garlic cloves, coarsely chopped

2 scallions, chopped

2 teaspoons soft brown sugar

1 tablespoon lime juice

2 tablespoons vegetable oil

1 Using a mortar and pestle, blender or food processor, blend together the ingredients for the jerk seasoning to make a smooth paste. Thinly brush or spread this mixture over both sides of the pork steaks and place, side by side, in a non-metallic shallow dish. Cover and leave to marinate in the refrigerator for at least 1 hour and up to 24 hours.

2 When you are ready to cook, preheat the grill to high. Remove the husks from the corn and trim the ends. Cut the corn in half crosswise. Add to a pot of boiling water. Bring back to a boil, then reduce the heat and simmer for 5–10 minutes until just tender. Drain well, then lightly brush them with the softened butter.

3 While the corn is cooking, top and tail the pineapple. Cut off the skin, then cut out any remaining hard "eyes." Slice the fruit into eight wedges and cut away the central core from each piece. Brush all over with the honey.

4 Place the pork on the grill tray. Cook for 3–4 minutes until the spicy crust is nicely browned, then turn and cook for another 3–4 minutes. Remove from the grill and keep warm.

5 Arrange the pineapple wedges and corn on the grill tray. Cook for about 5 minutes until the pineapple and corn are lightly singed. Turn the pineapple and corn frequently to prevent them from burning. Serve hot, with the pork, with paper napkins for sticky fingers.

EACH SERVING

13.5 g protein • 15.5 g fat of which 4 g saturates • 48 g carbohydrate • 6.5 g fibre • 395 Calories

• A compound in the seeds and membranes of chili peppers will cause burning pain should you inadvertently touch your eyes or lips, so be sure to wash your hands thoroughly after preparing chili peppers, or wear thin disposable plastic gloves.

• You can prepare this meal a day in advance. Prepare the corn and pineapple, then store in an airtight container in the refrigerator. The pork will benefit from the long marinating time. Cook everything just before you are ready to serve.

Fresh trout with walnut dressing

Plain grilled trout is dramatically transformed with the help of herbs and nuts, spiced vinegar and a pinch of paprika.

Serves 4

Preparation time 15 minutes

Cooking time 10 minutes

2 teaspoons canola oil

4 trout fillets

¼ teaspoon paprika

10 walnut halves

125 grams (4 oz) mixed greens

FOR THE DRESSING

1 shallot or 2 scallions

A few sprigs of fresh dill,
or celery leaves

2 tablespoons spiced rice vinegar,
or sherry vinegar

6 tablespoons walnut oil

Salt and black pepper

COOK'S TIP

• New potatoes go well with the flavours of this dish. Start boiling before you start cooking the trout.

1 Preheat the grill to the highest setting. To make the dressing, peel and finely chop the shallot, or rinse, trim and finely chop the scallions, and place them in a small bowl. Rinse, dry and chop the dill or celery leaves and add them to the bowl with the vinegar, walnut oil, salt and pepper. Mix well and set aside.

2 Grease the grill pan with half the canola oil and lay the trout fillets on top, skin sides down. Season them with salt and paprika. Grill the fish for 5–8 minutes, on one side only, until the flesh is opaque in the centre and delicately brown at the edges.

3 While the fillets are cooking, heat the remaining oil in a small frying pan and gently fry the walnuts, shaking and stirring constantly so that they colour but do not burn. Drain them on kitchen paper, then chop them roughly.

4 Rinse and dry the salad leaves and arrange on four plates. Lay a fillet of trout on each. Stir the dressing, spoon it over the fish, and scatter the walnuts on top.

EACH SERVING

37 g protein • 33 g fat of which 4 g saturates • 1 g carbohydrate
• 451 Calories

Chargrilled salmon with sherry and walnut dressing

Fresh salmon is ideal for quick cooking on a grill pan. Here it's served on a mixed leaf salad with grapefruit, walnuts and chargrilled zucchini ribbons. Serve with warm plain or olive ciabatta.

Serves 4

Preparation time 20 minutes,
*   plus overnight marinating*

Cooking time 20 minutes

¼ cup olive oil

1 tablespoon walnut oil

1 lemon, zest finely grated and juiced

¼ cup medium dry sherry

4 salmon steaks with skin (about 115 grams/4 oz each)

2 zucchini, pared into ribbons with a vegetable peeler

150 grams (5 oz) mixed salad greens, such as arugula, lamb's lettuce or baby spinach

1 pink grapefruit, peeled and cut into segments

2 tablespoons walnuts, roughly chopped

COOK'S TIPS
• *To make zucchini ribbons, use a vegetable peeler to peel off thin ribbons, drawing the peeler along the length of the zucchini until you are left with only a slim centre core, which can be discarded.*
• *If you don't have a grill pan, cook both the zucchini ribbons and the salmon under a preheated broiler.*

1 Mix together half the olive oil, the walnut oil, lemon zest and juice, and sherry in a shallow dish. Place the salmon fillets in the dish, turn to coat with the dressing, then cover and leave to marinate in the refrigerator overnight.

2 Place the zucchini ribbons in a large bowl, add the remaining oil and toss together. Set aside. Arrange the salad leaves on four serving plates, top with the grapefruit segments, then scatter the walnuts over the top. Set aside.

3 Heat a cast-iron, ridged grill pan over a high heat and cook the zucchini ribbons (in batches, if necessary) for 4–5 minutes, turning often, to produce charred stripes on the surface. Remove from the pan, set aside and keep warm.

4 Remove the salmon from the marinade, reserving the marinade. Reduce the heat to medium and put the salmon, skin-side down first, on the pan and cook for 4–5 minutes on each side until cooked through and firm to the touch.

5 Spoon some zucchini ribbons onto each portion of salad and top each with a piece of salmon. Pour the marinade into the grill pan and simmer on a high heat for 1–2 minutes until reduced slightly. Pour over the salmon and serve.

EACH SERVING

31 g protein • 32 g fat of which 5 g saturates • 5 g carbohydrate
• 2.5 g fibre • 452 Calories

Chargrilled tuna with summer herb crust

Perfect for summer lunches or an alfresco dinner party, this informal dish is simple to make and very healthy. Serve with slices of toasted ciabatta.

Serves **4**   *Preparation time* **15 minutes, plus 30 minutes marinating**
Cooking time **10 minutes**

4 tuna steaks (about 150 grams/5 oz each)

1 garlic clove, crushed

2 tablespoons olive oil

1/3 cup dry white wine

3/4 cup ciabatta breadcrumbs

1/4 cup pine nuts

2 tablespoons chopped fresh basil

2 tablespoons chopped fresh flat-leaf parsley

50 grams (1 3/4 oz) sun-dried tomatoes, drained and chopped

1 lemon, zest grated and juiced

4 beefsteak or other large tomatoes

8 large basil leaves

250 grams (1/2 lb) baby spinach leaves

1 Place the tuna steaks in a single layer in a non-metallic dish, sprinkle with the garlic, oil and wine, turning to coat evenly. Cover and leave to marinate in the refrigerator for about 30 minutes.

2 Meanwhile, prepare the crumb topping. Mix together the ciabatta crumbs, pine nuts, chopped basil and parsley, sun-dried tomatoes and lemon zest. Season to taste and put to one side. Make a deep, cross-shaped cut into the base of each tomato and tuck a couple of basil leaves deep into the cuts.

3 Preheat a cast-iron, ridged grill pan to hot. Lift the tuna steaks from the marinade and place onto the pan. Brush the tomatoes with a little of the marinade and add to the pan. Cook the tuna for about 4 minutes on one side, brushing with the remaining marinade occasionally. Turn carefully, spoon the crumbs on top of the tuna, and sprinkle a few crumbs over the tomatoes. Cook for a further 4 minutes until the tuna is just cooked but still slightly pink inside.

4 Spread the spinach leaves on a serving platter, arrange the tuna steaks and tomatoes on top and sprinkle with the lemon juice.

COOK'S TIP

• *The tuna can be left in its marinade for several hours or overnight in the refrigerator, along with the crumb topping and the basil-filled tomatoes. To make the crumbs, whizz day-old bread briefly in a food processor until crumbs form.*

EACH SERVING

45.5 g protein • 26.5 g fat of which 5 g saturates • 17.5 g carbohydrate • 7 g fibre • 523 Calories

Zucchini cakes with minted yogourt sauce

Chargrilled zucchini cakes, served with a cool sauce, make a refreshing dish.

Serves **4**   *Preparation time* **55 minutes**   *Cooking time* **10 – 20 minutes**

750 grams (1½ lbs) zucchini

Salt and black pepper

1 large egg, beaten

²/₃ cup matzo meal

Pinch of freshly grated nutmeg

FOR THE SAUCE

Finely grated zest and juice of ½ lemon

3–4 tablespoons chopped fresh mint

150 grams (6 oz) low-fat plain yogourt

Fresh sprigs of mint to garnish

1 Finely grate the zucchini into a colander, sprinkle with salt, mix well and allow to drain for 30 minutes. Rinse under running water and squeeze dry with your hands, then place in a clean dish towel and squeeze again.

2 Transfer the zucchini to a bowl and add the egg, matzo meal, nutmeg, and pepper to taste. Mix together until well combined, then allow to stand for 20 minutes for the flavours to develop.

3 To make the sauce, combine the lemon zest and juice, mint and yogourt in a bowl, then cover and chill until ready to serve.

4 Heat a ridged cast-iron grill pan or nonstick frying pan over medium heat. Place tablespoons of the zucchini mixture onto the pan, flattening each to form a thick cake. Dry-fry the cakes for 4–5 minutes on each side, until they are firm and browned. (You may need to cook them in two batches.) Garnish with the mint and serve hot, with the chilled sauce on the side.

EACH SERVING

8 g protein • 3 g fat of which 1 g saturates • 18 g carbohydrate • 2 g fibre • 129 Calories

Chargrilled vegetable platter

These colourful grilled vegetables, topped with a fresh tomato and basil salsa and creamy Camembert cheese, make a wonderful vegetarian main course. Enjoy with toasted ciabatta slices and a green salad.

Serves 4

Preparation time 15 minutes

Cooking time 30 minutes

1 small butternut squash, peeled, deseeded and cut into slices

¼ cup olive oil

2 red onions, thickly sliced

2 zucchini, thickly sliced

1 eggplant, thickly sliced

1 red pepper, deseeded and cut into wide strips

1 yellow pepper, deseeded and cut into wide strips

200 grams (7 oz) asparagus, trimmed

2 large flat mushrooms, thickly sliced

4 small ripe tomatoes, finely chopped

2 garlic cloves, crushed

1 tablespoon chopped fresh basil

150 grams (5 oz) Camembert cheese, cut into small pieces

COOK'S TIP

• You can grill all the vegetables up to 3 hours ahead and keep, covered, at room temperature. Or, they can be chilled for up to 2 days to serve cold. Add the cooled salsa and Camembert cheese just before serving.

1 Bring a pot of lightly salted water to a boil. Add the squash and cook for about 3 minutes until slightly softened. Drain.

2 Preheat a large cast-iron, ridged grill pan. Pour the oil into a small pot. Using a pastry brush, very lightly coat the onions with oil and chargrill for about 2 minutes on each side. Transfer to a large platter and keep warm. Oil and chargrill the zucchini and eggplant in the same way, then add to the platter.

3 Chargrill the peppers, without oil, for 3–4 minutes on each side until charred and slightly softened. Transfer to the platter. Lightly oil the asparagus and chargrill, turning occasionally, for about 4 minutes. Add to the platter.

4 Very lightly oil the mushrooms and parboiled squash and chargrill for about 3 minutes, turning once. Add to the platter.

5 To make the salsa, add the tomatoes, garlic and basil to the oil remaining in the small pan. Heat through gently and season to taste. Pour the salsa over the grilled vegetables and scatter the Camembert over the top.

EACH SERVING

17 g protein • 25 g fat of which 8 g saturates • 20 g carbohydrate • 13.5 g fibre • 394 Calories

Polenta and vegetable salad

Grilled Mediterranean vegetables, combined with plump olives and a chili pepper, garlic and lemon dressing, make an exciting topping for polenta.

Serves **4**

Preparation **10 minutes, plus cooling**

Cooking time **30 minutes**

3 1/3 cups 1% milk

40 grams (1 1/2 oz) butter

1 1/2 cups instant polenta

1 large eggplant, thinly sliced lengthwise

1/4 cup olive oil

2 red peppers, halved and deseeded

200 grams (7 oz) shallots, halved but not peeled

1 red chili pepper, halved lengthwise and deseeded

1 garlic clove, unpeeled

1 tablespoon lemon juice

1/2 cup (75 g) pitted black olives

40 grams (1 1/2 oz) Parmesan cheese, shaved

1 tablespoon fresh basil leaves

1 Put the milk, butter and a pinch of salt into a pot. Heat the milk until almost boiling, then turn the heat down and pour in the polenta in a slow, steady stream while stirring continuously with a wooden spoon. Keep stirring for 5 minutes until it thickens. Spoon into a 20 x 30 cm tray lined with baking paper. Smooth the top with a spatula. Allow to cool completely, then cut into slices.

2 Heat a grill until it is very hot. Brush the eggplant slices on both sides using 1 tablespoon of the oil and lay, side by side, on a baking tray. Add the peppers, skin-side up, and the shallots, skin-side down. Grill for 15 minutes, turning the eggplants over halfway through, until the pepper and shallot skins are blackened all over. Set aside until cool enough to handle.

3 Arrange the chili pepper, cut-side down, unpeeled garlic and polenta slices on the baking tray. Brush the polenta on both sides with 1 tablespoon of the oil. Grill for about 6 minutes, then remove the chili pepper and garlic and turn the polenta over. Grill for a further 6–8 minutes until the polenta is golden.

4 Scrape the flesh from the chili pepper and garlic, mash and mix with the remaining oil and the lemon juice in a small bowl. Peel the skins from the peppers and slice the flesh. Peel the shallots. Arrange the polenta slices around a wide platter. Pile the peppers, shallots, eggplant and olives in the centre and spoon over the chili pepper dressing. Top with Parmesan and basil.

EACH SERVING

20.5 g protein • 28 g fat of which 9.5 g saturates • 54.5 g carbohydrate • 6.5 g fibre • 571 Calories

VARIATION
• Tzatziki is a mixture of yogourt, cucumber, mint
and garlic. If you prefer, use reduced-fat hummus
mixed with a little low-fat plain yogourt. Or, for a
really low-fat dressing, combine ½ cup low-fat plain
yogourt with ¼ cup chopped fresh mint.

Middle Eastern kibbeh

Lebanese-style meatballs are great for a relaxed family supper. They're made with lean ground lamb, bulgur, herbs and spices, then grilled on skewers and served in pita bread pouches with crisp salad.

Step 1

Step 3

Step 4

Serves **4**

Preparation time **25 minutes, plus cooling**

Cooking time **15 minutes**

¾ cup bulgur

1²⁄₃ cups diluted salt-reduced or homemade vegetable stock (page 29), hot

400 grams (14 oz) lean ground lamb

1 red onion, grated

¼ cup pine nuts, toasted and roughly chopped

¼ cup chopped cilantro

¼ teaspoon ground allspice

½ teaspoon ground cumin

½ teaspoon ground cinnamon

½ teaspoon chili powder

4 whole wheat pita breads

1 baby romaine lettuce, shredded

1 carrot, peeled and grated

¼ English cucumber, thinly sliced

8 radishes, thinly sliced and tossed in 1 tablespoon lemon juice

²⁄₃ cup tzatziki

1 Put the bulgur in a pot and pour over the hot stock. Cover and leave to stand for 15 minutes. Meanwhile, soak eight bamboo skewers in cold water (to prevent them from burning on the grill). Remove the lid from the pan and cook the bulgur over a low heat for 4–5 minutes, stirring frequently, until the excess liquid has evaporated, but the mixture is still moist. Tip onto a tray, spread out and leave to cool.

2 Tip the cooled bulgur into a bowl. Add the lamb, onion, pine nuts, cilantro and dry spices and season to taste. Thoroughly mix together with your hands. If you prefer a smoother-textured kibbeh, transfer the mixture to a food processor and blend for a few seconds. (You may need to do this in batches.)

3 Preheat the grill to medium. Divide the lamb mixture into 16 pieces and shape into oval-shaped balls (kibbeh). Thread the kibbeh onto the soaked wooden skewers, putting two on each skewer. Arrange, side by side, on a foil-lined grill tray and grill for 4–5 minutes on each side until well browned and cooked through. Remove and wrap loosely in the foil to keep warm.

4 Put the pita breads on the grill tray and grill for about 30 seconds on each side to warm them; don't let them brown or cook for any longer, or they will be too brittle to split open. Run a knife down one long edge of each pita and gently open out to make a pocket.

5 Half-fill the pita bread pockets with the shredded lettuce, carrot, cucumber and radishes. Slide the kibbeh off the skewers and divide among the pita pockets. Add more salad to taste. Drizzle each one with a spoonful of tzatziki and serve immediately.

EACH SERVING

40 g protein • 26 g fat of which 9.5 g saturates • 53 g carbohydrate • 11 g fibre • 622 Calories

Chimichurri pork kebabs

Kebabs are always a favourite, particularly for casual entertaining. Here, lean pork is marinated in a punchy Argentinian-style sauce, then threaded onto skewers and grilled with wedges of sweet potato and slices of corn.

Serves 4   Preparation time 15 minutes, plus at least 20 minutes marinating
Cooking time 35 minutes

500 grams (1 lb) pork tenderloin, trimmed of all excess fat and cut into 2 cm slices

2 orange sweet potatoes, scrubbed

1 fresh ear of corn

CHIMICHURRI MARINADE

5 garlic cloves, finely chopped

½ cup chopped fresh parsley

⅓ cup red wine vinegar

¼ cup extra virgin olive oil

1 teaspoon dried oregano

½ teaspoon ground cumin

½ teaspoon paprika

Tabasco, to taste

4 lime wedges

1 To make the marinade, put all the ingredients in a large non-metallic bowl, adding Tabasco to taste. Add the pork and stir around to coat, then set aside to marinate for at least 20 minutes.

2 Meanwhile, bring a large pot of lightly salted water to a boil over a high heat. Add the sweet potatoes and boil in their skins for 12–15 minutes until just beginning to soften. Use a slotted spoon to remove them and set aside to cool. Add the corn cob to the water and boil for 5 minutes until the kernels are tender. Drain well and set aside until cool enough to handle.

3 When the vegetables have cooled, peel off the sweet potato skins, then cut the sweet potatoes first in half lengthwise, then widthwise into 3 cm thick wedges. Cut the corn into slices. Preheat the grill.

4 Thread pork, sweet potato and corn in turn onto four long or eight shorter metal skewers and brush the marinade mixture onto the vegetables. Broil or barbecue the kebabs, turning frequently and basting with any remaining marinade, for about 15 minutes until the pork is cooked through. Serve with lime wedges.

COOK'S TIP
• *The pork can be left to marinate for up to 1 day in the refrigerator and the vegetables prepared up until the end of step 3 a day in advance.*

VARIATION
• *If you prefer, replace the corn with wedges of green or red pepper.*

EACH SERVING

30 g protein • 17 g fat of which 3 g saturates • 15.5 g carbohydrate • 3.5 g fibre • 343 Calories

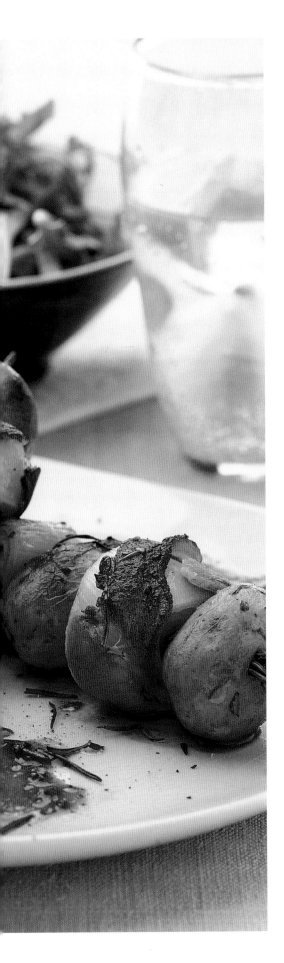

Rosemary-skewered vegetables with bacon

Fresh rosemary stalks make excellent skewers and flavour the ingredients they hold (you can use metal skewers if you prefer). This is a stylish way of cooking and serving simple, healthy ingredients. Serve with a leafy salad.

Serves **4**   *Preparation time* **10 minutes, plus 30 minutes marinating**
Cooking time **30 minutes**

24 even-sized baby new potatoes

8 strong, fresh rosemary stalks, each about 20 cm long

2 tablespoons olive oil

⅓ cup balsamic vinegar

1 tablespoon Dijon mustard

⅓ cup apple juice

4 thick leeks, trimmed

4 strips of bacon

1 Cook the potatoes in a pot of lightly salted boiling water for about 10 minutes until tender, then lift out with a slotted spoon. Put the pot back on the heat to return the water to a boil.

2 Meanwhile, strip the leaves from the rosemary stalks, leaving a tuft at the top. Set the stalks aside. Chop enough of the leaves to make 1 tablespoon; discard the rest. Mix together the oil, vinegar, mustard, chopped rosemary and apple juice in a large bowl. Add the hot cooked potatoes and stir to coat them. Set aside to marinate for 30 minutes.

3 While the potatoes are marinating, cut each leek into eight chunks, each about 2.5 cm long. Put the leeks in the pot of boiling water, cover and cook gently for about 8 minutes until just tender. Drain well in a colander and set aside.

4 Stretch the bacon with the back of a knife, then cut each strip in half. Use a metal skewer to make a hole through the leek pieces. Wrap pieces of bacon around about half of them.

5 Preheat the grill to high. Drain the potatoes, reserving any leftover marinade, and make a hole in each one. Divide the potatoes and leek pieces (both unwrapped and bacon-wrapped) among the rosemary stalk skewers, threading them on alternately.

6 Place the kebabs on the grill tray and grill for 8–10 minutes until nicely browned, carefully turning the skewers halfway through cooking and brushing them with the reserved marinade. Serve immediately.

EACH SERVING

15 g protein • 13.5 g fat of which 2.5 g saturates • 28 g carbohydrate
• 6.5 g fibre • 311 Calories

Citrus chicken and pineapple kebabs

Lemon zest and crushed cardamom seeds add a lovely flavour to marinated, grilled chicken kebabs, threaded with juicy chunks of fresh pineapple and grape tomatoes and served with crunchy pita chips.

Serves 4

Preparation time 35 minutes, plus 1–2 hours marinating

Cooking time 20 minutes

KEBABS

1 lemon, zest grated and juiced, plus 1 lemon, juiced

¼ cup olive oil

1 tablespoon honey

4 green cardamom pods, crushed and pods discarded

2 tablespoons chopped cilantro

500 grams (1 lb) skinless boneless chicken breasts, cut into 2.5 cm cubes

1 pineapple, peeled, cored and cut into chunks

24 cherry tomatoes

PITA CHIPS

4 white or whole wheat pita breads

2 tablespoons olive oil

1 large garlic clove, crushed

1 tablespoon chopped fresh mixed herbs or 2 teaspoons dried mixed herbs

1 Mix together the lemon zest and juice, oil, honey, cardamom seeds and chopped cilantro in a shallow dish. Season with freshly ground black pepper. Add the chicken and toss to coat well, then cover and leave to marinate in the refrigerator for 1–2 hours. Soak 12 bamboo skewers in cold water (to prevent them from burning on the grill).

2 To make the pita chips, preheat the grill to medium. Cut each pita bread across in half, then split into two layers. Mix together the oil, garlic and herbs and lightly brush each piece of pita on both sides with the oil mixture. Place the pita on the rack in a grill tray (you may need to do this in two batches). Grill for 4–5 minutes or until lightly browned and crisp, turning once. Place on a plate and keep warm, or transfer to a wire rack to cool.

3 Thread the chicken, pineapple and tomatoes alternately onto the skewers, dividing the ingredients evenly. Grill for 10–15 minutes, turning occasionally, until the chicken is cooked through and tender. Brush the kebabs regularly with the marinade to prevent them from drying out. Serve with the pita chips.

EACH SERVING

30.5 g protein • 30 g fat of which 5 g saturates • 44.5 g carbohydrate • 8.5 g fibre • 590 Calories

Thai-style chicken skewers

Packed with fresh, zesty Thai flavours, these little ground chicken skewers are grilled and served with baby corn, pepper and scallion skewers for a healthy, nutritious meal. Serve with an Asian-style salad for extra vegetables.

Serves 4   Preparation time 25 minutes   Cooking time 25 minutes

24 baby corn	1 garlic clove, crushed
1 large yellow pepper, halved and deseeded	¼ cup chopped cilantro
8 scallions	2 teaspoons fish sauce
500 grams (1 lb) ground chicken or pork	1 lemon grass stalk, chopped
1 small egg white	1 tablespoon vegetable oil
2.5 cm piece fresh ginger, peeled and chopped	2 teaspoons sesame oil
	1 teaspoon sesame seeds
	½ cup sweet chili sauce

1 Soak 16 bamboo skewers in cold water (to prevent them from burning under the broiler). Cut the pepper into 2.5 cm chunks. Cut six of the scallions into 4 cm lengths. Thread the vegetables onto half of the skewers, alternating the corn with the pepper and scallions. Set aside. Preheat the broiler.

2 Chop the remaining scallions and put in a food processor bowl with the chicken, egg white, ginger, garlic, cilantro, fish sauce and lemon grass. Process until chopped and beginning to bind together, but not completely smooth.

3 Divide the mixture into eight and use your hands to shape each piece around the remaining skewers. Arrange on a foil-lined grill tray. Mix the vegetable and sesame oils and lightly brush onto the chicken and vegetable skewers. Add the sesame seeds to any remaining oil.

4 Broil the chicken skewers for 15–20 minutes, turning occasionally, until golden. After 10 minutes, add the vegetable skewers and cook for 10 minutes, turning occasionally, until tender and golden. Brush over the remaining oil with the seeds for the last minute of cooking. Serve with sweet chili sauce for dipping.

COOK'S TIP
• *To prepare ahead, make up the mixture for the chicken skewers, then cover with plastic wrap. Keep chilled and cook within 2 days.*

EACH SERVING

27 g protein • 19 g fat of which 4 g saturates • 10 g carbohydrate • 3 g fibre • 325 Calories

COOK'S TIP
• *You can prepare this up until the end of step 2 a day in advance.*

VARIATIONS
• *Other citrus fruits would be good in the marinade, such as 1 small orange with 1 lemon, or 3 limes in place of the lemons.*
• *If you have some button mushrooms, they could also be threaded onto the skewers or used instead of the cherry tomatoes.*

Skewered swordfish with charred zucchini

A real summer dish of cubes of marinated swordfish and lemon wedges, chargrilled (or barbecued) with baby zucchini. Swordfish has firm flesh, ideally suited to cooking on skewers. Serve with warm focaccia.

Step 2

Step 3

Step 4

Serves 4

Preparation time 20 minutes, plus 10 minutes marinating

Cooking time 15 minutes

500 grams (1 lb) swordfish steaks

3 lemons

¼ cup olive oil

1 garlic clove, crushed

15 grams (½ oz) fresh basil

500 grams (1 lb) small zucchini, trimmed

1 Soak four bamboo skewers in cold water (to prevent them from burning). Meanwhile, using a sharp knife cut any skin away from the fish steaks, then cut the steaks into 2 cm cubes.

2 Grate the zest and squeeze the juice from one of the lemons. Combine this zest and juice with the olive oil and garlic. Finely chop the basil leaves and mix into the marinade. Cut each of the remaining lemons into four wedges.

3 Halve the zucchini lengthwise and score the white flesh with the tip of a sharp knife to make a crisscross pattern.

4 Lightly brush the cut surfaces of the zucchini with some of the marinade, then set aside. Mix the swordfish cubes into the rest of the marinade and leave for 5–10 minutes to absorb the flavours.

5 Thread the swordfish cubes and the lemon wedges onto the soaked skewers. Arrange on a cast-iron, ridged grill pan along with the zucchini. Sprinkle with coarsely ground black pepper then cook for 10–15 minutes, turning the skewers occasionally to make sure they are thoroughly cooked. Baste with the remaining marinade. (Alternatively, grill on a rack under a preheated barbecue.)

EACH SERVING

25 g protein • 19 g fat of which 3 g saturates • 2 g carbohydrate • 2.5 g fibre • 295 Calories

• Change the flavour of this dish by altering the marinade. For an Asian flavour, use the zest and juice of 1½ limes instead of the lemon, use cilantro instead of basil, and add chopped red chili pepper to taste.

Use lime wedges on the skewers, and grill quartered red and green peppers alongside the fish instead of the zucchini.
• Other fish that work well in this recipe include salmon and raw jumbo shrimp.

Tofu satay

Spicy satay sauce works well with tofu and diced eggplant in these delicious kebabs, served on a crisp baby corn, sprout and cucumber salad.

Serves **4**

Preparation time **40 minutes**

Cooking time **15 minutes**

400 grams (14 oz) firm tofu

1 eggplant

1 red onion

8 baby corn, halved
on the diagonal

½ English cucumber

3½ cups bean sprouts

2 tablespoons unsalted peanuts

SATAY SAUCE

⅓ cup crunchy peanut butter

1 teaspoon salt-reduced soy sauce

1 teaspoon honey

1 teaspoon Chinese rice vinegar
or cider vinegar

1 large garlic clove, peeled

1 scallion, chopped

⅓ cup light coconut milk

1 tablespoon sweet chili sauce

1 Soak 12 bamboo skewers in cold water (to prevent them from burning). Meanwhile, to make the satay sauce, combine the peanut butter, soy sauce, honey, vinegar, garlic, scallion, coconut milk and chili sauce in a blender or food processor. Blend or process to make a thick, almost smooth mixture.

2 Preheat a medium grill pan or barbecue. Cut the tofu and eggplant into 2.5 cm cubes. Cut the red onion into chunks about the same size.

3 Cut the cucumber into thin sticks about 5 cm long. Arrange the bean sprouts, cucumber sticks and corn on a large platter and scatter the peanuts over the top. Set aside while you cook the tofu and vegetable skewers.

4 Thread the tofu, eggplant and onion onto the soaked skewers, spacing the pieces slightly apart. Place on a ridged grill or barbecue grate. Brush with some of the satay sauce, then grill for 10–12 minutes, turning the skewers frequently and brushing with the satay sauce. Gently heat the remaining satay sauce in a small pot or in a dish in the microwave until warm.

5 Set the skewers on top of the salad, spoon the remaining satay sauce over the top and serve.

EACH SERVING

25 g protein • 22 g fat of which 3.5 g saturates • 14 g carbohydrate
• 9 g fibre • 373 Calories

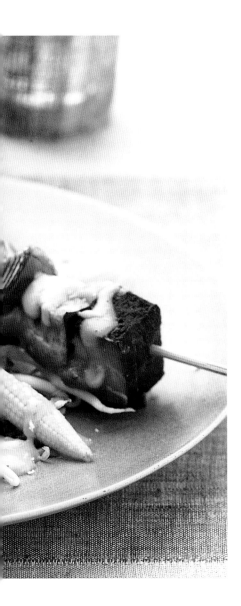

Fish, shrimp and prosciutto brochettes

Sumptuous seafood on skewers with cheerful yellow pepper, baby tomatoes and cubes of bread makes an attractive meal, great for entertaining. A fresh basil and lime mayonnaise completes the dish. Serve with a mixed green or asparagus salad.

Serves **4** *Preparation time* **30 minutes** *Cooking time* **10 minutes**

2 limes

2 tablespoons olive oil

1 yellow pepper, deseeded and cut into 2.5 cm squares

24 raw shrimp, peeled

350 grams (12 oz) firm white fish steak, cut into 2.5 cm cubes

75 grams (2²/₃ oz) prosciutto, cut into strips 2.5 cm wide

24 grape or cherry tomatoes

16 cubes of bread, such as ciabatta or rustic-type loaf

BASIL MAYONNAISE

¹/₃ cup light mayonnaise

1 tablespoon chopped fresh basil

1 Soak eight bamboo skewers for the brochettes in cold water (to prevent them from burning under the broiler). Squeeze the juice from one of the limes. Put 1 tablespoon of the lime juice into a bowl with the oil and whisk together, seasoning with a little freshly ground pepper. Reserve the remaining lime juice and cut the other lime into four wedges, then set aside.

2 Add the pepper pieces to the marinade (there should be about 16 squares) and toss until coated, then remove and set aside, leaving as much marinade as possible behind. Do the same with the shrimp and, finally, the fish.

3 Wrap each fish cube in a strip of prosciutto; the two ends should just overlap, leaving the sides of the fish showing, so trim if necessary.

4 Preheat the broiler. Thread the prosciutto-wrapped fish onto the skewers, alternating with the shrimp, pepper and tomatoes. Make sure that there is still about 10 cm left at the top of each skewer to add the bread.

5 Grill the brochettes for 1¹/₂ minutes on each side. Add the cubes of bread to the end of the skewers and grill for a further 3–4 minutes, turning as needed, until all the ingredients are golden brown and cooked through.

6 Meanwhile, combine the mayonnaise, basil and reserved lime juice. Serve two brochettes per person with some basil mayonnaise and a wedge of lime.

EACH SERVING

30.5 g protein • 14.5 g fat of which 2.5 g saturates • 13 g carbohydrate • 2.5 g fibre • 284 Calories

COOK'S TIP
• *Tofu comes in many forms. The best variety to use for this recipe is the organic, naturally smoked tofu, found in coolers in health-food stores and some supermarkets.*

VARIATION
• *In the salad, replace half the bean sprouts with thin green beans, trimmed and steamed or blanched in boiling water for 3 minutes.*

Roasts and braises

Ideal for family get-togethers and cozy winter evenings, roasts and braises make the most of tender cuts of meat and fish, without requiring constant attention. Succulent and flavourful, traditional Sunday roasts are always a treat, while more modern interpretations ensure there's always something new to enjoy. Meat, poultry and fish are all suitable for roasting and braising, and you can make the meal as light or as hearty and as simple or as impressive as you like.

Mediterranean roasted lamb

Just a few fresh ingredients, simply cooked, make a warmly satisfying meal. Eggplants and shallots, whose flavours intensify with roasting, make perfect partners for tender, succulent lamb. Serve with warm, crusty bread.

Serves 4

Preparation time 20 minutes,
   plus several hours marinating

Cooking time 45 minutes

¼ cup olive oil

1 teaspoon balsamic or red wine vinegar

4 lean lamb fillets, trimmed of all excess fat

2 teaspoons black peppercorns

1 teaspoon cumin seeds

250 grams (8 oz) shallots, unpeeled

2 large eggplants

2 garlic cloves, crushed

400 grams (14 oz) cherry tomatoes, pricked

1 tablespoon chopped cilantro

VARIATION

• For a vegetarian version, use cheese instead of lamb fillets. First roast the eggplant and shallot mixture, sprinkled with cumin seeds, for 25–30 minutes, turning once, then scatter with the tomatoes and roast for a further 5 minutes. Finally, top with 250 grams (½ lb) thinly sliced mozzarella cheese and return to the oven for 5 minutes. Scatter with olives or pine nuts.

1 Mix 1 tablespoon of the oil with the vinegar and lightly brush this marinade over both sides of the fillets. Crush the peppercorns and add the cumin seeds. Sprinkle the mixture over the fillets, pat it in gently and then place the fillets in a non-metallic dish. Set aside, or cover and refrigerate for several hours.

2 Preheat the oven to 400°F (200°C). Put the shallots in a large, heatproof bowl and pour over enough boiling water to cover. Leave for 2–3 minutes, then drain. Peel off the skins, then return them to the bowl.

3 Trim the ends from the eggplants and cut them into 2.5 cm chunks. Add these to the shallots. Drizzle the remaining oil over the vegetables. Add the crushed garlic, then toss to lightly coat the vegetables with oil.

4 Heat a large, heavy-based roasting pan over a medium–high heat on the stove. Sear the fillets for about 1 minute on each side, then remove and set aside in the original marinade dish.

5 Tip the vegetables into the hot pan and spread them out. Place in the oven and roast for 15–20 minutes until softened. Lay the lamb fillets over the vegetables and drizzle any juices left in the dish over the lamb. Return to the oven to roast for 10 minutes.

6 Scatter the tomatoes into the pan and return to the oven for a further 8–10 minutes until the lamb is cooked to your liking and the vegetables are tender. Season to taste and serve sprinkled with chopped cilantro.

COOK'S TIP

• You can prepare all the ingredients up until the end of step 4 a day ahead of time and keep, covered, in the refrigerator. Bring all the ingredients to room temperature for 30 minutes before cooking and preheat the roasting pan in the oven for about 10 minutes.

EACH SERVING

30 g protein • 22 g fat of which 5.5 g saturates • 8 g carbohydrate • 5.5 g fibre • 360 Calories

Persian-style lamb shanks with figs

Roasting lamb shanks before slowly braising them removes much of the fat and gives a wonderful flavour, which perfectly complements the fragrant vegetable mix here.

Serves 4

Preparation time 30 minutes

Cooking time about 2 hours

2 lamb shanks

2 tablespoons olive oil

6 shallots, quartered

3 garlic cloves, chopped

2 sprigs of fresh rosemary

1 bay leaf

500 grams (20 oz) tomatoes, peeled and quartered

1 1/2 cups green lentils

2 tablespoons pomegranate molasses

1 tablespoon honey

3 1/2 cups diluted salt-reduced or homemade beef or vegetable stock (pages 28–29), or as needed

8 dried figs, quartered

2 zucchini, thickly sliced

2 tablespoons roughly chopped cilantro

1 Preheat the oven to 425°F (220°C). Put the lamb shanks in a large flameproof casserole dish and roast for 25 minutes until they are a rich brown colour on the outside. Drain on paper towel. Reduce the oven temperature to 325°F (160°C).

2 Heat the oil in the casserole dish over a medium heat. Add the shallots and cook for 5 minutes, stirring until lightly browned. Stir in the garlic, rosemary, bay leaf and tomatoes and cook for 1 minute. Stir in the lentils, then add the lamb shanks, pushing them down into the vegetable mixture.

3 Stir the pomegranate molasses and honey into the stock, then pour over the lamb. Slowly bring to a boil, then cover the casserole dish with a tight-fitting lid and bake for 45 minutes.

4 Remove the casserole from the oven, add a little more stock if needed and stir in the figs and zucchini (this is easier if you lift out the lamb shanks first, then return them after stirring). Cover and bake for a further 45 minutes or until the lamb is very tender. Lift out the lamb and carve the meat from the shanks. Discard the bones and return the meat to the casserole. Gently stir, then serve scattered with cilantro.

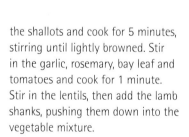

EACH SERVING

52.5 g protein • 27 g fat of which 9 g saturates • 54.5 g carbohydrate • 13.5 g fibre • 689 Calories

Braised Asian beef

Asian flavours are often associated with stir-fries, but as this delicious meal shows, they can be used to good effect in a hearty braise. Lemon grass, star anise and cinnamon add an exotic edge to braised beef. Serve with steamed rice or noodles.

Serves 4–6   Preparation time 15 minutes   Cooking time about 2 hours

2 tablespoons canola oil

1 onion, diced

3 garlic cloves, smashed with the side of a cleaver

2 lemon grass stalks, white part only, bruised

1 kg (2 lbs) lean stewing beef, cut into 3–4 cm cubes

1 tablespoon curry powder

2 cups diluted salt-reduced or homemade beef stock (page 28)

1½ cups water

4 star anise

1 cinnamon stick

1½ tablespoons sugar

2½ tablespoons ground bean sauce

2 tablespoons tomato paste

3 carrots, peeled and sliced into 1 cm thick chunks

2 scallions, cut into 2 cm lengths

1 Heat the oil in a large flameproof casserole dish over a medium heat and cook the onion, garlic and lemon grass for 2 minutes or until the onion is softened and the ingredients are aromatic.

2 Increase the heat to high and add the beef, stirring well to brown slightly. Add the curry powder and toss for a further 1 minute. Add the stock, water, star anise, cinnamon stick, sugar, bean sauce and tomato paste. Bring it to a boil, then cook over a low heat and allow to simmer, uncovered, for about 1½ hours or until the meat is tender.

3 Add the carrots to the casserole dish and cook for a further 30 minutes. The meat should be very tender at this stage. Just before serving, toss in the scallion lengths.

COOK'S TIP
• Pomegranate molasses is made with concentrated pomegranate juice. If your supermarket doesn't stock it, dry a delicatessen or gourmet food store.

COOK'S TIP
• Ground bean sauce (sometimes labelled ground bean paste) is available in the Asian section of some supermarkets, or in Asian food stores.

EACH SERVING (6)

44.5 g protein • 17.5 g fat of which 5 g saturates • 13 g carbohydrate • 3 g fibre • 394 Calories

Roast beef with thyme and fennel crust

A crunchy deep crust of herb-flavoured breadcrumbs ensures a succulent roast beef. It's roasted with a selection of tasty root vegetables and served with a rich gravy, made using the pan juices.

Serves 4

Preparation time 25 minutes

Cooking time about 2 hours

1½ cups fresh whole wheat breadcrumbs

1 tablespoon fennel seeds

6 large sprigs of fresh thyme

¼ cup olive oil

2 tablespoons low-fat milk

1.25 kg (2¾ lbs) beef round roast, trimmed of all excess fat

1 tablespoon whole-grain mustard

1 celeriac, peeled

2 orange sweet potatoes, peeled

4 carrots, peeled

300 grams (10 oz) shallots, peeled

7 tablespoons medium sweet sherry, Madeira or port

1¼ cup water

VARIATIONS
• *If you like, add some finely chopped garlic to the crumb mixture. Fresh oregano could be used instead of thyme.*
• *Spread horseradish sauce over the meat in place of the whole-grain mustard.*
• *Use 1½ cups red wine to deglaze the roasting pan.*

1 Preheat the oven to 375°F (190°C). Mix the breadcrumbs and fennel seeds in a bowl with the leaves from two of the thyme sprigs and seasoning to taste. Sprinkle 2 tablespoons of the olive oil and the milk over the crumbs and mix thoroughly with a spoon until they are moist and clump together.

2 Place the beef in a large, lightly oiled roasting pan and spread the meat with the mustard. Press the crumb mixture on the top of the meat, pressing it firmly all over with both hands to make a neat, firm crust. Roast for about 1¾ hours for a medium result or about 2 hours for well cooked but juicy meat. Cover the crust loosely with a piece of foil after 1 hour, to prevent overbrowning, then remove the foil for the final 5 minutes of cooking.

3 Meanwhile, cut the celeriac and sweet potatoes into 3.5 cm chunks and place in a large bowl. Halve the carrots lengthwise, then cut them across into chunky sticks. Add to the bowl along with the shallots and the remaining thyme leaves and oil. Mix well.

4 The vegetables require about 1 hour for roasting, so put them in the oven when the beef has been cooking for 45 minutes to 1 hour. Arrange the vegetables around the meat, placing any that won't fit in a separate roasting pan or large ovenproof dish, if necessary. Turn the vegetables and liberally baste them once during cooking.

5 Remove the meat and vegetables to a warmed serving dish and cover with foil. Pour the water into the roasting pan and bring to a boil on the stove, stirring and scraping up all the browned cooking residue on the bottom of the pan. Add the sherry, Madeira or port and boil steadily for 5–7 minutes, stirring from time to time, until the liquid is reduced by about half. Season to taste, then strain the gravy into a jug.

6 Slice the meat and serve with the roast vegetables and gravy. Any pieces of crust that break off as the meat is sliced can be divided among the plates.

COOK'S TIP
• *Calculate the cooking time for the beef at 55 minutes per kg, plus 45 minutes for medium, or 65 minutes per kg, plus 45 minutes for well-done meat that's still juicy.*

EACH SERVING

76 g protein • 25 g fat of which 7 g saturates • 38 g carbohydrate • 10 g fibre • 720 Calories

Beef olives

This updated version of a traditional recipe is ideal for entertaining. Slices of beef are wrapped around a mushroom stuffing to make rolls, which are then braised with vegetables.

Serves 4   Preparation time 20 minutes, plus 20 minutes soaking
Cooking time 50 minutes

500 grams (1 lb) beef round, cut into 8 very thin slices

2 tablespoons olive oil

1 tablespoon coarsely crushed black peppercorns

1 onion, thinly sliced

2 celery stalks, sliced

400 grams (14 oz) new potatoes, scrubbed and cut into 5 mm slices

2 carrots, peeled and sliced

600 grams (1 1/3 lbs) tomatoes, chopped

1 1/4 cups diluted salt-reduced or homemade beef stock (page 28)

1/3 cup dry sherry

1 bay leaf

2 tablespoons chopped fresh parsley

MUSHROOM STUFFING

15 grams (1/2 oz) dried porcini mushrooms

2 tablespoons olive oil

1 small onion, finely chopped

1 garlic clove, finely chopped

200 grams (7 oz) cremini mushrooms, finely chopped

1/4 cup fine fresh breadcrumbs (made from day-old bread)

1/3 cup finely chopped fresh flat-leaf parsley

1 teaspoon dried thyme

1 lemon, zest finely grated

pinch of cayenne pepper

1 To make the stuffing, put the porcini mushrooms in a heatproof bowl, cover with boiling water and soak for 20 minutes. Drain and chop, then set aside.

2 Heat the oil for the stuffing in a large frying pan over a medium heat. Add the onion and garlic and cook gently, stirring frequently, for 5–8 minutes, until golden. Add the cremini mushrooms and fry for 5 minutes, stirring occasionally, then stir in the chopped porcini mushrooms and the remaining stuffing ingredients. Season, then set aside to cool slightly. Wipe out the pan.

3 Lay the beef slices between sheets of plastic wrap and pound as thinly as possible using a rolling pin. Place, side by side, on a board. Divide the stuffing among them, then roll up each slice and secure with wooden toothpicks. Lightly brush the beef with some of the oil, then roll in the peppercorns.

4 Heat the remaining oil in the pan, add the beef olives and fry over a medium heat to brown all over. Remove using a slotted spoon and set aside.

5 Add the onion and celery to the pan and cook for 5 minutes until softened. Add the potatoes, carrots and tomatoes and stir for a couple of minutes, then return the beef olives to the pan. (If your pan is not big enough, transfer everything to a large flameproof casserole dish.)

6 Pour in the stock and sherry and add the bay leaf. Slowly bring to a boil, then reduce the heat to low, cover and simmer for 20–25 minutes until the meat and vegetables are tender.

7 Lift out the beef olives using a slotted spoon and keep warm. Boil the liquid in the pan over a high heat to reduce to the desired consistency. Season to taste. Put the beef olives back into the pan and serve sprinkled with parsley.

EACH SERVING

35.5 g protein • 23 g fat of which 4.5 g saturates • 24.5 g carbohydrate • 8.5 g fibre • 484 Calories

COOK'S TIP
• *To prepare this meal in advance, follow the recipe to the end of step 5, and chill the braise for up to a day in the refrigerator. Then continue from step 6, allowing 5 minutes extra cooking time.*

Sausages with French green lentils

Meaty sausages are simple to cook, succulent and juicy, and when combined with diced vegetables and tender lentils they make a hearty meal with a healthy balance of nutrients.

Serves 4   Preparation time 15 minutes   Cooking time 50 minutes

2 large onions, chopped	1 tablespoon olive oil
4 garlic cloves, thinly sliced	6 good-quality, thin pork sausages
350 grams (12 oz) carrots, peeled and diced	1 1/3 cups French green lentils, rinsed
1 large fennel bulb, chopped	1 1/4 cups red wine
2 bay leaves	1/3 cup currant jelly
4 sprigs of fresh thyme	1 tablespoon Dijon mustard
1 orange, zest grated and juiced	1 orange, cut into eight small wedges

1 Preheat the oven to 375°F (190°C). Put the onions, garlic, carrots, fennel, bay leaves and thyme in a fairly deep roasting pan and stir until mixed together. Add the orange zest and olive oil and mix thoroughly.

2 Place the sausages on top of the vegetables. Bake for about 25 minutes until the sausages are lightly browned on top.

3 Meanwhile, place the lentils in a large pot and cover with boiling water. Bring to a boil, then reduce the heat, partly cover the pan and boil for 15 minutes until just tender. Drain well.

4 Lift the sausages out of the roasting pan and set aside. Stir the wine, currant jelly, mustard and orange juice into the vegetables in the pan, then add the lentils and stir in with a fork. Reposition the sausages on top, turning them browned-sides down.

5 Bake for a further 20–25 minutes, until the sausages are well browned and the vegetables and lentils are cooked. Remove the sausages to a board and thickly slice them on the diagonal. Discard the herbs from the lentil mixture, then lay the sausages back on top and serve garnished with orange wedges.

EACH SERVING

22 g protein • 25 g fat of which 8.5 g saturates • 46 g carbohydrate • 12 g fibre • 559 Calories

Stuffed roast pork with prunes

Pork and prunes is a classic French combination, and here it is given an extra flavour boost with ginger and orange. Cooked with a variety of vegetables it makes an easy roast meal and can be prepared ahead and kept in the refrigerator ready for cooking.

Step 1

Step 2

Step 3

Serves 4

Preparation time 25 minutes

Cooking time about 1 hour

2 small pork tenderloins

1 large orange

1/3 cup sliced prunes

3 knobs stem ginger in syrup, drained and thinly sliced

6 lean bacon strips

400 grams (14 oz) new potatoes, scrubbed and cut into 5 mm slices

2 leeks, trimmed and thickly sliced

2 carrots, peeled and thickly sliced

2 red apples

2 cups dry alcoholic cider

2 tablespoons chopped fresh flat-leaf parsley

COOK'S TIP

• *To prepare this meal in advance, follow the recipe up to the end of step 3 and leave in the refrigerator for a few hours or overnight.*

1 Preheat the oven to 400°F (200°C). Put the pork tenderloins on a chopping board and cut each in half lengthwise, without cutting all the way through. Open the tenderloins like a book and press down to flatten slightly.

2 Finely grate the zest from the orange and set aside. Using a small, serrated knife, cut away all the white pith from the orange, then slice down between the membranes to remove the orange segments. Arrange the orange segments over the cut surface of one tenderloin. Top with the sliced prunes and ginger, sprinkle with the orange zest, then season to taste.

3 Place the second tenderloin, cut-side down, on top and gently press the two tenderloins together. Wrap the bacon strips around the pork and secure in place with kitchen string. Set aside.

4 Spread the potatoes over the bottom of a large roasting pan, then scatter over the leeks and carrots. Core and thickly slice the apples, then add to the pan. Place the pork package on top and pour in the cider. Roast for 1 hour or until the potatoes and carrots are tender and clear juices come out of the pork when it is pierced with the tip of a knife. Lift out the pork and vegetables, cover with foil and leave to rest and keep warm for 10 minutes.

5 Meanwhile, put the roasting pan on the stove and boil the cooking liquid over a high heat until it is reduced to about 2/3 cup. Add the parsley and season to taste. Slice the pork and serve with the vegetables and the cooking juices spooned over the top.

EACH SERVING

37 g protein • 8.5 g fat of which 3 g saturates • 54 g carbohydrate • 7.5 g fibre • 488 Calories

Pork with red cabbage and pears

For this slow-cooked dish, lightly browned pork steaks are braised on top of a delicious mixture of red cabbage, baby beets, sliced pears and lentils.

*Serves **4*** *Preparation time **30 minutes*** *Cooking time **2 hours***

1½ tablespoons canola oil

2 teaspoons balsamic vinegar

4 pork steaks, trimmed of all excess fat

1 red onion, thinly sliced

1 garlic clove, crushed

500 grams (1 lb) red cabbage, shredded

250 grams (½ lb) raw baby beets, peeled and cut into six wedges

2 pears, ripe but firm, quartered, cored and thinly sliced

1 orange, zest finely grated and juiced

1½ tablespoons soft brown sugar

398 ml can green lentils, drained and rinsed

⅓ cup diluted salt-reduced or homemade chicken or vegetable stock (pages 28–29)

1 teaspoon whole-grain mustard

1 Preheat the oven to 350°F (175°C). Mix 2 teaspoons of the oil and 1 teaspoon of the vinegar. Lightly brush over the pork and season. Set aside to marinate.

2 Heat 3 teaspoons of the oil in a flameproof casserole dish with a capacity of at least 3 litres. Add the onion and fry gently for 3 minutes. Add the garlic, cook for a few seconds, then remove from the heat. Add the cabbage, beet wedges, pear slices, orange zest and juice, remaining vinegar and sugar to the casserole. Lightly season, then stir the ingredients together. Cover the dish with a tight-fitting lid and cook in the oven for 1½ hours or until the cabbage is just tender, stirring halfway through the cooking time. Towards the end of the cooking time, pat the marinated pork steaks dry on paper towel.

3 Heat a heavy-based frying pan and brush with the remaining oil. Add the pork steaks and cook for 2 minutes on each side over a medium–high heat until browned. (The steaks will still be undercooked at this stage.)

4 Stir the lentils into the red cabbage mixture, then place the steaks on top. Blend together the stock and mustard and drizzle over the top. Re-cover and return to the oven for 15–20 minutes until the cabbage is tender and the pork cooked through. Serve at once.

EACH SERVING

33.5 g protein • 13 g fat of which 3 g saturates • 31.5 g carbohydrate • 11 g fibre • 396 Calories

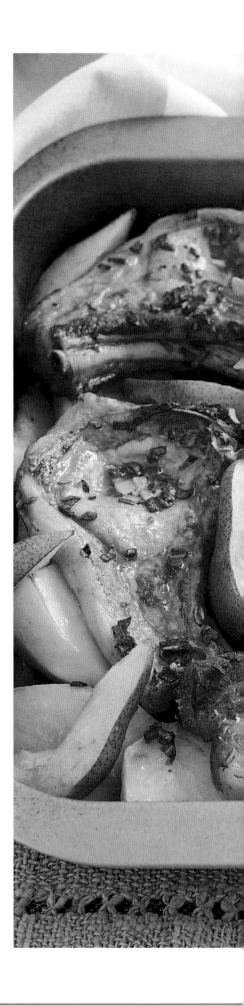

Pork chops with parsnips and maple pear wedges

A superb combination of flavours, conveniently roasted all in one big pan. The pork is best marinated ahead, if time allows. A spicy fruit relish would make a great accompaniment.

Serves 4   Preparation time 20 minutes, plus 1 hour marinating
Cooking time 55 minutes

4 lean pork chops, trimmed of all excess fat

2 tablespoons olive oil

2 garlic cloves, finely chopped

2 tablespoons chopped fresh sage

½ teaspoon fennel seeds, roughly crushed

¼ cup balsamic vinegar

2 red onions, quartered

4 potatoes (about 500 grams/1 lb in total), peeled and quartered

2 large parsnips, peeled and quartered lengthwise

1 large pear, ripe but firm

2 tablespoons maple syrup

a few sprigs of fresh sage (optional)

1 Place the chops in a wide dish. Sprinkle over the oil, garlic, sage, fennel seeds and 2 tablespoons of the balsamic vinegar. Turn to coat evenly, then cover and place in the refrigerator to marinate for 1 hour.

2 Preheat the oven to 400°F (200°C). Combine the onions, potatoes and parsnips in a large roasting pan. Add the pork chops with their marinade and turn the vegetables to coat evenly. Spread out the vegetables in a single layer, with the chops on top. Season to taste. Roast for about 40 minutes until the vegetables are tender and golden.

3 Core the pear and cut into eight slices. Toss in the remaining balsamic vinegar and the maple syrup. Remove the roasting pan from the oven and arrange the pear slices over the chops, spooning over the syrup mixture.

4 Return to the oven and roast for a further 10–12 minutes until the pears are tender. Serve the pork chops topped with the pear slices and juices, with the roasted vegetables alongside and, if you like, sage leaves scattered over the top.

COOK'S TIP
• *To prepare this meal in advance, you can marinate the meat overnight and chop all the vegetables, keeping them covered in the refrigerator.*

EACH SERVING

31 g protein • 15 g fat of which 3 g saturates • 38.5 g carbohydrate • 6 g fibre • 423 Calories

Tarragon chicken with creamy vegetables

Potatoes and carrots are baked in a luxuriously creamy, sour cream sauce, flavoured with garlic and tarragon, with marinated chicken breasts cooked on top. Serve with cherry tomatoes and a green salad.

Serves 4

Preparation time 35 minutes

Cooking time 1 hour 25 minutes

750 grams (1²/₃ lb) new potatoes, scrubbed

4 large carrots, peeled

4 skinless chicken breasts (about 150 grams/5 oz each)

1 teaspoon olive oil

1 tablespoon lemon juice

¹/₄ cup chopped fresh tarragon or 2 teaspoons dried tarragon

³/₄ cup light sour cream

²/₃ cup diluted salt-reduced or homemade chicken stock (page 28)

1 garlic clove, crushed

4 scallions, finely chopped

VARIATION

• *If you like, you can replace the carrots with parsnips.*

1 Put the potatoes in a pot of lightly salted boiling water. Bring back to a boil, then reduce the heat and simmer for 7 minutes. Add the carrots and simmer for a further 5 minutes. Drain and leave until cool enough to handle.

2 Meanwhile, place the chicken breasts in a shallow dish. Mix together the oil, lemon juice and 1 tablespoon of the chopped fresh tarragon (or 1 teaspoon dried) with a little salt and pepper. Drizzle this over the chicken and turn to coat. Cover and set aside to marinate in the refrigerator while preparing and cooking the vegetables. Preheat the oven to 375°F (190°C).

3 Peel and thinly slice the potatoes. Thinly slice the carrots. Whisk the sour cream into the stock, then stir in the garlic, scallions and half the remaining fresh tarragon or remaining 1 teaspoon of dried tarragon.

4 Roughly layer the potatoes and carrots alternately in a lightly greased, shallow ovenproof dish, spooning a little of the sour cream mixture over each layer. Finish with potato slices covered with the last of the sour cream mixture. Cover the dish with foil and bake for 35–40 minutes.

5 Arrange the chicken on top of the potatoes and re-cover with foil. Bake for 25–30 minutes until the chicken is cooked through (the juices will run clear when the chicken is pierced with a skewer). Scatter over the remaining tarragon.

EACH SERVING

40 g protein • 19.5 g fat of which 9 g saturates • 31 g carbohydrate • 7 g fibre • 476 Calories

Braised chicken with beans

This is a great way to cook good-value drumsticks, so that they are moist and tender. A simple barbecue sauce and a mixture of vegetables and beans makes a healthy dish children will love. Serve with a leafy side salad.

Serves 4

Preparation time 15 minutes

Cooking time 50 minutes

2 tablespoons canola oil

4 garlic cloves, crushed

½ teaspoon dried marjoram

8 chicken drumsticks, skinned

500 grams (1 lb) leeks, trimmed, split lengthwise and sliced

250 grams (½ lb) carrots, peeled and diced

1 celery stalk, diced

1¼ cups diluted salt-reduced or homemade chicken stock (page 28)

2 cups frozen corn kernels

398 ml can white kidney beans, drained and rinsed

1 tablespoon dark brown sugar

2 tablespoons cider vinegar

1 teaspoon chili sauce, or to taste

¼ cup tomato sauce

2 tablespoons whole-grain mustard

1 Heat the oil in a large, deep frying pan or flameproof casserole dish. Add the garlic, marjoram and chicken and cook over a medium heat for 5 minutes, turning the drumsticks to lightly brown all over. Transfer the chicken to a plate.

2 Add the leeks, carrots and celery. Cook for 5 minutes until the leeks are softened. Stir in the stock and replace the drumsticks, shuffling them among the vegetables. Reduce the heat, cover and simmer for 30 minutes until the drumsticks are tender. Use a slotted spoon to transfer the drumsticks to a plate.

3 Add the corn and white kidney beans and heat through for 1 minute. Then, using the slotted spoon, transfer the vegetables to a serving dish. Cover and set aside to keep hot.

4 Bring the liquid in the pan to a boil. Stir in the sugar, vinegar, chili sauce, tomato sauce and mustard. Boil hard for about 5 minutes until it has reduced to a slightly syrupy, shiny sauce.

5 Put the drumsticks in the sauce and heat through, turning them to coat evenly. Serve the drumsticks on the vegetables, pouring over all the sauce.

EACH SERVING

39.5 g protein • 20 g fat of which 4 g saturates • 35 g carbohydrate • 10 g fibre • 492 Calories

Middle Eastern roast chicken with saffron couscous

Here chicken is roasted with a fig and pistachio couscous stuffing and basted with a spicy lemon marinade to keep the meat deliciously moist. A leafy salad with fresh oranges would make a great side dish.

Serves 4–6
Preparation time 30 minutes
Cooking time 1 hour 25 minutes

1 large chicken (about 1.5 kg/3 lbs)

1 lemon, zest grated and juiced

1 tablespoon honey

2 tablespoons olive oil

½ teaspoon ground ginger

½ teaspoon ground cinnamon

1 teaspoon ground cumin

3 small red onions, each cut into six wedges

COUSCOUS STUFFING

1²/3 cups couscous

¼ teaspoon saffron threads

2 cups diluted salt-reduced or homemade chicken or vegetable stock (pages 28–29), hot

⅓ cup coarsely chopped dried figs

⅓ cup shelled unsalted pistachios, coarsely chopped

VARIATION
• For an Indian-style recipe, replace the couscous with basmati rice, slightly under-cooked. Omit the saffron and stock, replace the pistachios with toasted cashews, and use a chopped beefsteak tomato in place of the figs. Flavour with ½ teaspoon garam masala, 1 tablespoon chopped cilantro and plenty of pepper.

1 Rinse the chicken inside and out under cold running water and dry with paper towel. Put into a large, lightly greased roasting pan. Mix the lemon zest and juice with the honey, olive oil, ginger, cinnamon, cumin and freshly ground black pepper to taste. Brush some of this mixture generously inside the cavity of the bird, then over the outside. Leave to marinate while making the stuffing or for longer, if convenient. Reserve the rest of the marinade.

2 Preheat the oven to 350°F (180°C). Put the couscous into a heatproof bowl. Stir the saffron into the stock, then pour over the couscous. Cover and leave to stand for 5 minutes or until all the stock has been absorbed. Stir in the figs and pistachios. Season to taste.

3 Spoon some of the couscous mixture into the neck end of the chicken. Fold the neck skin over and secure with the wing tips or with a wooden toothpick. Put the onion wedges into the cavity of the body (or, if you prefer, arrange them in the pan around the bird after it has been roasting for 40 minutes). Spoon the rest of the spiced lemon juice mixture over the chicken and roast for 1 hour.

4 Spoon the remaining couscous around the chicken and roast for a further 25 minutes. To test if the bird is cooked, pierce the thickest part of the thigh: the juices should run clear.

5 Transfer the chicken to a serving platter, loosely cover with foil to keep warm and leave to rest for 10 minutes before carving. Remove the skin before serving. Serve with the couscous and onions.

COOK'S TIP
• The chicken can be marinated a day in advance and the couscous stuffing prepared ahead of time. Don't stuff the chicken until just before you are ready to cook it.

EACH SERVING (6)

52.5 g protein • 30 g fat of which 7.5 g saturates • 23.5 g carbohydrate • 3 g fibre • 579 Calories

Braised duck breasts with celery and orange

Try this stylish dish for entertaining. Duck breasts are full of succulent flavour and when you remove the skin, you reduce the fat.

Serves 4

*Preparation time 20 minutes,
    plus at least 1 hour marinating*

Cooking time 45 minutes

6 oranges

4 skinless duck breasts
(about 175 grams/6 oz each)

2 tablespoons canola oil

2 onions, thinly sliced

4 celery stalks, sliced

1 large garlic clove, crushed

500 grams (1 lb) small new
potatoes, scrubbed and halved

²/₃ cup diluted salt-reduced or
homemade chicken stock (page 28)

1 red chili pepper, deseeded and
thinly sliced (optional)

1 tablespoon chopped fresh
flat-leaf parsley

1 Finely grate the zest, then juice 4 of the oranges. Arrange the duck in a single layer in a dish, sprinkle with the zest and pour over the juice, then turn several times. Cover with plastic wrap and marinate in the refrigerator for at least 1 hour.

2 Bring the duck to room temperature. Preheat the oven to 350°F (180°C). Peel the remaining oranges and cut each into segments.

3 Heat the oil in a shallow flameproof casserole dish over a medium heat. Add the onions and celery and stir for 3 minutes. Add the garlic and fry for 1 minute until the onions are soft but not brown. Using a slotted spoon, remove from the pan and set aside.

4 Lift the duck breasts out of the marinade and transfer to the casserole dish. Spoon the onions and celery over them, then pour over the marinade. Add the potatoes and half the orange segments, scattering them around the duck breasts. Pour over the stock, add the chili pepper, if using, and bring to a boil.

5 Cover the dish and bake for 40 minutes until the duck and potatoes are tender. Season to taste.

6 Remove the duck breasts from the casserole and slice them. Spoon the onions and celery into soup bowls and scatter the potatoes around the side. Top each portion with sliced duck, then spoon the juices over. Garnish with reserved orange and sprinkle with parsley.

EACH SERVING

37 g protein • 19 g fat of which 3.5 g saturates • 33.5 g carbohydrate
• 6 g fibre • 466 Calories

Orange roast chicken with vegetables

Here's a roast meal, cooked in one pan, that even makes its own gravy — the pan juices are so full of flavour that no other accompaniment is needed. Use a large roasting pan, so that the vegetables cook in a single layer.

Serves 4   Preparation time 15 minutes   Cooking time about 2 hours

2 oranges

4 garlic cloves

1 chicken (about 1.5 kg/3 lbs)

3 cinnamon sticks

4 sprigs of fresh rosemary

1 bay leaf

2 cups diluted salt-reduced or homemade chicken stock (page 28) or water

2 orange sweet potatoes

2 fresh ears of corn

2 red onions

1 Preheat the oven to 350°F (180°C). Cut each orange into eight wedges and tuck half of them and an unpeeled garlic clove into the cavity of the chicken.

2 Place the cinnamon sticks, rosemary, bay leaf and remaining garlic in a large roasting pan and set the chicken on top. Pour half the stock or water into the pan. Place in the oven and roast for 1 hour, basting the chicken with the pan juices after 30 minutes.

3 Meanwhile, peel the sweet potatoes and cut into 3–4 cm chunks. Cut each corn cob across into four pieces. Peel the onions and cut each into four wedges. Remove the pan from the oven and add the vegetables and remaining orange wedges, turning them in the pan juices to coat evenly.

4 Add the remaining stock or water to the pan and return to the oven to roast for a further 50–60 minutes until the chicken is cooked and the vegetables are tender. Baste with the pan juices halfway through the roasting time.

5 Remove the chicken from the pan and place on a warmed serving dish. Lift out the vegetables with a slotted spoon and arrange around the chicken. Discard the cinnamon, rosemary, bay leaf and garlic cloves. Skim any excess fat from the juices and heat until boiling, then serve with the chicken.

VARIATIONS

• *For a dish that cooks in under 1 hour, replace the chicken with chicken quarters or Cornish hens, and cook all together with the vegetables.*
• *If sweet potatoes are not available, use butternut squash.*

EACH SERVING

75.5 g protein • 29 g fat of which 9 g saturates • 59 g carbohydrate • 11 g fibre • 820 Calories

VARIATIONS

• *Pork steaks would also work well in this dish. Trim off all the excess fat and cook them for 20 minutes.*
• *This is a great dish to try in the spring with ruby-coloured blood oranges.*

Roast vegetables with pears and bacon

A warming autumnal dish of roasted root vegetables with eggplant, sweet pears and salty bacon. Roasting brings out the sweetness of the vegetables and, unlike boiling, retains all the goodness.

Serves 4

Preparation time 20 minutes

Cooking time 50 minutes

1 eggplant, cut into eight pieces lengthwise

3 orange sweet potatoes, peeled and cut into eight pieces lengthwise

3 parsnips, quartered lengthwise

150 grams (5 oz) baby leeks, trimmed

2 tablespoons olive oil

2 tablespoons chopped fresh thyme or 2 teaspoons dried thyme

2 firm pears, cored and quartered

8 slices back bacon

1 tablespoon balsamic vinegar

COOK'S TIP

• *If you arrange all the vegetables parallel in the pan, they are easier and quicker to brush with oil.*

VARIATIONS

• *When quinces are in season, they can be used instead of the pears.*
• *If baby leeks are not available, replace them with ordinary leeks, sliced on the diagonal or, alternatively, use wedges of red onion instead.*

1 Preheat the oven to 400°F (200°C). Arrange the eggplant, sweet potatoes, parsnips and leeks in a single layer in a wide roasting pan. Use a pastry brush to coat them lightly with oil.

2 Sprinkle the thyme over the vegetables and season with freshly ground black pepper. Bake for 25–30 minutes until the vegetables are almost tender, then turn the vegetables and add the pear wedges, turning to coat lightly in oil. Arrange the bacon rashers over the vegetables.

3 Return the pan to the oven for 15–20 minutes until the vegetables and pears are tender and the bacon is lightly browned. Drizzle the balsamic vinegar over the roast vegetables and serve hot.

EACH SERVING

19 g protein • 14 g fat of which 3 g saturates • 75 g carbohydrate • 13 g fibre • 522 Calories

Mustard-roast ham with parsnips

This is an excellent way of cooking all your vegetables with a joint of meat in one pan. Parsnips as well as zucchini and red onions provide a colourful and delicious mixture that goes beautifully with ham. It is high in sodium, so make it an occasional treat.

Serves 8

Preparation time 25 minutes

Cooking time 2 hours

1 boneless, unsmoked ham, with its skin on (soaked if necessary)

1 bay leaf

12 large parsnips, quartered lengthwise

2 red onions, each cut into six wedges

¼ cup canola oil

20 cloves

1 tablespoon Dijon mustard

1 tablespoon honey

1 tablespoon soft brown sugar

3 zucchini, thickly sliced

1 tablespoon sesame seeds

1 Put the ham in a large pot with the bay leaf and enough cold water to cover it. Slowly bring to a boil, skimming off any scum that rises to the surface. Reduce the heat, cover and gently simmer for 40 minutes. Remove from the pot of water and set aside on a board.

2 Preheat the oven to 350°F (180°C) and put a large roasting pan in to heat. Add the parsnips and onions to the simmering water, bring back to a boil and cook for 2 minutes, then drain in a colander. Leave to cool for a few minutes, then return to the pan. Drizzle with 2½ tablespoons of the oil and toss to coat. Tip the vegetables into the roasting pan; roast for 20 minutes.

3 Meanwhile, use a sharp knife to cut the rind off the ham, leaving a thin, even layer of fat. Score deep

lines across the fat, cutting into the flesh slightly so the glaze can penetrate, then score the fat in the opposite direction to make neat diamond shapes.

4 Stud the ham with cloves (one per diamond). Blend the mustard, honey and sugar together into a paste, then spread over the fat. Push the vegetables aside of the roasting pan and put the ham in the middle. Roast for 10 minutes.

5 Increase the oven temperature to 425°F (220°C). Toss the zucchini in the remaining oil. Add to the pan, turning the roasted vegetables at the same time, then roast for a further 30 minutes until the ham is well glazed and golden. Check that the ham is cooked by inserting a fine skewer into the centre for a few seconds — when removed the juices should run clear.

6 Remove the ham, cover with foil and leave in a warm place. Turn the vegetables, then sprinkle the sesame seeds and a little freshly ground black pepper over them. Roast for a final 5 minutes until tender and nicely browned. Thickly slice the ham and serve hot with the vegetables.

EACH SERVING

30.5 g protein • 12.5 g fat of which 2 g saturates • 22.5 g carbohydrate • 5 g fibre • 335 Calories

Lentil and cashew nut roast

Not only are low-fat lentils richer in protein than many other legumes, but their slightly smoky flavour makes a great base for this tasty nut roast, packed with colourful vegetables and served with a quick tomato sauce.

Serves **4** *Preparation time* **20 minutes** *Cooking time* **1¼ hours**

1 cup split red lentils

2 cups diluted salt-reduced or homemade vegetable stock (page 29)

1 bay leaf

¾ cup unsalted cashews

1½ tablespoons olive oil

1 large onion, finely chopped

1 large or 2 small leeks, trimmed and finely chopped

1 red pepper, deseeded and chopped

100 grams (3½ oz) mushrooms, chopped

1 garlic clove, crushed

1 tablespoon lemon juice

¾ cup fresh whole wheat breadcrumbs

¼ cup chopped fresh flat-leaf parsley

⅔ cup grated mature cheddar cheese

1 egg, lightly beaten

TOMATO SAUCE

1 tablespoon tomato paste

½ teaspoon paprika

398 ml can chopped tomatoes

⅔ cup red wine or diluted salt-reduced or homemade vegetable stock (page 29)

¼ teaspoon dried mixed herbs

1 Rinse the lentils in a sieve under cold running water. Drain, then tip into a pot. Add the stock and bay leaf and bring to a boil. Reduce the heat to a gentle simmer, then cover and cook for 15 minutes until the lentils are soft and pulpy and the stock has been absorbed. Stir once or twice towards the end of the cooking time to prevent the lentils sticking. Discard the bay leaf.

2 Meanwhile, put the cashews in a frying pan and toast over a medium heat until lightly browned, stirring often. Cool, then coarsely chop. Preheat the oven to 375°F (190°C). Line the bottom of a 1.4 litre loaf pan with parchment.

3 Add the oil to the frying pan and cook the onion over a medium heat for 5 minutes. Remove half the onion and reserve for the sauce. Add the leeks, pepper, mushrooms and garlic to the pan and cook for 5 minutes, stirring occasionally, until tender. Stir in the lemon juice.

4 Tip the lentils and vegetables into a bowl. Stir in the breadcrumbs, nuts and 2 tablespoons of the parsley, followed by the cheese and egg. Season, then spoon into the loaf pan. Level the top and cover with a piece of lightly oiled foil.

EACH SERVING

22.5 g protein • 29.5 g fat of which 8 g saturates • 37 g carbohydrate • 9 g fibre • 545 Calories

5 Bake the loaf for 30 minutes, then remove the foil and bake for a further 30 minutes or until a skewer inserted into the centre comes out clean. Remove from the oven and leave to cool in the pan for 15 minutes before carefully turning out and cutting into thick slices.

6 Meanwhile, make the sauce. Put the reserved onion and remaining ingredients in a small pot. Bring to a boil, then reduce the heat and simmer for 20 minutes, until slightly reduced. Stir in the remaining parsley before serving with the loaf.

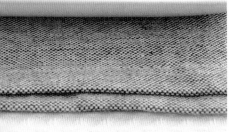

COOK'S TIPS
• If you don't have a loaf
pan in this size, use an
alternative pan with a
similar capacity. The
mixture should come to
a depth of 4–5 cm.
• The mixture should be
warm, not steaming hot
when adding the egg. If
necessary, allow it to cool
for a few minutes.

Fish boulangère

Firm white fish lends itself to gentle oven-braising on a bed of vegetables. Sliced potatoes and onion provide the vegetable base while peas and cherry tomatoes are scattered on top.

Serves 4   *Preparation time* 25 minutes   *Cooking time* 1 hour 10 minutes

750 grams (1²/₃ lbs) Yukon Gold potatoes, peeled and thinly sliced

1 onion, thinly sliced

1 teaspoon fresh thyme

15 grams (¹/₂ oz) fresh chives, snipped

1 lemon, zest grated and juiced

1²/₃ cups diluted or homemade fish stock (page 29), hot

4 thick firm white fish steaks (about 500 grams/1 lb in total)

2 cups shelled fresh or frozen peas, thawed if necessary

200 grams (7 oz) cherry tomatoes, halved

1 Preheat the oven to 375°F (190°C). Layer the sliced potatoes and onion in a large, greased ovenproof dish, adding the thyme and half the chives plus a little seasoning between each layer. Mix the lemon zest and juice with the stock and pour over the vegetables. Cover the dish with foil, then bake for 45 minutes or until the potatoes are almost tender.

2 Meanwhile, cut the fish into large, bite-sized chunks, discarding any skin and bones. Uncover the ovenproof dish and arrange the fish on top of the potatoes in a single layer. Re-cover the dish and return it to the oven. Bake for a further 15 minutes.

3 Uncover the dish and scatter the peas over the fish and potatoes. Finish with the tomatoes, cut-side up, then sprinkle with coarsely ground black pepper. Cover the dish and return it to the oven for a final 10 minutes.

4 Scatter the rest of the snipped chives over the fish and vegetables as a garnish, then serve.

VARIATIONS
• *Replace the onion with a thinly sliced bulb of fennel.*
• *Fresh or frozen fava beans can be used instead of peas.*

EACH SERVING

40 g protein • 4 g fat of which 1.5 g saturates • 31 g carbohydrate
• 8.5 g fibre • 341 Calories

Braised whole sea bass with chermoula

Sea bass makes an impressive meal, and its delicious flesh is moist, tender and sweet. Here it's stuffed with an exotic Moroccan-style fresh herb and spice mixture called chermoula, then braised on a bed of vegetables.

Step 1

Step 2

Step 3

Serves 4

Preparation time 20 minutes,
  plus at least 30 minutes
  marinating
Cooking time 55 minutes

1 whole sea bass, salmon or firm white fish (about 1 kg/2 lbs), cleaned

4 garlic cloves

1 small red chili pepper, deseeded

40 grams (1 1/2 oz) cilantro

1 teaspoon paprika

1/2 teaspoon ground cumin

1/4 cup canola oil

1 lemon, juiced

175 grams (6 oz) thin green beans, halved

600 grams (1 1/4 lbs) russet potatoes, peeled

2 scallions, finely chopped

250 grams (1/2 lb) grape or cherry tomatoes

1/3 cup pitted black olives

1 1/4 cups diluted or homemade fish stock (page 29), hot

1 Cut about six deep, diagonal slashes in the flesh on each side of the fish. Place it in a wide, non-metallic dish.

2 Put the garlic, chili pepper, cilantro, paprika, cumin, oil and lemon juice in a food processor and process until blended and finely chopped. Season to taste. Spread about half of this "chermoula" inside the fish and into the slashes. Cover the fish and the remaining chermoula, and leave in the refrigerator for at least 30 minutes to marinate.

3 Preheat the oven to 400°F (200°C). Drop the beans into a pot of boiling water and blanch for 1 minute, then drain and refresh in cold water. Thinly slice the potatoes and spread in a shallow layer with the scallions in a wide, deep ovenproof dish. Scatter the beans, tomatoes and olives over the top.

4 Pour the stock over the vegetables and place the fish on top. Cover with foil and cook in the oven for 40–50 minutes until the potatoes are tender and the fish flakes easily when tested with a fork.

5 Serve the whole fish with the vegetables on a platter, with the reserved chermoula as a sauce.

EACH SERVING

38.5 g protein • 27.5 g fat of which 4.5 g saturates • 21.5 g carbohydrate • 5 g fibre • 500 Calories

VARIATION

• If you prefer, use 4 small fish, or 4 steaks. Cook
the vegetables on their own for 30 minutes, then
arrange the whole fish or steaks on top and cook for
a further 20 minutes or until the fish flakes easily.

Casseroles and curries

Wholesome, warming casseroles and exotic, spicy curries are the ultimate, adaptable one-dish meals. They can often be prepared ahead and doubled in quantity, then reheated or frozen for later. Long, slow cooking is ideal for tenderizing cuts of meat and poultry; it develops a rounded flavour and maintains all the nutrients in a delicious sauce. Try these healthy versions of the classics, knowing that while you're enjoying every mouthful, your body is relishing the healthy nutrients.

Lancashire hot-pot

This modern version of the popular favourite, Lancashire hot-pot, is still slow-cooked for maximum flavour, but is lighter, using lean lamb and more vegetables than the original recipe. If you like, sprinkle the top with a little cheddar cheese at the end of cooking.

Serves 4

Preparation time 20 minutes

Cooking time about 2 hours

500 grams (1 lb) lean lamb, trimmed of all excess fat, then sliced

1 garlic clove, crushed

2 tablespoons Worcestershire sauce

1 onion, thinly sliced

2 leeks, trimmed and thinly sliced

3 carrots, peeled and sliced

250 grams (1/2 lb) button mushrooms, halved

1 bay leaf

1 small bunch of fresh thyme

1 sprig of fresh rosemary

500 grams (1 lb) new potatoes, scrubbed and thickly sliced

2 tablespoons tomato paste

1 2/3 cups diluted salt-reduced or homemade beef or chicken stock (page 28), hot

50 grams (1 3/4 oz) cheddar cheese, crumbled (optional)

1 Preheat the oven to 350°F (180°C). Toss the lamb pieces together with the garlic and Worcestershire sauce in a bowl.

2 Spread a layer of onion, leeks and carrots in the bottom of a large casserole dish. Top with a layer of meat and mushrooms and season lightly, then repeat the layers until the ingredients are all used up.

3 Make a bouquet garni by tying together the bay leaf, thyme and rosemary with kitchen string. Tuck it into the centre of the casserole. Top with a thick layer of overlapping potato slices.

4 Mix the tomato paste into the hot stock and pour the mixture over the potatoes. Cover tightly with a lid and bake for 1 1/2 hours or until the meat and potatoes are tender.

5 Remove the lid and sprinkle the cheddar cheese over the potatoes, if using. Increase the oven temperature to 450°F (230°C) and bake, uncovered, for a further 25-30 minutes until golden.

COOK'S TIP
• *You can prepare the hot-pot ahead of time up until the end of step 4 and leave it in the refrigerator for a few hours or even overnight, if more convenient.*

EACH SERVING

38 g protein • 13.5 g fat of which 6.5 g saturates • 28 g carbohydrate • 8.5 g fibre • 403 Calories

VARIATION
• *Instead of sliced potatoes, top the hot-pot with a layer of coarsely grated potato, or mix potato half-and-half with grated parsnips. Bake in the same way as in the main recipe, topping with Parmesan cheese if you like.*

Lamb tagine with dried fruit

An aromatic North African-style casserole, richly flavoured with dried fruits and warmly spiced with ginger and cinnamon. The sweetness of the honey tempers the fiery harissa, and chickpeas add high-fibre carbohydrate to the dish.

Serves **4**

Preparation time **30 minutes**

Cooking time **about 2 hours**

2 tablespoons olive oil

500 grams (1 lb) lean boneless lamb (such as leg), cubed

1 onion, chopped

¼ teaspoon saffron threads

2 cups diluted salt-reduced or homemade vegetable stock (page 29), hot

1 tablespoon tomato paste

1 orange, zest cut into strips

¼ teaspoon ground ginger

1 teaspoon ground cinnamon

½ teaspoon ground coriander

½ teaspoon harissa, or to taste

1 tablespoon honey

16 pickling onions or small shallots, peeled

⅔ cup pitted dried dates

1 cup dried apricots

2 x 398 ml cans chickpeas, drained and rinsed

2 tablespoons chopped walnuts

COOK'S TIP

• *You can prepare ahead up to the end of step 4, then cool and chill. Freeze if you like. Thaw and reheat gently until piping hot throughout, adding a little extra stock if necessary.*

VARIATION

• *You could replace the pickling onions, dates and apricots with 2 tablespoons raisins, 1 large zucchini, diced, and 1 chopped tomato, plus a slice of pumpkin, peeled, cored and diced.*

1 Heat the oil in a large, deep saucepan or flameproof casserole dish. Add the lamb and fry until lightly browned. Push the meat to one side and add the chopped onion to the pan. Fry for 5–10 minutes, stirring frequently, until golden.

2 Stir the saffron into the hot stock, then pour into the pan. Add the tomato paste, strips of orange zest and spices. Stir well, then bring to a boil. Reduce the heat, cover and leave to simmer gently for 1½ hours.

3 Uncover the pan and take out about a cup of the sauce. Stir the harissa and honey into the reserved sauce, then stir the mixture back into the pan.

4 Add the pickling onions or shallots, dates, apricots and chickpeas and mix. Simmer gently, uncovered, for a further 20 minutes, stirring occasionally.

5 Season to taste and scatter the chopped walnuts over the top, then serve. Put a little extra harissa on the table for those who like more heat.

EACH SERVING

40 g protein • 21.5 g fat of which 5.5 g saturates • 67 g carbohydrate • 17 g fibre • 650 Calories

Lamb and eggplant curry

A spicy, high-fibre and very satisfying curry that combines lots of vegetables with lean, tender lamb chunks and lentils. Serve with whole wheat chapattis or nan.

Serves 4

Preparation time 30 minutes,
*   plus at least 2 hours marinating*

Cooking time 40 minutes

1 teaspoon cumin seeds

1 teaspoon coriander seeds

1 teaspoon fennel seeds

½ teaspoon black mustard seeds

4 green cardamom pods, crushed and pods discarded

1 teaspoon chili flakes

375 grams (¾ lb) lean leg of lamb, cut into 2.5 cm cubes

1 tablespoon vegetable oil

1 onion, sliced

2 red peppers, deseeded and cut into 2 cm chunks

1 eggplant, cut into 2 cm chunks

½ cup split red lentils

1⅔ cups diluted salt-reduced or homemade beef stock (page 28)

1 cinnamon stick

¼ cup flaked almonds, toasted

1 Place the cumin, coriander, fennel, mustard and cardamom in a mortar and crush with a pestle. Add the chili flakes. Place the lamb in a bowl, add the spices and toss to coat evenly. Cover and chill for about 2 hours, or overnight.

2 Heat the oil in a large, deep saucepan or flameproof casserole dish and fry the onion, peppers and eggplant for about 10 minutes, stirring occasionally, to soften.

3 Add the spiced lamb and lentils, then stir in the stock and cinnamon. Bring to a boil, then stir, reduce the heat and cover. Simmer gently for about 30 minutes until the meat is tender. Serve scattered with toasted flaked almonds.

COOK'S TIP

• *Curries improve in flavour if made ahead, allowing time for the flavours to mingle. Chill for a few hours or overnight, then reheat gently until thoroughly heated through. This would also freeze well.*

EACH SERVING

28.5 g protein • 15 g fat of which 3.5 g saturates • 9.5 g carbohydrate • 4.5 g fibre • 291 Calories

• The filling mixture can be made up to 1 day ahead, then covered and kept in the refrigerator. Allow to come to room temperature before using to fill the pastry-lined basin.

• For vegetarians, you could replace the steak and kidney with 250 grams (¹/₂ lb) button mushrooms, browning them lightly first. The steaming time could then be reduced to 2 hours.

Steak and kidney pie

This is a lighter version of the delicious traditional pie. The richly flavoured casserole filling is mixed with sweet root vegetables and the herbed pastry is made with vegetable shortening.

Step 1

Step 3

Step 4

Serves 4–6

Preparation time 35 minutes

Cooking time 3 hours 20 minutes

FILLING

250 grams (½ lb) lean stewing beef, cubed

100 grams (3½ oz) beef kidney, cut into small pieces

2 teaspoons vegetable oil

2 leeks, trimmed and sliced

200 grams (7 oz) rutabaga, peeled and cubed

175 grams (6 oz) carrots, peeled and thickly sliced

2 teaspoons plain flour

1¼ cup diluted salt-reduced or homemade beef stock (page 28)

PASTRY

2 small slices whole wheat bread

1 cup self-raising flour

½ teaspoon dried thyme

100 grams (3½ oz) vegetable shortening, cut into small pieces

3–5 tablespoons cold water

1 To make the filling, heat a non-stick frying pan over a high heat. Add the beef and fry, stirring occasionally, for 4 minutes until browned on all sides. Transfer to a bowl, add the kidney and set aside.

2 Heat the oil in the pan, then add the leeks. Stir, then cover and cook gently for 4 minutes until starting to soften. Stir in the rutabaga and carrots, cover and cook for a further 4 minutes until lightly browned. Add the beef and kidney; season to taste, then add the flour and toss well to coat. Pour in the stock and bring to a boil, stirring. Simmer for 2 minutes. Remove the pan from the heat and set aside.

3 To make the pastry, tear the bread into small pieces and put into a food processor. Pulse until fine crumbs are formed. Add the flour, thyme and vegetable shortening and season with a little salt and pepper. Pulse again to combine, then, with the motor running, pour in enough of the cold water to form a soft dough.

4 On a lightly floured surface, roll out three-quarters of the dough, to a circle large enough to line a 1 litre pie basin. Line the basin carefully, then fill with the steak and kidney mixture. Trim the excess pastry. Roll out the remaining pastry to form a lid, wet the edges of the dough and place on top of the filling, sealing the edges well with your fingers.

5 Cover the basin with a double thickness of foil, pleated in the middle and secured with string. Steam the pie over simmering water for 3 hours. Serve the pie hot.

EACH SERVING (6)

17 g protein • 19 g fat of which 9 g saturates • 27 g carbohydrate • 4 g fibre • 357 Calories

Beef in beer casserole

Beef provides plenty of iron and minerals. It makes a mouth-watering casserole when cooked with beer and hearty winter vegetables.

Serves **4**

Preparation time **30 minutes**

Cooking time **about 1³/4 hours**

500 grams (1 lb) lean stewing beef, cubed

2 tablespoons oatmeal, coarsely chopped

2 tablespoons extra virgin olive oil

2 onions, finely chopped

2¹/₂ cups good-quality beer

3–4 sprigs of fresh thyme

3 juniper berries, crushed

2 good pinches of allspice

200 grams (7 oz) baby shallots or small pickling onions, peeled

275 grams (10 oz) baby carrots, scrubbed and trimmed

275 grams (10 oz) baby parsnips or baby turnips, scrubbed and trimmed, or mature ones, scrubbed and cubed

1 baguette

1 Preheat the oven to 325°F (160°C). Toss the pieces of steak in the oatmeal to lightly coat, then shake to remove any excess.

2 Heat the oil in a heavy flameproof casserole and briefly cook the beef until lightly coloured. Transfer to a plate. Add the chopped onions to the casserole and cook gently over a low heat, stirring frequently, for about 10 minutes until softened and golden.

3 Add the beer, thyme, juniper berries and allspice plus a little seasoning to taste, and bring to a boil, stirring constantly.

4 Stir in the shallots or onions, whole baby carrots, parsnips or turnips, and the beef and any meat juices. When the liquid comes to a boil, cover the casserole and put into the oven. Cook, stirring occasionally, for about 1¹/₂ hours until the meat is really tender.

5 Towards the end of the cooking time, cut the bread stick into slices about 2.5 cm thick and lay on a baking tray. Bake for about 15 minutes until they are lightly brown and crisp. Arrange the toasted bread on top of the meat and vegetables and cook, uncovered, for a further 5 minutes. Serve hot, straight from the casserole dish.

EACH SERVING

40 g protein • 20 g fat of which 4.5 g saturates • 78 g carbohydrate • 7.5 g fibre • 713 Calories

COOK'S TIPS
• *To prepare ahead, cook up to the end of step 4, then cool and store in the refrigerator for up to 48 hours, or freeze. Thaw, if frozen, then reheat thoroughly before adding the toasted bread.*
• *Shallots and pickling onions are easy to peel if you make a small cut in the skin at the top and then soak in boiling water for 2 minutes.*

VARIATION
• *If you like, use 2 cups beer with ¹/₂ cup beef stock instead of just beer.*

Greek stifado

A tempting beef casserole — with artichoke hearts, fava beans, new potatoes and juicy, purple-skinned kalamata olives — that is ideal for a family Sunday lunch or easy entertaining, and needs only a green salad alongside.

Serves **4**

Preparation time **20 minutes**

Cooking time **about 1¾ hours**

300 grams (10 oz) pickling onions or shallots

1 tablespoon olive oil

500 grams (1 lb) lean stewing beef, cut into chunks

2 garlic cloves, crushed

½ teaspoon ground cumin

½ teaspoon ground cinnamon

398 ml can chopped tomatoes

1⅔ cups red wine

1 bay leaf

350 grams (12 oz) new potatoes

398 ml can artichoke hearts, drained and halved

1¼ cups frozen fava beans, thawed

⅓ cup kalamata olives, pitted and roughly chopped

COOK'S TIPS

• You can make the whole stew up to 3 days ahead, just leaving out the artichoke hearts, beans and olives. Allow to cool, then cover and keep in the refrigerator. When ready to serve, allow to come to room temperature, then add the remaining ingredients and reheat gently over a low heat until bubbling hot.
• If more convenient, cook the casserole slowly in an oven preheated to 350°F (180°C).

VARIATION

• You can replace the artichoke hearts and olives with 200 grams (7 oz) button mushrooms added with the potatoes.

1 Cut the ends from the onions or shallots and place in a large bowl. Cover with boiling water and allow to stand for about 2 minutes to loosen the skins.

2 Heat the oil in a large flameproof casserole dish over a medium heat. Add the beef and brown evenly, stirring occasionally, for about 8 minutes.

3 Meanwhile, slip the skins from the onions or shallots. Add the peeled onions or shallots to the casserole dish to brown lightly, stirring frequently, for about 5 minutes. Stir in the garlic with the ground spices.

4 Pour in the tomatoes with their juice, and the red wine and bring to a boil. Add the bay leaf, reduce the heat to low, cover the casserole dish and simmer gently for 1 hour.

5 Stir the potatoes into the casserole and continue to simmer for a further 30 minutes, covered, until the meat and potatoes are tender. Add the artichoke hearts, beans and olives and cook for a final 5 minutes to heat through. Season to taste.

EACH SERVING

35 g protein • 12 g fat of which 3.5 g saturates • 24 g carbohydrate • 8 g fibre • 427 Calories

Beef in ale with horseradish dumplings

A hearty beef and vegetable casserole that can be left to cook or made ahead and then reheated before serving. Cook the dumplings on top shortly before serving.

Step 1

Step 2

Step 4

Serves **4**

Preparation time **35 minutes**

Cooking time **about 2½ hours**

2 tablespoons olive oil

500 grams (1 lb) lean stewing beef, cubed

2 onions, sliced

1 tablespoon plain flour

2½ cups well-flavoured dark beer

1 tablespoon currant jelly

1 teaspoon whole-grain mustard

1 bay leaf

6 carrots, peeled and thickly sliced

200 grams (7 oz) baby or small turnips, trimmed and quartered if necessary

4 large portobello mushrooms, thickly sliced

DUMPLINGS

1¼ cups self-rising flour

6 sprigs of fresh flat-leaf parsley

⅓ cup cottage cheese

2 teaspoons horseradish sauce

2 tablespoons 1% milk, or as needed

1 Preheat the oven to 325°F (160°C). Heat the oil in a large, heavy flameproof casserole dish and briefly fry the pieces of beef until they are nicely browned. Lift the meat out of the casserole dish with a slotted spoon and set aside on a plate. Add the onions to the pan, reduce the heat to medium and fry gently for about 10 minutes until golden.

2 Sprinkle the flour over the onions, stir well and cook for 1 minute. Pour in the beer and bring to a boil, stirring well to dislodge any bits of food stuck to the base of the dish.

3 Add the currant jelly, mustard and bay leaf, then return the meat to the casserole dish, followed by the carrots, turnips and mushrooms. Cover and transfer to the oven. Cook for 2 hours or until the meat is very tender.

4 Shortly before the end of the cooking time, make the dumplings. Put the flour, a little seasoning and the parsley sprigs into a food processor. Process briefly to chop the parsley. Mix the cottage cheese with the horseradish and milk and add to the processor. Mix to make a soft dough, adding a little more milk if necessary. (Alternatively, chop the parsley, then mix everything together in a mixing bowl.) Turn the dough out onto a lightly floured work surface and divide into eight equal portions. Roll each into a ball with floured hands.

5 Increase the oven temperature to 350°F (180°C). Uncover the casserole dish, stir and season to taste. Gently place the dumplings on top of the meat and vegetables, but do not submerge them. Cover, return to the oven and cook for a further 20 minutes. Serve at once.

EACH SERVING

38 g protein • 19.5 g fat of which 6 g saturates • 53 g carbohydrate • 7 g fibre • 611 Calories

- *You can prepare ahead up until the end of step 3, if more convenient. Keep in the refrigerator, then reheat thoroughly before adding the dumplings.*
- *If you are freezing this meal, freeze it without the dumplings — make them just before serving.*

- *For a more sophisticated meal, use stewing venison instead of beef, and replace the turnips with chunks of rutabaga or pickling onions.*
- *You can use 200 grams (7 oz) smaller brown mushrooms instead of portobellos.*

Chinese pork with plums

All the family will love this sweet and sour casserole that makes the most of seasonal fresh plums. It's traditionally flavoured with ginger, five-spice, vinegar, soy and scallions, and the addition of water chestnuts and cubes of sweet potato turn it into a complete, low-fat dish.

Serves **4**

Preparation time **30 minutes**

Cooking time **about 45 minutes**

2 tablespoons vegetable oil

4 lean pork loin steaks

800 grams (1³/₄ lbs) plums, halved, stoned and coarsely chopped

4 scallions, cut into 2 cm lengths

4 orange sweet potatoes, peeled and cut into 1 cm cubes

230 gram can water chestnuts, drained and rinsed, then sliced

3 cm piece fresh ginger, peeled and grated

2 garlic cloves, crushed

1 red chili pepper, deseeded and finely chopped (optional)

2 teaspoons sugar

1 tablespoon salt-reduced soy sauce

1 tablespoon cider vinegar

2 tablespoons Chinese rice wine or dry sherry

¹/₄ teaspoon five-spice powder

2 tablespoons chopped cilantro

1 Preheat the oven to 350°F (180°C). Heat the oil in a large flameproof casserole dish, then briefly fry the pork steaks on both sides until lightly browned. Add the plums, scallions, sweet potatoes and water chestnuts to the casserole dish, then stir everything together.

2 Put the ginger into a small bowl. Add the garlic, chili pepper if using, sugar, soy sauce, vinegar, wine or sherry and the five-spice powder. Mix well, then spoon the mixture over the ingredients in the casserole dish. Cover with the lid, then cook in the oven, stirring occasionally, for about 45 minutes until the meat is tender and the sauce has thickened.

3 Taste the sauce and add more sugar or vinegar if needed, depending on the flavour of the plums, to give a good balance of sweet and sour tastes. Scatter the chopped cilantro over the top and serve.

EACH SERVING

38 g protein • 15 g fat of which 3 g saturates • 91 g carbohydrate
• 15 g fibre • 697 Calories

Beef bourguignon

This dish is best started overnight to maximize the rich flavour of the beef and red wine. It's worth using a good-quality red in the dish — you'll appreciate the superior flavour.

Serves **4** *Preparation time* **20 minutes, plus at least 4 hours marinating**
Cooking time **about 2 hours**

4 sprigs of fresh thyme

2 bay leaves

6 sprigs of fresh flat-leaf parsley

1 kg (2 lbs) lean stewing beef, trimmed of all excess fat and cubed

2½ cups red wine

3 garlic cloves, bruised

40 grams (1½ oz) butter

300 grams (10 oz) shallots

2 strips of bacon, sliced

200 grams (7 oz) button mushrooms

1 onion, chopped

2 carrots, peeled and cut into chunks

2 tablespoons plain flour

¾ cup water

1 tablespoon chopped fresh thyme

1 Using a piece of kitchen string, tie together the thyme, bay leaves and parsley into a bouquet garni. Place into a non-metallic bowl with the beef, wine and garlic cloves. Marinate for at least 4 hours, preferably overnight. Remove the meat from the marinade with a slotted spoon and set aside on a plate, then strain the liquid, reserving the marinade.

2 Preheat the oven to 350°F (180°C). Heat a large flameproof casserole over medium heat with 20 g of the butter. Cook the shallots or onions, and bacon for 5–6 minutes until the bacon is crisp and the shallots or onions lightly browned, then add the mushrooms and cook for a further 2–3 minutes. Remove from the dish and set aside. Add the remaining butter to the dish and cook the chopped onion and carrots for 1–2 minutes until softened.

3 Increase the heat to high, add the strained meat and cook for about 3 minutes until the meat is well sealed. Add the flour, tossing well to coat, then add the reserved marinade along with the bouquet garni and water. Bring the mixture to a boil, mixing well.

4 Place the lid on the dish and place into the oven. Cook for about 1¼ hours, stirring from time to time.

5 Return the bacon, mushrooms and shallots or onions to the casserole , and cook for a further 30 minutes or until the meat is very tender. Before serving, discard the bouquet garni and season to taste if you like. Serve garnished with chopped fresh thyme.

EACH SERVING

53 g protein • 26.5 g fat of which 13 g saturates • 11 g carbohydrate • 4 g fibre • 606 Calories

COOK'S TIPS
• *This dish can be prepared a day ahead of time and refrigerated. Reheat gently before serving, sprinkled with the cilantro.*
• *You can find bottles of Chinese rice wine in the Asian section of large supermarkets or in Asian food stores.*

VARIATION
• *This recipe would work equally well with skinless chicken thighs.*

COOK'S TIP
• Soak dried mushrooms in boiling water for
20 minutes to rehydrate, then drain. The soaking
liquid makes a tasty stock but needs to be strained
through a fine sieve to remove any gritty bits.

VARIATION
• Omit the scallions and instead stir 75 grams
(2 ³/₄ oz) bean sprouts into the hot juices just before
adding the rice noodles. Garnish with chopped
cilantro instead of scallion curls.

Chinese slow-cooked pork

Star anise, soy and ginger add wonderful flavours to this deliciously tender pork joint casserole, simmered with shallots, carrots and mushrooms. Vegetables and rice noodles cooked in exotic, rich juices make this into a complete meal.

Step 2

Step 3

Step 4

Serves **4**

Preparation time **15 minutes**

Cooking time **about 1¼ hours**

500 grams (1 lb) lean, boneless loin of pork with skin, tied firmly

1²/₃ cups diluted salt-reduced or homemade chicken stock (page 28), hot

2 tablespoons salt-reduced soy sauce

2 tablespoons Chinese rice wine or dry sherry

2 tablespoons honey

2 garlic cloves, crushed

15 grams (½ oz) fresh ginger, peeled and finely chopped

3 star anise

4 shallots, halved

2 large carrots, peeled and sliced on the diagonal

6 scallions

30 grams (1 oz) dried Chinese mushrooms, soaked to rehydrate

125 grams (4 oz) oyster mushrooms, sliced or halved

250 grams (½ lb) dried flat rice noodles

1 Place the pork in a large flameproof casserole and pour over enough boiling water to cover. Bring back to a boil on the stove, then pour off the water. Add the stock, soy sauce, rice wine or sherry, honey, garlic, ginger, star anise, shallots and carrots to the casserole dish and bring to a boil. Thickly slice four of the scallions, roughly chop the drained Chinese mushrooms and add both to the casserole. Reserve the strained mushroom soaking liquid.

2 Cover and simmer gently on a very low heat for 1–1¼ hours, stirring the vegetables and basting the meat occasionally until everything is tender. Add the oyster mushrooms for the last 20 minutes of the cooking time. If necessary, top up using the reserved mushroom soaking liquid or more stock or water.

3 Meanwhile, cut the remaining scallions into 6 cm lengths, then cut lengthwise into fine shreds. Place in a bowl of iced water and leave to curl. Soak the rice noodles in a bowl of boiling water for 4 minutes or until softened, then drain well.

4 Carefully lift the meat out of the casserole with a slotted spoon and keep hot. Bring the juices to a boil on the stove, then add the rice noodles and remove the dish from the heat. Turn and stir the noodles to coat with the juices. Slice the pork thinly.

5 Spread the noodles on a large shallow serving platter, using a slotted spoon to lift them from the casserole. Arrange the sliced meat and vegetables on top, then spoon over the casserole juices. Scatter the scallion curls over the top as a garnish.

EACH SERVING

34 g protein • **6 g fat of which 2 g saturates** • **58 g carbohydrate** • **4.5 g fibre** • **438 Calories**

Mussels with Pernod

The combination of Pernod and fennel adds a wonderful anise flavour to this popular seafood dish, which just needs some crusty whole wheat bread to mop up the tasty juices. Mussels are low in fat and rich in many minerals, including iron and zinc.

Serves **4**

Preparation time **35 minutes**

Cooking time **25 minutes**

30 grams (1 oz) unsalted butter

2 leeks, trimmed and thinly sliced

1 fennel bulb, trimmed and thinly sliced

1 garlic clove, crushed

½ cup diluted salt-reduced or homemade vegetable stock (page 29)

⅓ cup Pernod or other licorice-flavoured liqueur

2 kg (4 lbs) fresh mussels in the shell, cleaned

⅓ cup light thickened cream

2 tablespoons chopped fresh flat-leaf parsley

COOK'S TIP

• *To clean mussels, scrub them well using a small, stiff brush under cold running water, to remove any grit, sand and barnacles. Pull off and discard the hairy "beard" protruding from the side of the shells. Sharply tap any open mussels with the back of a knife, and discard any that don't close. Rinse and drain the mussels once again before use.*

VARIATION

• *Instead of Pernod, use Greek ouzo or dry white wine.*

1 Melt the butter in a saucepan large enough to hold the mussels. Add the leeks, fennel and garlic and fry gently for 5 minutes.

2 Add the stock and bring to a boil, then cover and cook gently for about 10 minutes until the vegetables are softened. Stir in the Pernod or other liqueur and bring back to a boil.

3 Add the mussels to the pan, cover tightly again and cook over a medium heat for 4–5 minutes until the shells open, shaking the pan occasionally. Discard any unopened mussels.

4 Carefully pour the cooking liquid into a small pan and set the covered pan of mussels aside. Stir the cream and chopped parsley into the cooking liquid and heat gently, without boiling. Season to taste with freshly ground black pepper. Tip the mussels and vegetables into a large, warmed dish or tureen and pour over the sauce. Serve at once.

EACH SERVING

15 g protein • 10.5 g fat of which 6 g saturates • 19 g carbohydrate • 3 g fibre • 285 Calories

Mediterranean chicken with olives

This is a dish of bright, vivid colour and bold flavours. Onions, tomatoes and red peppers make a chunky vegetable sauce for chicken pieces, with spicy chorizo sausage, sun-dried tomatoes, rosemary and olives adding tastes of the Mediterranean. Serve with crusty bread so you don't waste any of the delicious juices.

Serves 4

Preparation time 15 minutes

Cooking time about 1 hour

2 tablespoons olive oil

2 onions, roughly chopped

2 garlic cloves, crushed

1 tablespoon chopped fresh rosemary

40 grams (1½ oz) chorizo sausage, skinned and diced

2 large red peppers, deseeded and roughly chopped

⅓ cup sun-dried tomatoes, roughly chopped

398 ml can chopped tomatoes

¼ cup dry white wine

4 skinless boneless chicken breasts or large thighs (about 500 grams/ 1 lb in total)

⅓ cup pitted olives (black, green or a mixture)

1 Heat the oil in a large, heavy flameproof casserole or deep frying pan. Add the onions, garlic and rosemary and cook gently, stirring frequently, for about 15 minutes until soft and golden.

2 Add the chorizo and peppers and cook over a medium heat, stirring frequently, for a couple of minutes or until the sausage turns slightly golden.

3 Add the sun-dried tomatoes, the canned tomatoes with their juice, and the wine. Season with freshly ground black pepper (salt should not be needed), then stir well and bring to a simmer.

4 Add the chicken and stir to coat with the sauce. Bring to a boil, then reduce the heat so the sauce simmers. Cover and cook for 25–30 minutes until the chicken is tender and the sauce is thick.

5 Just before serving, stir in the pitted olives and cook for just long enough to heat them through.

COOK'S TIP

• *You can prepare ahead up until the end of step 4. Keep refrigerated or frozen, then thaw and reheat gently. Add the olives before serving.*

EACH SERVING

31.5 g protein • 19.5 g fat of which 4.5 g saturates • 13 g carbohydrate • 4 g fibre • 372 Calories

Coq au vin avec légumes

This lighter version of the great French classic, chicken in red wine sauce, is lower in fat and includes more vegetables. It just needs some crusty, rustic-style bread and perhaps a light green salad to serve it with. The dish is better if made a full day ahead so the flavours can mature.

Step 1

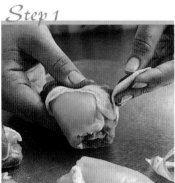

Step 3

Step 4

Serves **4**

Preparation time **20 minutes**

Cooking time **about 1 hour**

8 large skinless chicken thighs

8 thin slices pancetta or lean, thinly cut streaky bacon

2 tablespoons olive oil

3 large garlic cloves, chopped

1 large red onion, halved and sliced

2 carrots, peeled and thickly sliced

1 fennel bulb or 3 celery stalks, thinly sliced

1 turnip, peeled and cut into chunks

2–3 tablespoons water (optional)

2 bay leaves

3–4 sprigs of fresh thyme

1½ cups red wine

1 tablespoon currant jelly

2 tablespoons brandy (optional)

2 cups diluted salt-reduced or homemade chicken or vegetable stock (pages 28–29)

8 pickling onions or shallots

250 grams (½ lb) button mushrooms

¼ cup cornstarch blended with ½ cup water

2 tablespoons chopped fresh flat-leaf parsley

1 Trim any excess fat from the chicken thighs, then wrap each one in a thin slice of pancetta or bacon, securing with wooden toothpicks if necessary. Heat 1 tablespoon of the oil in a large flameproof casserole and add the chicken, join-side down, and brown for 2–3 minutes. Turn the chicken to brown the other side, then remove to a plate.

2 Add the remaining oil to the casserole dish and gently fry the garlic, onion, carrots, fennel or celery and turnip, stirring a couple of times, until softened. If you need to moisten, add the water, not extra oil.

3 Add the herbs, red wine, currant jelly and brandy, if using, and simmer for 5 minutes. Stir in the stock and bring to a boil.

4 Meanwhile, blanch the pickling onions or shallots in boiling water for 2 minutes, then cool and peel. Add to the casserole with the chicken thighs and season to taste. Cover and cook very gently for about 30 minutes.

5 Add the mushrooms, stir well and cook for a further 15 minutes. Add the cornstarch mixture and simmer for about 2 minutes until the sauce has thickened slightly. Remove from the heat and allow to cool for about 10 minutes. If you used cocktail sticks, remove these, then serve, sprinkled with the parsley.

EACH SERVING

41 g protein • 24.5 g fat of which 6 g saturates • 13 g carbohydrate • 6 g fibre • 501 Calories

• *For maximum flavour, prepare the dish a day in advance. Reheat the casserole over a medium heat before serving.*
• *To freeze the casserole, prepare up until the end of step 4. Add the mushrooms when you reheat it.*

Creamy vegetable fricassee

For this fricassee, a selection of colourful vegetables is lightly cooked in a tarragon-flavoured stock, which is finished with sour cream to make a wonderful, creamy coating sauce. Serve with whole-grain or seeded bread, for a delicious, satisfying meal.

Serves 4

Preparation time 10 minutes

Cooking time 25 minutes

1 tablespoon olive oil

250 grams (½ lb) carrots, peeled and cut into sticks

250 grams (½ lb) new potatoes, scrubbed and halved or quartered (depending on size)

150 grams (5 oz) button mushrooms, halved

1⅔ cups diluted salt-reduced or homemade vegetable stock (page 29)

2 tablespoons dry white wine

2 teaspoons fresh tarragon or ½ teaspoon dried tarragon

1 cup frozen fava beans

150 grams (5 oz) asparagus, trimmed

¼ cup light sour cream

½ cup unsalted cashews

1 tablespoon fresh tarragon

COOK'S TIP

• *You can partly prepare this dish up to 6 hours ahead. Cook the vegetables up to the end of step 2 and allow them to cool. When ready to serve, reheat gently and finish as described in the main recipe.*

1 Heat the oil in a large flameproof casserole dish over a medium heat. Add the carrots, potatoes and mushrooms, and cook, stirring frequently, for about 4 minutes until lightly browned.

2 Pour in the stock with the white wine and stir in the tarragon. Bring to a boil, then reduce the heat, cover and simmer gently for about 10 minutes until the vegetables are almost cooked.

3 Stir in the fava beans and lay the asparagus on top. Cover and simmer for a further 6 minutes or until the vegetables are tender.

4 Lift out the vegetables onto a plate, using a slotted spoon. Stir the sour cream into the liquid in the casserole dish and heat through gently, then season to taste. Return the vegetables to the casserole dish, coating them with the sauce. Scatter the nuts and tarragon leaves over the top, then serve.

EACH SERVING

10 g protein • 15 g fat of which 4 g saturates • 18.5 g carbohydrate • 7 g fibre • 266 Calories

Mixed bean cassoulet

A vegetarian version of the hearty French country dish, this uses canned beans for a quick and easy one-pot. It's finished in the traditional way, with a crunchy breadcrumb and herb topping, plus nuts for extra protein.

Serves **4**

Preparation time **20 minutes**

Cooking time **55 minutes**

1 tablespoon olive oil

1 onion, chopped

2 garlic cloves, crushed

1 butternut squash, peeled, deseeded and cut into 1.5 cm cubes

1¼ cups diluted salt-reduced or homemade vegetable stock (page 29), hot

398 ml can chopped tomatoes

1 tablespoon tomato paste

2 bay leaves

2 sprigs of fresh thyme

398 ml can lima beans, drained and rinsed

398 ml can pinto beans, drained and rinsed

BREADCRUMB CRUST

¾ cup whole wheat breadcrumbs

⅓ cup mixed nuts, coarsely chopped

2 tablespoons chopped fresh flat-leaf parsley

COOK'S TIP

• *Use any combination of canned beans available, such as red kidney, white kidney or mixed beans, to suit your preference.*

1 Preheat the oven to 400°F (200°C). Heat the oil in a flameproof casserole and gently fry the onion for 6–7 minutes until softened. Add the garlic and butternut squash and cook for a further minute, stirring all the time.

2 Add the stock, tomatoes with their juice, tomato paste, bay leaves, thyme and beans. Stir well (the mixture may look slightly dry at this stage, but the squash will produce extra juices as it cooks), then slowly bring to a boil. Cover the casserole with a lid and transfer to the oven to cook for 25 minutes.

3 Meanwhile, mix together the breadcrumbs, nuts and parsley. Remove the casserole from the oven and season to taste. Scatter the top with the breadcrumb mixture and return to the oven, uncovered, for a further 20 minutes or until the crust is lightly browned.

EACH SERVING

21 g protein • 15 g fat of which 2.5 g saturates • 63 g carbohydrate • 11.5 g fibre • 513 Calories

Shrimp and mango balti

A tasty curry with a spicy kick, mellowed with reduced-fat coconut milk. The addition of fresh mango not only adds to the colour and appeal, but boosts the vitamin content of the dish. Serve with warm nan bread and a favourite Indian chutney.

Serves **4**   *Preparation time* **20 minutes**   *Cooking time* **25 minutes**

1 tablespoon vegetable oil

1 onion, finely chopped

1 red chili pepper, deseeded and thinly sliced

¼ cup balti curry paste

1 cup light coconut milk

2 vine-ripened tomatoes, peeled and chopped

1 ripe mango, peeled, stoned and diced

24 large raw shrimp, peeled and deveined (about 250 grams prepared weight)

2 tablespoons chopped cilantro

1 Heat the oil in a large frying pan, add the onion and cook, stirring, over a medium heat for about 5 minutes until softened. Add the chili pepper and curry paste and cook for 1–2 minutes, taking care not to allow the paste to burn on the base of the pan.

2 Pour the coconut milk into the pan and stir well, then add the chopped tomatoes and stir again. Cook over a low–medium heat for about 10 minutes or until the tomatoes have softened and the sauce has thickened slightly, stirring occasionally.

3 Stir the mango into the curry and cook for 1–2 minutes, then add the shrimp and simmer gently for about 5 minutes until the shrimp are pink, tender and cooked through. Stir in the chopped cilantro and serve immediately.

COOK'S TIPS
• *If you regularly eat chili pepper, you may like to increase the heat of this curry by adding more chili peppers.*
• *You can experiment by using different curry pastes in the recipe.*

EACH SERVING

21 g protein • 12 g fat of which 2 g saturates • 18.5 g carbohydrate • 4 g fibre • 274 Calories

Kashmiri chicken with fruit

Sweet bananas, exotic lychees and creamy Greek yogourt are combined with chicken and spicy seasonings to make a luscious, yet healthy dish. Serve with warm nan bread.

Serves **4**   *Preparation time* **20 minutes**   *Cooking time* **30 minutes**

2 tablespoons vegetable oil

1 cinnamon stick

2 teaspoons fennel seeds

1 tablespoon cumin seeds

50 grams (2 oz) fresh ginger, peeled and chopped

2 red chili peppers, deseeded and chopped

1 green pepper, deseeded and chopped

2 carrots, peeled and diced

2 celery stalks, diced

4 skinless boneless chicken breasts (about 500 grams/1 lb in total), cut into 2.5 cm chunks

300 ml diluted salt-reduced or homemade chicken stock (page 28)

¾ cup dried apricots, roughly chopped

¾ cup Greek-style yogourt

4 small firm bananas, sliced

398 ml can lychees, drained and halved

⅓ cup flaked almonds, toasted

1 Heat the oil in a large, deep frying pan and add the cinnamon, fennel and cumin. Cook over a medium heat for 1–2 minutes. Add the ginger, three-quarters of the chili peppers, the green pepper, carrots and celery. Stir well, then cover and cook gently over a low heat for 5 minutes or until the vegetables begin to soften.

2 Push the vegetables to the side of the pan, then add the chicken and increase the heat slightly. Cook, stirring occasionally, for 4–5 minutes until the chicken begins to brown. Pour in the stock, add the apricots and bring to a boil. Reduce the heat, cover and simmer gently for 10–15 minutes until the chicken and vegetables are cooked.

3 Stir in the yogourt, bananas and lychees and heat through gently without boiling. Scatter the toasted flaked almonds and remaining chili pepper over the top just before serving.

COOK'S TIP

• *To prepare this dish ahead of time, make up to the end of step 2, then cool and keep chilled in the refrigerator. Reheat gently before adding the yogourt and fruit.*

EACH SERVING

40.5 g protein • 29 g fat of which 6.5 g saturates • 48 g carbohydrate • 8 g fibre • 623 Calories

Thai chicken curry

It is easy to keep the fat content low in a tangy Thai curry as there is no need to pre-fry the ingredients; instead they are simply simmered in light coconut milk and stock with potatoes, peas and tomatoes.

Serves **4**

Preparation time **10 minutes**

Cooking time **25 minutes**

1²/₃ cups light coconut milk

³/₄ cup diluted salt-reduced or homemade chicken stock (page 28)

2 tablespoons Thai green curry paste

4 skinless boneless chicken breasts (about 500 grams/1 lb in total), cut into thin strips

350 grams (12 oz) new potatoes, scrubbed and cut into chunks

6 scallions, sliced on the diagonal

2 tablespoons lime juice

³/₄ cup shelled fresh or frozen peas, thawed if necessary

8 grape or cherry tomatoes, halved

¹/₃ cup chopped cilantro

COOK'S TIP

• *If you find it hard to squeeze the juice out of limes, put them in the microwave for a few seconds — the heat will make them easier to juice.*

1 Put the coconut milk, stock and Thai curry paste in a wok or large frying pan, stir together and heat until boiling. Stir in the chicken strips and potatoes, then bring back to a boil.

2 Reduce the heat and simmer, uncovered, for about 15 minutes until the chicken and potatoes are just tender.

3 Stir in the scallions, lime juice, peas and tomatoes and simmer for a further 3–4 minutes. Stir in the cilantro and season to taste.

EACH SERVING

51 g protein • 16.5 g fat of which 4.5 g saturates • 29 g carbohydrate • 6 g fibre • 486 Calories

Red Thai curry with tofu

This great-tasting, medium-hot curry is made with tofu — an exceptionally nutritious and protein-rich ingredient that soaks up the fragrant flavour of the spice paste.

Serves **4**   *Preparation time* **15 minutes**   *Cooking time* **20 minutes**

1 tablespoon vegetable oil

1 large onion, finely chopped

1 tablespoon Thai red curry paste, or to taste

6 baby corn, halved lengthwise

1/3 cup plus 2 tablespoons diluted salt-reduced or homemade vegetable stock (page 29)

1 tablespoon salt-reduced soy sauce

1 1/4 cups light coconut milk

100 grams (3 1/2 oz) broccoli, cut into small florets

100 grams (3 1/2 oz) thin green beans, trimmed

1 red pepper, quartered, deseeded and sliced

350 grams (12 oz) firm tofu, drained and cut into 2 cm cubes

300 grams (10 oz) Hokkien noodles

2 tablespoons coarsely chopped cilantro

1 Heat the oil in a wok or large, deep frying pan, preferably non-stick. Add the onion and stir over a medium heat for 7–8 minutes until softened. Stir in the curry paste and cook for a few more seconds.

2 Add the baby corn and stir to coat in the curry paste. Gradually add the stock, soy sauce and coconut milk. Bring to a gentle simmer and cook for 1 minute. Carefully stir in the remaining vegetables and tofu cubes. Bring back to simmering point, then cover and cook for 5–6 minutes until the vegetables are just tender.

3 Add the noodles to the vegetable mixture and cook, stirring, for a further minute. Stir in the chopped coriander and serve straight away.

COOK'S TIP
• *Thai red curry paste often includes shrimp so this dish is not suitable for strict vegetarians.*

VARIATION
• *This dish would also work well made with 2 large chicken breasts, cut into 2.5 cm cubes, instead of tofu. Lightly brown the chicken with the onion in a mixture of sesame and vegetable oils.*

EACH SERVING

22 g protein • 14.5 g fat of which 2.5 g saturates • 31 g carbohydrate • 5 g fibre • 359 Calories

VARIATION
• *For a change of flavour, replace the new potatoes with the same amount of diced eggplant.*

Pork korma with potatoes and spinach

Thickened with ground almonds and yogourt, this ground meat dish is rich and creamy yet not as indulgent as traditional Indian korma curries that are full of cream and ghee (clarified butter). Serve with warm chapattis or nan to mop up the delicious, aromatic sauce.

Serves **4**

Preparation time **10 minutes**

Cooking time **55 minutes**

1 tablespoon vegetable oil

2 large onions, sliced

500 grams (1 lb) lean ground pork

2 garlic cloves, crushed

8 green cardamom pods, crushed and pods discarded

1 tablespoon cumin seeds

2½ cups diluted salt-reduced or homemade chicken stock (page 28), hot

800 grams (1¾ lb) small new potatoes, scrubbed and halved

2 teaspoons cornstarch

1 cup low-fat plain yogourt

¾ cup ground almonds

250 grams (½ lb) baby spinach leaves

¼ cup flaked almonds, lightly toasted

COOK'S TIP

• *This dish is even better if made ahead of time, then reheated. Make up to the end of step 4, then cool and chill. Reheat gently, then complete the dish with the spinach.*

1 Heat the oil in a large, heavy-based saucepan or flameproof casserole dish. Add the onions and cook over a medium heat for 10 minutes. Transfer to a bowl.

2 Add the pork, garlic, cardamom and cumin seeds. Cook, stirring often, for 5 minutes until the meat has broken up and changed colour. Return about half the onions to the pan, pour in the stock and bring back to a boil. Reduce the heat, cover the pan and simmer for 15 minutes.

3 Stir in the potatoes and bring back to simmering point, then cover and cook for about 20 minutes until the potatoes are tender.

4 Meanwhile, blend the cornstarch with about ½ cup (130 g) of the yogourt and the ground almonds to make a paste. Stir this mixture into the curry and bring just to a boil, stirring. Reduce the heat and simmer for 1 minute until slightly thickened. Season to taste.

5 Fold the spinach leaves through the korma, reserving a few small leaves for garnishing, until they are just wilted and bright green. Mix the toasted flaked almonds with the remaining onions. Serve the curry drizzled with the remaining yogourt and topped with the almonds, onions and reserved spinach.

EACH SERVING

50 g protein • 34.5 g fat of which 6.5 g saturates • 36.5 g carbohydrate • 10 g fibre • 677 Calories

Sweet potato curry with paneer

A light, colourful curry that is very quick and easy to make, this is packed with antioxidant-rich vegetables. Sweet potatoes, in particular, are an excellent source of beta-carotene and provide good amounts of fibre, vitamins B_6 and C, potassium and folate. Serve with nan bread.

Serves **4**

Preparation time **10 minutes**

Cooking time **30 minutes**

1 tablespoon vegetable oil

1 onion, chopped

2 garlic cloves, crushed

500 grams (1 lb) orange sweet potatoes, peeled and cut into chunks

1 tablespoon mild curry powder

1 tablespoon finely chopped fresh ginger

398 ml can chopped tomatoes

1/3 cup plus 2 tablespoons diluted salt-reduced or homemade vegetable stock (page 29)

1 cup shelled fresh or frozen peas, thawed if necessary

250 grams (1/2 lb) paneer or firm tofu, cut into 1.5 cm cubes

2 tablespoons chopped or whole fresh mint

COOK'S TIP
• *Paneer is a lightly pressed Indian cheese that is available in Indian grocery stores.*

1 Heat the vegetable oil in a large frying pan and fry the onion and garlic gently, stirring occasionally, for 4–5 minutes until softened.

2 Add the sweet potatoes and cook, stirring, for 2 minutes, then stir in the curry powder and ginger and cook for 30 seconds.

3 Stir in the tomatoes with their juice, and the stock. Bring to a boil, then reduce the heat, cover and cook gently for 12–15 minutes until the sweet potato is tender when pierced with a knife.

4 Stir in the peas and simmer for 3 minutes, then add the diced paneer or tofu and cook for a further 2 minutes until heated thoroughly. Season to taste, scatter with the chopped mint and serve hot.

EACH SERVING

13.5 g protein • 9.5 g fat of which 1.5 g saturates • 25.5 g carbohydrate • 8.5 g fibre • 258 Calories

Red lentil and vegetable dal

A dal is a dish of simmered lentils flavoured with aromatic spices and usually served as a sauce. But add extra vegetables and it becomes a light and easy vegetarian meal. Serve it with a selection of Indian-style breads and plain yogourt or raita.

Serves **4**

Preparation time **15 minutes**

Cooking time **30 minutes**

1 onion, chopped

2 large garlic cloves, crushed

1 green chili pepper, deseeded and chopped

1 carrot, peeled and grated

1 eggplant, chopped

1 tablespoon vegetable oil

2 tablespoons water

1 teaspoon ground cumin

1 teaspoon mild curry powder

2 teaspoons black mustard seeds

3/4 cup split red lentils

3 1/3 cups diluted salt-reduced or homemade vegetable stock (page 29), hot

1 zucchini, halved and sliced

1 large tomato, chopped

2 tablespoons chopped fresh cilantro

COOK'S TIP

• *This can be made a day in advance, then reheated. You may need to add a little more water if it has thickened too much. It is also suitable for freezing.*

1 Put the onion, garlic, chili pepper, carrot and eggplant into a flameproof casserole dish or large saucepan and stir in the oil and water. Heat until it starts to sizzle, then cover and cook gently for about 5 minutes until softened.

2 Uncover and stir in the spices. Cook for 1 minute, then stir in the lentils and stock. Bring to a boil, then add the zucchini and tomato.

3 Cover and simmer gently for 15 minutes, then uncover for a further 5 minutes, by which time the lentils should have burst open and thickened the liquid. Serve garnished with coarsely chopped cilantro.

EACH SERVING

6.5 g protein • 6 g fat of which 0.5 g saturates • 14.5 g carbohydrate • 7.5 g fibre • 152 Calories

Spiced potatoes and cauliflower with nuts

The warm, golden colour and flavour of saffron with a mild kick of ginger help to make this vegetable curry a real winner. Garlic is an important ingredient not just for flavour, but for its many health benefits. Serve with warm nan bread.

Serves **4** *Preparation time* **15 minutes** *Cooking time* **20 minutes**

400 grams (14 oz) potatoes, peeled and cut into 2 cm dice

pinch of saffron threads

15 grams (½ oz) fresh ginger, peeled and finely chopped

2 garlic cloves, crushed

1 small onion, chopped

⅔ cup low-fat plain yogourt

1 small cauliflower, cut into florets

⅔ cup diluted salt-reduced or homemade vegetable stock (page 29), hot

¼ cup ground almonds

2 teaspoons garam masala

⅓ cup unsalted cashews

2 tablespoons chopped cilantro

1 Place the potatoes in a large pot of boiling water and simmer for 5 minutes, then drain.

2 Dry the pot thoroughly, then heat the saffron gently until lightly toasted. Add the ginger, garlic, onion, yogourt, cauliflower and stock. Stir in the potatoes and ground almonds.

3 Bring to a boil, then reduce the heat, cover and simmer, stirring occasionally, for about 10 minutes until the vegetables are just tender. Stir in the garam masala and cook for a further 2 minutes.

4 Meanwhile, toast the cashews under a hot grill. Scatter the toasted cashews and cilantro over the curry and serve.

VARIATIONS
• *For a more authentic dal, use yellow split peas instead of the lentils. These will need to be soaked in cold water for about 2 hours first.*
• *Instead of a zucchini, add 250 grams baby spinach leaves at the end of step 3 and cook for about 2 minutes, until just wilted, before seasoning.*

COOK'S TIP
• *Toasting saffron helps to bring out the colour and flavour, but must be done very lightly to prevent scorching. Keep shaking the pan over the heat to keep the saffron moving.*

VARIATIONS
• *If you don't have saffron, ½ teaspoon ground turmeric will add a rich colour to the curry.*
• *Scatter 2 chopped hard-boiled eggs over the curry just before serving.*

EACH SERVING
10 g protein • 10 g fat of which 1.5 g saturates • 22 g carbohydrate • 5 g fibre • 231 Calories

Bakes and pies

Healthy bakes can often be prepared ahead and then just popped in the oven and left to cook — making them ideal for easy family meals or informal entertaining. Give your traditional favourites a healthy vegetable boost to bump up the nutrition. A range of pasta bakes, stuffed vegetables, hearty pies and fish cakes provide delicious comfort food that will go down well at any time of the year.

Lamb and sultana stuffed onions

Stuffing vegetables is a great way of using them to make a healthy one-dish meal. This tasty stuffing, of spiced lean lamb and bulgur, has a distinct Middle Eastern flavour.

Serves 4 (Makes 8)

Preparation time 30 minutes

Cooking time 1 hour

8 large onions, peeled and root end trimmed so the onions will stand upright

⅓ cup sultanas

⅓ cup bulgur

3 garlic cloves

1 tablespoon olive oil

400 grams (14 oz) lean ground lamb

2 teaspoons ground cumin

½ teaspoon ground cinnamon

1 teaspoon ground coriander

¼ teaspoon cayenne pepper

1 Preheat the oven to 375°F (190°C). Bring a large pot of water to a boil, add the onions, bring the water back to a boil and cook for 10 minutes. Drain well, reserving 1¼ cups of the water, then leave the onions to cool.

2 Put the sultanas and bulgur into a heatproof bowl. Pour in the hot onion water and soak for 20 minutes until the water is absorbed. Drain if necessary.

3 Meanwhile, slice off the top 1 cm of each onion. Scoop out the centre of each onion. Finely chop the onion lids, centres and the garlic.

4 Heat the oil in a non-stick frying pan over a medium heat. Add the lamb and fry for 5 minutes, stirring frequently, until the meat is lightly coloured.

5 Push the lamb to one side, reduce the heat and add the spices. Stir-fry for 20 seconds, then add the onion mixture and cook for 1 minute. Stir in the lamb and cook over a medium heat for 10 minutes. Stir in the bulgur mixture.

6 Sit the onions in a large, lightly greased roasting pan and fill with the lamb mixture. Cover with foil and bake for 20 minutes, then uncover and bake for a further 10 minutes. Serve immediately.

VARIATION

• *Large beefsteak tomatoes can be filled with the same mixture. Slice a lid off each tomato (allow 2 per serving) and scoop out the seeds and core. The tomatoes do not need to be cooked in boiling water. Chop the cores and add to the lamb mixture with 1 finely chopped onion.*

EACH SERVING

32 g protein • 18 g fat of which 7 g saturates • 36.5 g carbohydrate • 8 g fibre • 445 Calories

Peppers stuffed with beef and tomatoes

Choose large, firm peppers — they make the perfect container for a herby beef, tomato and fresh breadcrumb mixture, topped with cheese. Serve with a salad.

Serves 4 as a light meal

Preparation time 15 minutes

Cooking time 1 hour

³/4 cup fresh whole wheat breadcrumbs

4 large yellow peppers

1 tablespoon olive oil

1 onion, finely chopped

350 grams (³/4 lb) lean ground beef

1 garlic clove, crushed

³/4 cup canned chopped tomatoes

1 tablespoon chopped fresh sage or 1 teaspoon dried sage

1 teaspoon chopped fresh rosemary or ¹/2 teaspoon dried rosemary

1¹/4 cups diluted salt-reduced or homemade vegetable stock (page 29), hot

¹/4 cup grated aged cheddar cheese

2 fennel bulbs, cut into 5 mm slices lengthwise

VARIATION

• *Use the beef mixture to fill 4 large zucchini (about 200 grams/7 oz each). Halve them lengthwise and scoop out the centres with a teaspoon. Fill with the beef mixture. Arrange the zucchini in a baking dish, sprinkle with the cheese, then cover with foil and bake for 40 minutes. Remove the foil and bake for 10 minutes.*

1 Preheat the oven to 375°F (190°C). Spread the breadcrumbs on a plate and leave them to dry a little while preparing the rest of the ingredients.

2 Cut the tops off the peppers and scoop out the seeds and membranes. Blanch the peppers and their tops in boiling water for 1 minute. Lift out the peppers with a slotted spoon, then drain, cut-side down, on paper towel.

3 Heat the oil in a large frying pan over a medium heat. Add the onion and cook for 10 minutes, stirring frequently, until softened. Increase the heat, add the beef and garlic and fry, stirring, until browned and crumbly. Add the tomatoes, herbs and ¹/4 cup of the stock. Cook for a further minute, then remove from the heat and stir in the breadcrumbs. Season to taste.

4 Stand the peppers upright in a lightly oiled, large ovenproof dish, fill with the beef mixture and press down gently. Sprinkle with the cheese and replace the tops. Scatter the fennel around the peppers and pour in the rest of the stock.

5 Cover the dish with foil and bake for 40 minutes until the peppers and fennel are tender, basting halfway through with the stock. Serve hot or warm.

EACH SERVING

34 g protein • 17 g fat of which 6.5 g saturates • 25.5 g carbohydrate • 10.5 g fibre • 414 Calories

Healthiest-ever lasagna

Lasagna is everybody's favourite cold-weather meal, but it can be very high in fat, especially if store-bought. This version includes plenty of fresh vegetables and lean ground beef in its scrumptious filling, making it a healthy option. Serve with a crisp green salad.

Serves **4** *Preparation time* **20 minutes** *Cooking time* *about 1¾ hours*

2 tablespoons olive oil

1 large onion, finely chopped

4 carrots, peeled and finely chopped

2 celery stalks, finely chopped

2 garlic cloves, crushed

350 grams (¾ lb) lean ground beef

150 grams (5 oz) button mushrooms, chopped

1¼ cup diluted salt-reduced or homemade beef stock (page 28)

⅔ cup red wine

398 ml can chopped tomatoes

2 teaspoons tomato paste

1 teaspoon dried oregano or mixed herbs

¼ cup chopped fresh flat-leaf parsley

10 instant lasagna sheets

⅓ cup grated aged cheddar cheese

SAUCE

¼ cup cornstarch

2½ cups 1% milk

pinch of grated nutmeg

1 To make the meat sauce, heat the oil in a large pot over a low heat. Add the onion and fry gently for about 5 minutes, stirring occasionally. Add the carrots, celery and garlic and cook, stirring, for a further 5 minutes until the onion is soft and just beginning to colour.

2 Turn up the heat a little, then add the ground beef and cook, stirring and breaking up the meat with a wooden spoon, until browned and crumbly. Add the mushrooms and cook for 1 more minute. Add the stock, wine, tomatoes with their juice, tomato paste and dried herbs and stir together thoroughly. Bring the mixture to a boil, then cover with a lid and gently simmer over a low heat for 45 minutes, stirring occasionally. Stir in the parsley and season to taste.

3 Preheat the oven to 350°F (180°C). To make the sauce, mix the cornstarch to a smooth paste with a little of the milk in a small bowl. Heat the remaining milk to boiling point in a pot, then pour some of it onto the cornstarch mixture, stirring well. Return this to the milk in the pot. Bring to a boil, stirring until the sauce thickens, then simmer for 2 minutes. Stir in the grated nutmeg and season to taste.

EACH SERVING

43 g protein • 24.5 g fat of which 8 g saturates • 60 g carbohydrate • 7.5 g fibre • 665 Calories

4 Spoon half the meat sauce over the base of a 3 litre ovenproof dish or roasting pan. Cover with half the lasagna sheets, then spoon over the remaining meat sauce and cover with another layer of pasta. Pour over the white sauce to cover the lasagna completely. Scatter the grated cheddar cheese over the top of the lasagna.

5 Place the dish on a baking tray and bake for about 45 minutes until the lasagna is bubbling and the top is lightly browned. Remove from the oven and leave to rest for about 10 minutes before serving.

Lamb and vegetable bake

This hearty dish of lean lamb layered with delicious root vegetables and baked in a covered casserole is perfect for busy lives. Once assembled, it can simply be left to cook and won't be spoiled if left in the oven a little longer.

Serves **4**   *Preparation time* **20 minutes**   *Cooking time* **about 2 hours**

500 grams (1 lb) lean boneless lamb, trimmed of all excess fat

1 tablespoon canola oil

750 grams (1½ lb) potatoes, peeled

350 grams (12²⁄₃ oz) turnips, peeled

2 large leeks, trimmed

2 teaspoons chopped fresh thyme or ½ teaspoon dried thyme

2 tablespoons chopped fresh flat-leaf parsley

1 bay leaf

4 cups diluted salt-reduced or homemade beef or vegetable stock (pages 28–29), hot

1 Preheat the oven to 300°F (150°C). Cut the lamb into 3 cm chunks. Heat the oil in a large flameproof casserole, with a capacity of at least 2 litres, over a medium heat. Fry the lamb in batches until it is browned on all sides. Remove with a slotted spoon and set aside.

2 Cut the potatoes, turnips and leeks into slices about 4 mm thick. Using about half the vegetables, place a generous layer of potato slices over the base of the casserole, then top with a layer of turnip slices, followed by the leeks. Lightly season between the layers with a little salt and freshly ground black pepper and scatter with the thyme and half the parsley.

3 Place the lamb on top of the leeks, tucking in the bay leaf. Top with the remaining leeks, followed by the rest of the turnip slices. Finish with the remaining potato slices, arranging them so that they overlap slightly.

4 Pour over the stock – don't worry if it doesn't completely cover the vegetables as they will cook in the steam. Cover with a tight-fitting lid and bake for 2 hours or until the meat and vegetables are tender and cooked. Just before serving, sprinkle the top with the remaining chopped parsley.

COOK'S TIP
• *You can cook this ahead, then refrigerate or freeze. If necessary, thaw before reheating in a moderate oven.*

EACH SERVING

43.5 g protein • 18 g fat of which 7.5 g saturates • 30 g carbohydrate • 7.5 g fibre • 472 Calories

COOK'S TIP
• *You can prepare the lasagna ahead of time up until the end of step 4, then refrigerate or freeze. If you freeze it, thaw it before baking. You may need to add 10 minutes to the cooking time in step 5.*

Chicken and blue cheese gratin

A layered bake of sliced potatoes, celeriac and leeks with chicken, topped with cheese, makes a perfect dish for an autumn day. Serve with a tomato and green bean salad and some chunks of crusty bread.

Serves 4

Preparation time 20 minutes

Cooking time 45 minutes

750 grams (1½ lb) potatoes, peeled and thinly sliced

300 grams (10 oz) celeriac, peeled and thinly sliced

350 grams (12 oz) leeks, trimmed and sliced

250 grams (½ lb) skinless boneless chicken breast, cut widthwise into thin strips

1 tablespoon chopped fresh thyme or ½ teaspoon dried thyme

1 cup diluted salt-reduced or homemade chicken stock (page 28), hot

75 grams (2⅔ oz) firm blue cheese, crumbled

30 grams (1 oz) butter, cut into small pieces

1 Preheat the oven to 400°F (200°C). Place the potatoes and celeriac in a pot of lightly salted water, cover with a lid and bring to a boil over a medium heat. Remove the lid and simmer for 3 minutes or until starting to soften. Remove from the heat and drain well.

2 Neatly spread about one-third of the potato and celeriac slices over the bottom of a 2 litre baking dish, overlapping the slices. Scatter about half the leeks, chicken strips and thyme over the vegetable layer. Season with plenty of freshly ground black pepper.

3 Continue layering the potatoes and celeriac with the remaining leeks, chicken and thyme. Finish with a layer of the remaining potatoes and celeriac.

4 Pour over the stock, then scatter the crumbled cheese and butter over the top. Cover with foil and bake for 20 minutes.

5 Remove the foil from the dish and continue to bake for a further 20 minutes or until the cheese has melted and the top is golden and bubbling.

EACH SERVING

24.5 g protein • 14 g fat of which 7.5 g saturates • 30 g carbohydrate • 8 g fibre • 353 Calories

Sausage, pasta and mixed bean bake

This hearty, colourful and very nutritious main dish is perfect for an easy midweek meal, and can be rustled up quickly from ingredients you have in the pantry. Serve with a green salad.

Serves 4 Preparation time 10 minutes Cooking time 55 minutes

400 grams (14 oz) pork sausages

250 grams (½ lb) penne

1 large onion, diced

2 large celery stalks, sliced

398 ml can mixed beans, drained and rinsed

284 ml can corn kernels, drained

2 cups tomato sauce

1 tablespoon Worcestershire sauce

1 cup water

1 Preheat the oven to 400°F (200°C). Fry the sausages in a non-stick frying pan over a medium heat, turning occasionally, for 12–15 minutes, until golden brown. Remove and cool slightly, then slice thickly. Meanwhile, cook the pasta for about 7 minutes — you are only partly cooking the pasta at this stage. Drain the pasta.

2 Add the onion to the frying pan and fry, stirring often, for 4–5 minutes, until softened. Add the celery and fry for a further 2 minutes.

3 Combine the onion and celery, sausages, penne, beans and corn in a large ovenproof dish, about 33 x 25 cm in size. In a large pitcher, mix the tomato sauce, Worcestershire sauce and water. Pour over the ingredients in the dish.

4 Cover the dish closely with a lid or foil, then bake for 25–30 minutes until the pasta is tender and most of the liquid has been absorbed. Serve immediately as the pasta will go soggy if left to stand.

VARIATIONS
• *You could omit the sausages and replace with cheese, adding diced mozzarella to the mixture, and sprinkle the top with a little aged cheddar cheese.*
• *Instead of the canned mixed beans use a can of baked beans.*

EACH SERVING

25.5 g protein • 22 g fat of which 8.5 g saturates • 66.5 g carbohydrate • 14 g fibre • 598 Calories

VARIATION
• *In place of the chicken you could use the same amount of shredded sliced ham, or a mixture of ham and chicken.*

Chicken and broccoli pasta bake

A healthy, quick and easy family meal, this hearty bake combines ready-cooked chicken and whole wheat pasta in a cheesy sauce. Including little broccoli florets is a great way to encourage children to enjoy this super-nourishing vegetable as part of their daily diet.

Serves 4

Preparation time 10 minutes

Cooking time 35 minutes

250 grams (½ lb) whole wheat penne or other pasta shapes

250 grams (½ lb) broccoli

2 leeks, trimmed and sliced

4 cooked skinless boneless chicken breasts

2 cups 1% milk

¼ cup cornstarch

¾ cup grated aged cheese, such as gouda, smoked cheddar or old cheddar

12 cherry tomatoes, halved

¼ cup grated Parmesan cheese

1 teaspoon dried oregano

¼ cup dried whole wheat breadcrumbs

VARIATIONS

• Cubes of cooked ham could be used instead of the chicken and any other of your family's favourite vegetables substituted for the broccoli.

• For a vegetarian meal, replace the chicken with 2 x 398 ml cans of mixed legumes, drained and rinsed.

1 Preheat the oven to 375°F (190°C). Cook the pasta in a large pot of boiling water for 10–12 minutes or according to the package instructions, until tender. Trim the broccoli into small florets and slice the stalks. Add all the broccoli and the leeks to the pasta for the last 5 minutes or so of cooking.

2 When just tender, drain well, reserving about 1 cup of the cooking water. Tip the pasta and vegetables into a large ovenproof dish. Skin the chicken and cut into small chunks and add to the dish.

3 Blend a little of the milk with the cornstarch to a paste in a cup. Heat the remaining milk and reserved cooking water in the same pot until on the point of boiling. Pour about a cupful onto the cornstarch paste and stir well, then pour this into the simmering milky water and stir briskly with a wooden spoon until it thickens. Remove the pot from the heat and mix in the mature cheese. Season to taste.

4 Pour the sauce over the pasta, stirring gently with a fork. Nestle the tomato halves into the mixture, then sprinkle with the Parmesan, oregano and breadcrumbs. Bake for 20 minutes until bubbling and crispy on top. Serve hot.

EACH SERVING

47 g protein • 18.5 g fat of which 8 g saturates • 57 g carbohydrate • 13.5 g fibre • 595 Calories

Chicken parmigiana

An easy, Italian-style dish of chicken breasts, oven-baked with a low-fat, chunky vegetable sauce, with a Parmesan topping. Serve with warm ciabatta or baguette to mop up the delicious sauce.

Serves 4

Preparation time 10 minutes

Cooking time 55 minutes

2 tablespoons olive oil

1 small onion, finely chopped

2 garlic cloves, crushed

200 grams (7 oz) small mushrooms, quartered

1 large eggplant, diced

500 grams (1 lb) Roma tomatoes, coarsely chopped

15 grams (½ oz) fresh basil, torn into small pieces

4 skinless boneless chicken breasts

2 tablespoons grated Parmesan cheese

VARIATIONS

• *Replace the mushrooms with a 398 ml can of artichoke hearts, drained and quartered, or with 4 zucchini, diced.*
• *This dish would also work well using turkey escalopes.*

1 Preheat the oven to 375°F (190°C). Heat the oil in a flameproof casserole or deep frying pan, add the onion and garlic and cook, stirring, for 2 minutes over a medium heat. Add the mushrooms and cook for 3–4 minutes until lightly coloured, stirring frequently.

2 Stir in the eggplant, cook for 2 minutes, then add the tomatoes and stir over a medium-high heat for 2 minutes to combine. Reduce the heat and leave to simmer for 15 minutes until thick. Stir in the basil and season to taste.

3 If using a flameproof casserole, lay the chicken in the sauce. Alternatively, arrange the chicken in a single layer in a deep ovenproof baking dish or casserole and spoon the sauce over the top. Cover and bake for about 25 minutes or until the chicken is thoroughly cooked.

4 Towards the end of the cooking time, preheat the grill. Uncover the chicken and sprinkle the cheese over the top of the dish. Put the dish under the grill for 1–2 minutes until the cheese is melted and bubbling.

EACH SERVING

36.5 g protein • 20 g fat of which 4.5 g saturates • 5 g carbohydrate • 4.5 g fibre • 354 Calories

Crab and shrimp cakes

Homemade fish cakes are always a special treat. They are the ultimate all-in-one dish, as they contain fish, potato and vegetables. These can be made ahead and chilled, ready to bake when you need them. If you like, serve with baby spinach.

Serves 4

Preparation time 15 minutes, plus 30 minutes chilling

Cooking time 35 minutes

500 grams (1 lb) potatoes, peeled and cut into chunks

2 tablespoons low-fat ricotta cheese

125 grams (4 oz) peeled shrimp, thawed if frozen, coarsely chopped

170 g can white crabmeat, well drained

2 scallions, chopped

a few shakes of Tabasco, or to taste

125 grams (4 oz) spinach

4 large tomatoes

1 lemon, cut into four wedges

BREADCRUMB COATING

¼ cup whole wheat flour

1 egg, beaten

⅔ cup dried whole wheat breadcrumbs

1 teaspoon dried thyme or oregano

2 tablespoons olive oil, warmed

1 Cook the potatoes in a pot of boiling water for 12–15 minutes until tender. Drain and return to the pot over the heat to dry out a little, then mash until smooth. Beat in the ricotta. Season and set aside to cool completely.

2 Pat the shrimp dry with paper towel, then chop coarsely. Mix with the crab, chopped scallions and Tabasco.

3 Put the spinach in a covered bowl with just the rinsing water clinging to the leaves. Cook in the microwave until just wilted. Cool, then squeeze dry and chop roughly. Mix the potato with the seafood and spinach. Chill for 30 minutes.

4 Preheat the oven to 375°F (190°C). Shape the seafood mixture into four large cakes, dipping your hands in a little flour if necessary.

5 Put the flour in a shallow bowl, the beaten egg in another shallow bowl and the breadcrumbs mixed with the dried herbs in a third. Coat the fish cakes evenly first in flour, then in beaten egg and, finally, in the crumbs.

6 Halve the tomatoes and place around the fish cakes on a baking tray. Season and sprinkle with any leftover crumbs. Brush the fish cakes with the warmed oil, then bake for 20 minutes until they are crisp and the tomatoes soft. Allow to stand for 3–4 minutes before serving. Serve with lemon wedges.

EACH SERVING

21 g protein • 13 g fat of which 2.5 g saturates • 37.5 g carbohydrate • 7 g fibre • 368 Calories

Cheesy cod and potato bake

Here's a really simple supper dish of smoked cod with a crispy topping of sliced potatoes finished with cheese. Peas and leeks add vitamins, minerals and fibre.

Serves 4

Preparation time 15 minutes

Cooking time 50 minutes

600 grams (1⅓ lb) small new potatoes, scrubbed

500 grams (1 lb) skinless, smoked cod fillets

1 tablespoon snipped fresh chives

⅔ cup diluted or homemade fish stock (page 29), hot

1½ cups fresh shelled or frozen peas, thawed if necessary

4 small leeks, trimmed and thinly sliced

½ cup grated aged cheddar cheese

COOK'S TIP

• To prepare ahead, use chilled rather than hot stock to assemble the dish, then cover tightly and refrigerate for up to 12 hours before cooking. Add an extra 5 minutes to the cooking time.

1 Preheat the oven to 375°F (190°C). Put the potatoes in a pot, cover with boiling water and bring back to a boil. Reduce the heat and simmer for 10 minutes until just tender. Drain.

2 Using kitchen scissors, cut the fish into large chunks and arrange in the base of a greased, large shallow ovenproof dish. Season with pepper and sprinkle the chives over the top. Pour in the hot stock, then scatter with the peas and leeks.

3 Thinly slice the parboiled potatoes and arrange in an even layer over the fish and vegetables. Season again with freshly ground black pepper. (There's no need to season with salt as the fish is quite salty.) Cover with a lid or a piece of greased foil and bake for 30 minutes.

4 Remove the dish from the oven and increase the oven temperature to 450°F (230°C). Sprinkle the cheese over the potatoes, then return the dish to the oven and bake for a further 5–10 minutes until crisp and golden. Serve.

EACH SERVING

31.5 g protein • 6 g fat of which 3 g saturates • 25 g carbohydrate • 8 g fibre • 296 Calories

Tray-baked salmon

Succulent salmon steaks are rich in heart-healthy fats. Here they are oven-baked on a luscious bed of sliced tomatoes, eggplant and potatoes and served with a light lemon mayonnaise. If you like, serve with garlic bread.

Serves 4

Preparation time 15 minutes

Cooking time 50 minutes

500 grams (1 lb) potatoes, peeled and sliced

1 eggplant, thickly sliced

4 large ripe tomatoes, sliced

4 anchovy fillets, drained, rinsed and finely chopped

2 tablespoons olive oil

1 tablespoon bottled capers, rinsed and chopped

4 salmon steaks

LEMON MAYONNAISE

1/3 cup light mayonnaise

1/2 lemon, zest grated and juiced

VARIATIONS
- *If you prefer, replace the anchovies and capers with finely chopped lemon zest and 2 crushed garlic cloves.*
- *Prepare fresh tuna or swordfish steaks in the same way.*

1 Preheat the oven to 400°F (200°C). Cook the potatoes in a pot of boiling water for about 8 minutes until they are just tender, then drain.

2 Arrange the potato, eggplant and tomato slices in overlapping rings in a large, lightly oiled roasting pan.

3 In a small bowl, combine the anchovies with the oil and capers, then season well with pepper (no salt is needed). Pour the mixture over the vegetables. Cover the dish with foil and bake in the oven for 20 minutes.

4 Arrange the salmon steaks on top of the vegetables, re-cover with the foil and cook for 10 minutes. Remove the foil and cook for a further 10 minutes until the salmon and vegetables are cooked through.

5 Meanwhile, in a small bowl, mix the mayonnaise with the lemon zest and juice. Serve the mayonnaise with the cooked salmon and vegetables.

EACH SERVING

45.5 g protein • 26.5 g fat of which 5 g saturates • 28 g carbohydrate • 9 g fibre • 551 Calories

VARIATION

• For a change of flavour, use a smoked cod fillet instead of salmon and replace the asparagus with tiny broccoli florets (there is no need to cook them before layering), or even use half broccoli florets, half asparagus.

Salmon and asparagus lasagna

It's always interesting to try a few changes with a familiar dish. This is an attractive and healthy variation on lasagna, with flakes of tender salmon and chopped asparagus in a light lemon and herb sauce layered with the pasta. It's perfect for when asparagus is in season.

Step 1

Step 2

Step 4

Serves 4

Preparation time 20 minutes

Cooking time 50 minutes

400 grams (14 oz) skinless salmon fillet

2 cups diluted or homemade fish stock (page 29)

small bunch of fresh dill

6 black peppercorns

1 lemon, zest grated and juiced

750 grams (1½ lbs) asparagus, trimmed

1 tablespoon butter

¼ cup flour

1¼ cups 1% milk

¼ cup light sour cream

300 grams (10 oz) fresh lasagna (the number of sheets will depend on the brand)

2 tablespoons grated Parmesan cheese

1 Preheat the oven to 400°F (200°C). Put the salmon fillet in a shallow pan in which it fits snugly and add the stock, the stems from the dill (reserve the fronds for the sauce), the peppercorns and lemon juice. Bring to a boil, then simmer gently for 8–10 minutes until barely cooked. Remove the fish from the stock and, when cool enough to handle, break up into coarse flakes. Strain the stock and discard the flavourings. Set aside.

2 Steam the trimmed asparagus for about 3 minutes until barely tender. Cut off and reserve the tips, then chop the stalks into short pieces. Chop the reserved dill fronds.

3 To make the sauce, melt the butter in a pot and stir in the flour, then gradually stir in the reserved stock and the milk. Bring to a boil, stirring constantly, to make a smooth light sauce. Simmer for 1 minute, then remove from the heat. Add the lemon zest, the chopped dill fronds, sour cream and seasoning to taste. Stir in the salmon and chopped asparagus stalks.

4 Arrange enough sheets of lasagna to cover the bottom of a greased lasagna dish or large shallow ovenproof dish, of about 1.5 litre capacity. Spoon over one-quarter of the salmon mixture. Repeat the layers twice more, then cover with the remaining lasagna sheets. Top with the reserved asparagus tips and press them down gently all over. Top with the remaining salmon mixture.

5 Sprinkle with Parmesan, then bake for 30–35 minutes until the mixture is bubbling and the top is golden.

EACH SERVING

39.5 g protein • 19.5 g fat of which 8 g saturates • 35 g carbohydrate • 4 g fibre • 486 Calories

Jumbo mushrooms with Camembert and pine nuts

Large flat mushrooms are ideal for stuffing with your favourite filling. These ones are topped with slices of creamy cheese, sprinkled with pine nuts and served on toast for a smart, no-fuss light lunch or supper. If you like, add a salad.

Serves 2

Preparation time 15 minutes

Cooking time 15 minutes

4 large flat or portobello mushrooms

a little olive oil

80 grams (2³/4 oz) Camembert or brie cheese

2 tablespoons dried whole wheat breadcrumbs

2 tablespoons pine nuts

4 slices whole wheat or multigrain bread

1 ripe beefsteak tomato

1 Preheat the oven to 375°F (190°C). Pull out the mushroom stalks and discard, then wipe the tops with paper towel (don't wash or peel the mushrooms). Rub the tops of the mushrooms lightly with a little olive oil, then place them upside down in a non-stick, shallow roasting dish. Season with freshly ground black pepper and bake for 10 minutes. Remove from the oven.

2 Slice the cheese thinly and place in the mushroom cups. Mix together the breadcrumbs and nuts and sprinkle the mixture over the cheese. Return the mushrooms to the oven and bake for a further 5 minutes until the cheese just melts.

3 Meanwhile toast the bread. There's no need to butter the toast, but you can brush it with a little olive oil, if you like.

4 Trim the ends from the tomato, then cut it into four even slices. Lay a slice of tomato on each slice of toast, then top with a hot baked mushroom, cheese-side up, and serve at once.

EACH SERVING

18 g protein • 23 g fat of which 8 g saturates • 28 g carbohydrate • 7 g fibre • 404 Calories

COOK'S TIP
• *Choose either large, white, flat mushrooms or the firmer textured brown flat type, called portobello, which has a stronger, nuttier flavour.*

Goat's cheese, spinach and pesto lasagna

Fresh pasta needs only brief oven-baking. Used in a vegetarian lasagna it is layered with wilted fresh spinach and juicy cherry tomatoes, then baked with a creamy goat's cheese topping.

Serves 4   Preparation time 20 minutes   Cooking time 35 minutes

500 grams (1 lb) baby spinach

200 grams (7 oz) mild creamy goat's cheese

3/4 cup ricotta cheese

1 tablespoon pesto

pinch of grated nutmeg

250 grams (1/2 lb) fresh lasagna (about 9 sheets)

350 grams (12²/₃ oz) cherry tomatoes, halved

2 eggs, lightly beaten

1/2 cup 1% milk

3/4 cup fresh white breadcrumbs

2 tablespoons grated Parmesan cheese

1 Preheat the oven to 375°F (190°C). Put the spinach in a large pot, with just the rinsing water clinging to the leaves. Cover and wilt it over a low heat for about 5 minutes, turning it occasionally. Tip the spinach into a colander and allow to drain, but do not squeeze dry. Reserve 2 tablespoons of the juices.

2 Put the goat's cheese and ricotta in a large bowl and mix together, then take out half the mixture and set aside. Add the pesto and reserved spinach juice to the cheese in the bowl and blend until smooth. Stir in the spinach and nutmeg and seasoning to taste.

3 Lay the lasagna sheets in a roasting pan and pour over enough boiling water to cover. Leave for 5 minutes until softened, then carefully drain.

4 Spread one-third of the spinach mixture over the base of a 25 x 18 x 8 cm ovenproof dish. Scatter one-third of the tomatoes in an even layer over the spinach mixture, then cover with a layer of pasta, trimming to fit the dish. Add half of the remaining spinach mixture in a thin layer, top with half the remaining tomatoes and cover with pasta as before. Cover with the last of the filling and arrange the remaining pasta sheets over the top.

5 Whisk the reserved cheese mixture with the eggs, milk and seasoning. Pour over the lasagna, then sprinkle with a mixture of the breadcrumbs and Parmesan. Bake for 25 minutes until the topping is lightly set and browned. Serve while hot.

EACH SERVING

27.5 g protein • 21 g fat of which 11 g saturates • 31 g carbohydrate • 11 g fibre • 442 Calories

Vegetable moussaka

This is a clever variation on the traditional, meat-based Greek dish that is usually quite high in fat. The meat has been replaced with a selection of vibrantly coloured vegetables and the protein is supplied by pinto beans. The dish is topped in the traditional way but with a lighter yogourt-based sauce.

Step 1

Step 2

Step 4

Serves **4**

Preparation time **15 minutes**

Cooking time **55 minutes**

2 zucchini, sliced

1 eggplant, sliced

300 grams (10 oz) new potatoes, scrubbed and sliced

2 red peppers, deseeded and cut into thick strips

398 ml can pinto beans, drained and rinsed

4 ripe tomatoes, chopped

¼ cup coarsely chopped fresh basil

2 tablespoons olive oil

½ cup low-fat plain yogourt

1 egg, lightly beaten

⅓ cup grated Parmesan cheese

1 Preheat the oven to 350°F (180°C). Bring a large pot of salted water to a boil. Add the zucchini and cook for 2 minutes. Remove from the water with a slotted spoon and drain well on paper towel. Add the eggplant slices to the water and cook for 2 minutes, then remove and drain. Add the potato slices to the water and cook for about 8 minutes until just tender. Drain and set aside with the other blanched vegetables.

2 Meanwhile, heat a cast-iron, ridged grill pan over a high heat. Cook the pepper slices for about 5 minutes, turning occasionally, until slightly charred all over and starting to soften. Remove from the pan and roughly chop.

3 Combine all the cooked vegetables with the beans, chopped tomatoes and basil in a large baking dish. Drizzle the olive oil over the top, season to taste and stir together thoroughly.

4 In a bowl, stir together the yogourt, egg and Parmesan until blended. Spread this mixture over the top of the vegetables in an even layer (it may not cover the vegetables completely, depending on the shape of the dish).

5 Bake the moussaka for 40 minutes or until the vegetables are tender and the topping is golden brown.

EACH SERVING

17 g protein • 14 g fat of which 3.5 g saturates • 31 g carbohydrate • 8.5 g fibre • 355 Calories

COOK'S TIP
• You can prepare all the vegetables a day ahead of time, up to the end of step 3. Cover and refrigerate. When ready to use, allow to come to room temperature, then cover with the yogourt mixture and bake as described in the main recipe.

VARIATIONS
• For non-vegetarians, add 200 grams (7 oz) chopped cooked chicken to the vegetables in step 3 and omit the pinto beans.
• To save time, instead of grilling peppers, you can use bottled chargrilled peppers, cut into strips.

Cauliflower and broccoli gratin

A favourite vegetarian dish gets a new twist here, with super-healthy broccoli added to cauliflower, in a cheese sauce thickened with breadcrumbs. Crunchy walnuts on top make this mouth-wateringly good. It's just as good served on its own or as a side dish.

Serves **4**

Preparation time **20 minutes**

Cooking time **25 minutes**

1 large cauliflower

500 grams (1 lb) broccoli

3 scallions, sliced

¼ cup cornstarch

2¼ cups 1% milk

⅔ cup grated aged cheddar or Gruyère cheese

1 egg, beaten

1⅔ cups fresh breadcrumbs

¼ cup walnuts

1 Preheat the oven to 375°F (190°C). Trim away the leaves from the cauliflower, then cut off the florets from the main stem. Cut the broccoli florets away from the stem. Blanch both the cauliflower and broccoli florets in a large pot of boiling water for 1 minute, then drain thoroughly.

2 Put the scallions into the same pot. Mix the cornstarch with a little of the milk in a large heatproof bowl to make a smooth paste. Pour the rest of the milk into the pot with the scallions and bring the milk to a boil. Stir half of the hot milk into the bowl with the cornstarch paste, mix well, then return the entire mixture to the pot. Bring the mixture to a boil, stirring

frequently, to make a smooth white sauce.

3 Remove the white sauce from the heat and stir in the grated cheese, beaten egg and half the breadcrumbs. Stir in the blanched vegetables and season to taste with freshly ground black pepper.

4 Transfer the vegetable mixture to a greased, ovenproof baking dish or gratin dish. Scatter the rest of the breadcrumbs and the walnuts over the top of the vegetables, then bake for about 20 minutes until golden. Serve immediately.

EACH SERVING

24 g protein • 14 g fat of which 5 g saturates • 36 g carbohydrate • 7 g fibre • 378 Calories

Mushroom pasta bake

Using a variety of fresh and dried mushrooms combined with tasty artichoke hearts gives an exotic flavour to this tempting dish. A great addition to your repertoire.

Serves **4**   *Preparation time* **15 minutes**   *Cooking time* **50 minutes**

20 grams (³/₄ oz) dried porcini mushrooms

1 cup boiling water

2 tablespoons olive oil

2 onions, chopped

2 garlic cloves, crushed

¹/₃ cup red wine

1 teaspoon dried sage

500 grams (1 lb) mixed fresh mushrooms, trimmed and sliced

2 x 398 ml cans chopped tomatoes

¹/₂ teaspoon sugar

400 grams (14 oz) large shells

398 ml can artichoke hearts, drained and quartered

1 Put the dried mushrooms in a heatproof bowl, pour over the boiling water to cover and set aside to soak for 15 minutes.

2 Meanwhile, heat the oil in a large flameproof casserole. Add the onions and garlic and cook, stirring, for 5–7 minutes, until the onions are soft and just starting to brown.

3 Drain the soaked mushrooms in a sieve set over a pitcher to catch the soaking liquid. Line the sieve with paper towel and strain the liquid to remove any grit. Add the liquid to the onions, along with the red wine and sage. Bring to a boil, then reduce the heat. Add the fresh and soaked mushrooms and stir for 3–4 minutes until the mushrooms start to give off their juice.

4 Stir in the tomatoes with their juice, the sugar and seasoning to taste. Cover and simmer for 12–15 minutes until the sauce thickens and the tomatoes start breaking down. Meanwhile, preheat the oven to 375°F (190°C).

5 While the sauce is simmering, add the pasta to a large pot of boiling water and cook for just 5 minutes until the pasta is just beginning to become tender (do not cook until tender).

6 Drain the pasta well, then stir it into the sauce along with the artichokes. Taste and adjust the seasoning, if necessary. Place the casserole dish in the oven, uncovered, and bake for 20 minutes until the pasta is tender. Serve the bake straight from the dish.

VARIATIONS

• *Boost the fibre content by using whole wheat pasta shells.*
• *If you like, sprinkle the baked pasta with grated Parmesan cheese.*

EACH SERVING

16 g protein • 12.5 g fat of which 2 g saturates • 76 g carbohydrate • 13 g fibre • 519 Calories

VARIATIONS

• *Pine nuts are a good alternative to walnuts.*
• *You could also arrange 100 grams (3¹/₂ oz) halved cherry tomatoes, cut side up, on top of the vegetables in the sauce, before adding the breadcrumbs and nuts.*

Roasted vegetable crumble

Roasted vegetable crumble

Sweetly flavoured, roasted vegetables topped with a savoury crumble that includes
Parmesan, nuts, pumpkin seeds and sunflower seeds for added texture and protein
value, make an irresistible vegetarian meal.

Serves 4

Preparation time 20 minutes

Cooking time about 1¼ hours

6 small red onions, quartered

400 grams (14 oz) orange sweet
potatoes, cut into 3 cm chunks

2 tablespoons olive oil

1 garlic clove, crushed

2 teaspoons fresh thyme

2 large zucchini, cut into
3 cm slices

100 grams (3½ oz) baby button
mushrooms

350 grams (12⅔ oz) Roma
tomatoes, quartered lengthwise

CRUMBLE TOPPING

½ cup whole wheat flour

1 tablespoon butter, cooled and
diced

1 tablespoon cold water

⅔ cup fresh whole wheat
breadcrumbs

½ cup grated Parmesan cheese

¼ cup mixed chopped nuts

2 tablespoons sunflower seeds

2 tablespoons pumpkin seeds

VARIATION
• *Other root vegetables, such as
parsnips, carrots and beets, cut
into 3 cm chunks, are also good
cooked in this dish.*

1 Preheat the oven to 375°F (190°C). Put an ovenproof dish, preferably metal
and measuring about 30 x 20 x 4 cm, in the oven and allow it to heat for
10 minutes. Combine the onions and sweet potatoes in a bowl, drizzle with
1 tablespoon of the oil and gently toss to coat. Tip into the heated dish and
roast for 30 minutes, turning the vegetables after 15 minutes.

2 Blend the remaining oil with the garlic and 1 teaspoon of the thyme in the
bowl. Add the zucchini, mushrooms and tomatoes, and gently toss to coat.
Tip into the dish and roast for a further 20 minutes.

3 Meanwhile, put the flour in a bowl and rub in the butter using your fingertips. Add the water and mix together with a fork to make large crumbs. Stir
in the breadcrumbs, cheese, nuts, seeds, pumpkin seeds and remaining thyme.

4 Sprinkle the crumble mixture over the vegetables. Bake for 15–20 minutes
until the topping is golden brown and all the vegetables are tender. Remove
from the oven and leave to stand for 3–4 minutes before serving.

EACH SERVING

17 g protein • 28.5 g fat of which 7.5 g saturates • 37 g carbohydrate
• 10 g fibre • 488 Calories

288 bakes and pies

Cheesy vegetable gratin

A comforting, chunky vegetable stew is topped with a cheesy breadcrumb crust to evoke the flavours of traditional farmhouse cooking.

Serves 4

Preparation time 15 minutes

Cooking time 35 minutes

1 butternut squash, peeled, deseeded and cut into 1 cm dice

400 grams (14 oz) carrots, peeled and sliced

300 grams (10 oz) leeks, trimmed, halved lengthwise and sliced

2 garlic cloves, finely chopped

2 cups bottled chunky salt-reduced pasta sauce

1¼ cups water or diluted salt-reduced or homemade vegetable stock (page 29)

½ teaspoon sugar

6 sprigs of fresh thyme, tied together, or 2 teaspoons dried thyme

GRATIN TOPPING

40 grams (1½ oz) butter

1¼ cups fresh whole wheat breadcrumbs

2 tablespoons snipped fresh chives

⅓ cup grated aged cheddar cheese

1 Put the butternut squash, carrots, leeks and garlic in a flameproof casserole or large pot. Pour the pasta sauce and water or stock into the pot and add the sugar. Bring to a boil, stirring, then reduce the heat. Add the thyme and cook for 12–15 minutes until the vegetables are almost tender when pierced with the tip of a knife. Season to taste.

2 Meanwhile, preheat the oven to 400°F (200°C). For the gratin topping, melt the butter in a pot and stir in the breadcrumbs and chives. Remove the pan from the heat.

3 If you are not using a flameproof casserole dish, transfer the vegetables to an ovenproof dish. Spread the breadcrumb mixture over the vegetables and sprinkle the cheese evenly over the top. Bake for 20 minutes or until the gratin topping is crisp and golden.

EACH SERVING

14 g protein • 14 g fat of which 8.5 g saturates • 46.5 g carbohydrate • 8.5 g fibre • 384 Calories

Mexican vegetable bake

Turn a tray of roasted vegetables into a spicy meal by adding kidney beans, a tomato sauce and a cheesy topping. This should prove a popular dish for teenaged vegetarians and is great served with warmed soft tortillas.

Serves 4

Preparation time 15 minutes

Cooking time 40 minutes

1 red onion

2 large garlic cloves, chopped

1 large red or yellow pepper, deseeded and cut into chunks

1 small fennel bulb or 2 celery stalks, thinly sliced

1 large zucchini, thickly sliced

2 tablespoons olive oil

398 ml can artichoke hearts, drained

1 teaspoon dried oregano

1 teaspoon paprika or mild chili powder

½ teaspoon ground cumin

398 ml can chopped tomatoes

398 ml can red kidney or pinto beans, drained and rinsed

¾ cup ricotta cheese, drained

½ cup 1% milk

¾ cup grated aged cheddar cheese

2 tablespoons dried whole wheat breadcrumbs

1 Preheat the oven to 400°F (200°C). Halve the onion lengthwise, then cut into thin wedges. Place in a large plastic bag with the garlic, pepper chunks, fennel or celery, zucchini slices and oil. Toss together well, then tip out into a shallow ovenproof dish. Alternatively, you can mix everything together in a large bowl before tipping into the ovenproof dish.

2 Add the artichoke hearts to the vegetables, being careful not to break them up too much, then season with freshly ground black pepper. Sprinkle the oregano, paprika or chili, and cumin over the vegetables, then transfer to the oven and roast for 15 minutes.

3 Stir in the tomatoes with their juice, and the drained beans. Return the vegetables to the oven to bake for a further 10 minutes.

4 Meanwhile, stir the ricotta with the milk, to thin it to a thick cream. Drizzle the cheesy sauce over the vegetables. Mix the grated cheese and breadcrumbs together and scatter on top. Return to the oven to bake for a further 15 minutes until golden and bubbling.

EACH SERVING

21 g protein • 23 g fat of which 9 g saturates • 25 g carbohydrate • 10.5 g fibre • 408 Calories

VARIATIONS
• *For meat-eaters, add some stir-fried ground chicken instead of the beans.*
• *Try grated Spanish manchego or manchego-style cheese instead of the cheddar.*

Baked couscous tomatoes

Large beefsteak tomatoes make tasty, juicy containers for a spicy dried fruit and nut couscous mixture, served with creamy yogourt. All that's needed is some warm crusty bread to complete the meal.

Serves 4

Preparation time 30 minutes

Cooking time 25 minutes

8 large beefsteak tomatoes, tops cut off and the insides scooped out and reserved

½ cup chopped dried apricots

⅓ cup chopped dried dates

⅓ cup sultanas

1¼ cups hot diluted salt-reduced or homemade vegetable stock (page 29), or as needed

1 tablespoon olive oil

½ cup pine nuts

4 scallions, thinly sliced

½ teaspoon ground cumin

½ teaspoon ground coriander

1 cup instant couscous

2 tablespoons chopped fresh flat-leaf parsley

1 cup Greek-style yogourt or tzatziki

1 Preheat the oven to 400°F (200°C). Place the tomatoes in a single layer in a baking dish (if necessary, cut a very thin sliver from the base of each tomato so that it will sit flat). Put the seeds and scooped-out flesh in a sieve over a pitcher, and press to squeeze out the juices. Discard the seeds and flesh.

2 Put the fruit in a small bowl with ⅓ cup of the tomato juice. Stir, then leave to soak. Make up the remaining tomato juice to 1½ cups with stock.

3 Heat 2 teaspoons of the oil in a non-stick pot. Add the pine nuts and cook over a low heat, stirring all the time, for 2 minutes, until golden. Remove from the pan with a slotted spoon and set aside.

4 Add the remaining oil to the pot and cook the scallions for 2 minutes, until soft. Stir in the spices and cook for a few more seconds. Pour in the stock and bring to a rapid boil. Remove from the heat, then add the couscous in a steady stream, stirring constantly. Cover and leave to stand for 3 minutes.

5 Stir the fruit, pine nuts and parsley into the couscous, then season. Spoon the couscous mixture into the tomatoes and replace the tops. Bake for 15 minutes until tender. Rest for 5 minutes before serving with yogourt or tzatziki.

EACH SERVING

14 g protein • 28 g fat of which 5 g saturates • 54 g carbohydrate • 10.5 g fibre • 538 Calories

VARIATION
• *Dried peaches can be used instead of dried apricots, and almonds or hazelnuts instead of pine nuts.*

Goat's cheese and cherry tomato clafoutis

Traditionally a sweet pudding, this savoury version of the French clafoutis is made with soft goat's cheese and small cherry tomatoes taking the place of the usual cherries. Serve with a rustic, whole wheat bread and a mixed leaf salad with sliced mushrooms and hazelnuts.

Serves 4

Preparation time 10 minutes

Cooking time 40 minutes

350 grams (12 oz) cherry tomatoes

6 eggs, lightly beaten

1 cup 1% milk

¼ cup all-purpose flour

¼ cup snipped fresh chives

100 grams (3½ oz) soft goat's cheese

VARIATIONS

• *Vary the cheese to your own taste – grated Gruyère, cheddar, Parmesan and crumbled blue cheese would all be good choices in the clafoutis.*
• *Instead of cherry tomatoes, try chopped grilled peppers or sautéed button mushrooms.*

1 Preheat the oven to 350°F (180°C). Spread the cherry tomatoes in an even layer in the bottom of a lightly oiled, 23 cm round ovenproof dish, that is approximately 5 cm deep.

2 Place the eggs in a bowl and whisk in the milk. Add the flour and whisk to combine thoroughly. Add the chives and season to taste. Pour this batter over the tomatoes. Crumble the cheese over the top.

3 Bake for 35–40 minutes until the top is golden and the pie is almost set (it will continue cooking once removed from the oven). Leave to cool for a few minutes before serving as the tomatoes will be very hot inside.

EACH SERVING

17 g protein • 12 g fat of which 5 g saturates • 13 g carbohydrate • 2 g fibre • 230 Calories

Cheesy bread and butter bake

A popular, farmhouse-style recipe, but with the addition of leeks and sun-dried tomatoes for a healthier result. Excellent for brunch or for an easy lunch, served with a simple salad.

Serves 4   Preparation time 25 minutes, plus 20 minutes soaking
Cooking time 35 minutes

1 medium whole wheat loaf, unsliced

30 grams (1 oz) unsalted butter, softened

1 tablespoon Dijon mustard

300 grams (10 oz) small leeks, trimmed and very thinly sliced

²/₃ cup sun-dried tomatoes, drained and roughly chopped

2 cups 1% milk

4 eggs

2 strips of bacon

³/₄ cup grated reduced-fat cheddar cheese

1 Trim the crusts off the loaf, then cut the bread into slices about 1 cm thick. Mix the softened butter with the mustard and spread thinly over half the slices. Make sandwiches by putting the unbuttered slices on top of the buttered ones, then cut each sandwich in half. Place in a lightly greased, 2 litre shallow, ovenproof dish, arranged like a jigsaw so that they fit snugly.

2 Scatter the leeks and tomatoes evenly over the bread. Whisk the milk with the eggs and season with freshly ground black pepper. Pour over the bread and vegetables, then leave to soak for 20 minutes.

3 Meanwhile, preheat the oven to 375°F (190°C). Use a grill pan or frying pan to dry-fry or lightly grill the bacon until just cooked – they will cook further in the oven. (Alternatively, the bacon can be cooked in the microwave.) Drain on paper towel and leave to cool.

4 When ready to bake, chop the bacon into small pieces and scatter the pieces over the bread and vegetables. Sprinkle the grated cheese on top, then bake for 25–30 minutes until puffed and golden. Serve immediately.

VARIATION

• *For a fishy bake, replace the bacon with 200 grams (7 oz) smoked cod fillets, poached in milk, then skinned and flaked. For extra flavour use the poaching milk to mix with the eggs. Scatter the fish over the leeks before soaking in the milk and egg mixture.*

EACH SERVING

41 g protein • 21 g fat of which 9 g saturates • 75.5 g carbohydrate • 14 g fibre • 686 Calories

Polenta and corn bake

This is a satisfying, sunny yellow dish made with instant polenta and canned corn kernels baked in a cheesy batter. Serve with a chunky homemade tomato sauce (page 232).

*Serves **4** Preparation time **25 minutes** Cooking time **45 minutes***

2 tablespoons fresh or dried whole wheat breadcrumbs

2½ cups instant polenta

1 teaspoon mustard powder

1⅔ cups boiling water

2 large eggs, separated

398 ml can corn kernels, drained

8 scallions, chopped

2 tablespoons snipped fresh chives

⅔ cup coarsely grated aged cheddar cheese

⅔ cup buttermilk

1 Preheat the oven to 425°F (220°C). Lightly grease a large ovenproof baking dish of about 2.4 litre capacity, then sprinkle the breadcrumbs around the inside of the dish, including the sides.

2 Put the polenta in a large heatproof bowl and stir in the mustard, then pour in the boiling water and stir until smooth. Cool slightly, then stir in the egg yolks, corn, scallions, chives and about half of the cheese. Add the buttermilk and stir to form a thick batter.

3 Whisk the egg whites in a separate bowl until stiff peaks form. Beat 1 large spoonful of the egg whites into the batter to lighten it, then gently fold in the remaining egg whites.

4 Spoon the mixture into the prepared dish and sprinkle the remaining cheese over the top. Bake for 40–45 minutes until the top is set and golden brown. Serve at once, straight from the dish.

COOK'S TIP
• *Buttermilk, a tangy cultured milk product, contains 2 grams of fat per cup, the same as a cup of 1% milk. It is stocked next to the cream in the cooler at supermarkets. If you can't find any, you can substitute 1% milk mixed with 1 teaspoon lemon juice and left to stand for about 5 minutes before using.*

VARIATION
• *Boost the vegetable content by adding diced steamed carrots, sliced leeks or frozen peas (no need to thaw) with the corn in step 2.*

EACH SERVING

19.5 g protein • 13 g fat of which 5.5 g saturates • 71 g carbohydrate • 5 g fibre • 492 Calories

Stuffed zucchini

In this delicious vegetarian dish, thick slices of large zucchini are hollowed out and filled with a tasty stuffing based on creamy white kidney beans and fennel. A crispy topping of breadcrumbs and walnuts makes the perfect finishing touch. Serve with extra bread and a seasonal salad.

Serves 4

Preparation time 15 minutes

Cooking time 1 hour

6 large zucchini

1½ tablespoons walnut or canola oil

1 garlic clove, crushed

2 shallots or ½ small onion, finely chopped

1 fennel bulb, finely chopped

398 ml can chopped tomatoes

398 ml can white kidney beans, drained and rinsed

¼ cup chopped cilantro

½ teaspoon chili flakes (optional)

⅓ cup diluted salt-reduced or homemade vegetable stock (page 29)

BREADCRUMB TOPPING

½ cup whole wheat breadcrumbs

½ cup walnuts, roughly chopped

½ cup grated Parmesan cheese

1 Preheat the oven to 375°F (190°C). Trim the ends from the zucchini, then peel off thin strips of skin, lengthwise, to achieve a striped effect. Cut across into pieces 4 cm long and remove the soft centre flesh by hollowing out with an apple corer or small sharp knife, making sure not to cut all the way through to the base. Finely dice the removed zucchini flesh and set aside.

2 Put the zucchini rings in a bowl and pour over enough boiling water to cover. Leave for 2 minutes, then drain in a colander and arrange them, upright, in a single layer in a large ovenproof dish.

3 Heat the oil in a frying pan and gently cook the garlic and shallots or onion for 3–4 minutes, until they are beginning to soften. Add the fennel and diced zucchini flesh and continue cooking over a low heat for a further 5 minutes until the fennel is almost tender. Remove the pan from the heat. Stir in the chopped tomatoes with their juice, the white kidney beans, cilantro and chili flakes (if using), then season to taste.

4 Spoon the bean mixture into the zucchini rings, piling it up on top. Pour the stock into the dish around them. Cover with a "tent" of foil, tightly sealing around the edge, but allowing space for the zucchini to steam. Bake the zucchini for 30 minutes.

5 Remove the foil and sprinkle the tops with a mixture of the breadcrumbs, walnuts, cheese and a little freshly ground black pepper, if you like. Return to the oven and bake, uncovered, for a further 15–20 minutes until the zucchini are very tender and the tops are crisp and brown.

EACH SERVING

17 g protein • 17 g fat of which 3.5 g saturates • 25.5 g carbohydrate
• 13 g fibre • 343 Calories

COOK'S TIP
• *The easiest way to remove the strips of zucchini peel is to use a vegetable peeler.*

Liver, bacon and mushroom pie

Nothing beats the smell of a pie baking in the oven, and this one is even more aromatic than most with its rosemary-flavoured crust.

Serves **4**

Preparation time **35 minutes**

Cooking time **40 minutes**

FILLING

350 grams (12 oz) lamb's liver, cut into 1 cm thick strips

2 tablespoons all-purpose flour

2 tablespoons olive oil

2 strips bacon

150 grams (5 oz) shallots, peeled and cut into wedges

250 grams (8 oz) carrots, peeled and diced

150 grams (5 oz) button mushrooms, sliced if large

1 garlic clove, crushed

1 teaspoon finely chopped fresh rosemary

1¼ cups diluted salt-reduced or homemade beef or vegetable stock (pages 28–29), hot

2 tablespoons dry sherry

PASTRY

¾ cup self-rising flour

1¼ cups fresh white breadcrumbs

1 teaspoon finely chopped fresh rosemary

50 grams (2 oz) vegetable shortening

about ⅓ cup cold water

COOK'S TIP

• *This recipe can be made ahead then cooled, covered and chilled for up to 48 hours. Reheat in a preheated 350°F (180°C) oven for 20 minutes before serving. Make sure the filling is piping hot.*

1 Preheat the oven to 350°F (180°C). Toss the liver in the flour and a little seasoning to lightly coat. Heat the oil in a heavy, deep frying pan, then stir-fry the liver and bacon until lightly browned. Transfer to a plate and set aside.

2 Add the shallots and carrots to the pan and cook, stirring frequently, until lightly coloured. Add the mushrooms and cook, stirring often, for 2 minutes, then add the garlic, rosemary, stock and sherry. Bring to a boil, stirring.

3 Return the liver and bacon to the pan and stir well. Transfer to a 1 litre pie dish, mounding the filling in the centre, then cool while making the pastry.

4 Combine the flour, breadcrumbs, rosemary, shortening and seasoning in a bowl. Stir in enough cold water to make a soft (not sticky) dough. Turn out onto a lightly floured surface and roll out to be slightly larger than the pie dish.

5 Dampen the rim of the dish, then gently lift the pastry over the filling and press the pastry to the rim to seal. Trim off any excess pastry with a sharp knife, make a steam hole in the middle and press the back of a fork or your thumb onto the pastry rim. Bake for 30–35 minutes until golden, then serve hot.

EACH SERVING

37 g protein • 34 g fat of which 12 g saturates • 44 g carbohydrate • 5 g fibre • 650 Calories

Phyllo shepherd's pie

An updated version of an old favourite. This pretty pie combines lean meat with lots of fresh vegetables, all topped with crisp and light phyllo pastry.

Serves 4
Preparation time 20 minutes
Cooking time about 1 hour

500 grams (1 lb) lean boneless lamb, trimmed of all excess fat and cut into 2 cm cubes

2½ tablespoons flour

2½ tablespoons canola oil

250 grams (8 oz) shallots, peeled

2 garlic cloves, crushed

4 carrots, peeled and thickly sliced

1 celery stalk, sliced

½ cup red wine

1½ cups diluted salt-reduced or homemade beef or vegetable stock (pages 28–29)

1 tablespoon Worcestershire sauce

1 tablespoon whole-grain mustard

1 bouquet garni

2 leeks, trimmed, halved lengthwise and thickly sliced

2 tablespoons chopped fresh parsley

3 sheets phyllo pastry

1 Toss the meat with the flour to coat lightly. Heat 1½ tablespoons of the oil in a large flameproof casserole dish or a deep frying pan over a medium heat. Fry the lamb in batches until browned all over. Remove using a slotted spoon.

2 Add the shallots to the fat left in the pan and fry, stirring frequently, for 5–8 minutes until lightly browned.

3 Add the garlic, carrots and celery to the pan. Stir in the wine, turn up the heat and cook until the wine has almost evaporated. Add the stock, Worcestershire sauce, mustard and bouquet garni. Return the lamb to the pan along with any juices. Bring to a boil, then reduce the heat, cover and simmer for 20 minutes.

4 Preheat the oven to 375°F (190°C). Stir in the leeks, cover and simmer for 10 more minutes. Season to taste. Remove and discard the bouquet garni, then spoon the mixture into a 1.75 litre ovenproof dish and stir in the parsley.

5 Cut the phyllo pastry into squares between 9 and 12 cm, depending on the size of your phyllo sheets. Lightly brush each square on one side with a little of the remaining oil, then crumple them up loosely and place them, oiled-side up, over the filling. Bake for 25–30 minutes until the pastry is crisp and golden.

EACH SERVING

30 g protein • 22 g fat of which 6.5 g saturates • 20 g carbohydrate • 5 g fibre • 426 Calories

Chicken cobbler

A richly flavoured combination of chicken and mixed vegetables, cooked in cider, with a topping of light, herby scones, makes a great dinner, particularly in winter.

Serves 4

Preparation time 15 minutes

Cooking time 50 minutes

500 grams (1 lb) chicken, diced

2 tablespoons all-purpose flour

1½ tablespoons olive oil

2 onions, finely chopped

2 cups dry alcoholic cider

1 bay leaf

4 carrots, peeled

150 grams (5 oz) button mushrooms, halved

3 zucchini, trimmed

⅔ cup frozen corn kernels

COBBLER TOPPING

1¼ cups self-rising flour

1 tablespoon chopped fresh parsley

1 tablespoon snipped fresh chives

1 tablespoon chopped fresh oregano

30 grams (1 oz) unsalted butter, chilled and diced

½ cup 1% milk

1 Preheat the oven to 400°F (200°C). Toss the chicken in the flour mixed with a little seasoning to coat. Heat 1 tablespoon of the oil in a deep frying pan. Add the chicken and fry over a medium heat, stirring frequently, for about 3 minutes. Stir in the remaining oil and the onions, reduce the heat and cook for a further 5 minutes until the onions are golden.

2 Stir in the cider and bay leaf and bring to a boil. Quarter the carrots lengthwise, then chop into 2 cm chunks and add to the pan with the mushrooms. Reduce the heat and simmer gently for 20 minutes.

3 Meanwhile, cut the zucchini into quarters lengthwise, then cut across into chunks, about the size of the carrots. Mix with the corn and set aside.

EACH SERVING

30.5 g protein • 20.5 g fat of which 7 g saturates • 55 g carbohydrate
• 8.5 g fibre • 572 Calories

4 To make the cobbler topping, combine the flour, herbs and a little seasoning in a bowl. Using your fingertips, rub in the butter until the mixture looks like fine crumbs, then stir in the milk until the ingredients come together to make a soft dough. Turn out onto a floured surface and press out with floured fingers until about 1 cm thick. Using a floured 6 cm round cookie cutter, cut out eight rounds, re-using the trimmings.

5 Stir the zucchini and corn into the chicken mixture and season. Transfer to an ovenproof dish and arrange the "cobblers" on top. Bake, uncovered, for 20 minutes until the topping is golden. Serve hot.

Mediterranean chicken with oaty crumble

This colourful dish contains chunks of tender chicken breast, first roasted with eggplant, zucchini and red pepper, then baked in a herby tomato and olive sauce with a crumbly oat crust.

Serves 4 Preparation time 20 minutes Cooking time about 1 hour

3 chicken breasts on the bone (skin on)

3 small sprigs of fresh rosemary

1 eggplant, cut into 2 cm cubes

2 zucchini, cut into 2 cm thick slices

1 red pepper, deseeded and cut into 2 cm pieces

1 tablespoon olive oil (or oil from the jar of sun-dried tomatoes)

398 ml can chopped tomatoes

12 pitted black olives

OATMEAL CRUMBLE

1¼ cups rolled oats

30 grams (1 oz) butter, chilled and diced

½ cup sun-dried tomatoes in oil, drained

2 teaspoons chopped fresh oregano

1 Preheat the oven to 375°F (190°C). Loosen the skin on each chicken breast and tuck a sprig of rosemary underneath, between the skin and the flesh. Place the chicken in a large roasting pan and roast for 5 minutes.

2 Combine the eggplant, zucchini and red pepper in a bowl. Drizzle the oil over the vegetables, then toss to coat. Push the chicken portions to one side in the roasting pan, then add the vegetables. Roast the vegetables and chicken for 20 minutes, then turn the vegetables. Roast for a further 5–10 minutes until the vegetables are well browned and tender and the chicken is cooked through.

3 Meanwhile, make the crumble topping. Put the oats in a food processor and pulse briefly to make a fairly fine "flour." Add the butter, then pulse again until the mixture comes together in small lumps. Pat the sun-dried tomatoes on paper towel to blot up excess oil, then snip into small pieces with kitchen scissors. Stir into the crumble mixture with the oregano.

4 Transfer the roasted vegetables to a baking dish, and stir in the tomatoes with their juice, and the black olives. Season to taste. Cover and cook in the oven for 10 minutes. Meanwhile, discard the chicken skin and rosemary sprigs, then remove the chicken meat from the bone and cut into large bite-sized pieces.

5 Stir the chicken into the vegetable mixture, then scatter the crumble topping over the top, making sure to cover any vegetables that are already browned. Bake, uncovered, for 20 minutes until the topping is crisp and golden, then serve.

EACH SERVING

35 g protein • 24 g fat of which 7.5 g saturates • 34 g carbohydrate • 9 g fibre • 512 Calories

COOK'S TIPS
• *To prepare ahead, cook the chicken and vegetables, then cool and chill. Reheat gently, then top with the cobbler topping and bake.*
• *You can make the cobbler dough in a food processor if you prefer.*

Seafood pie with potato pastry

A very special fish pie that is sure to please everyone. The recipe uses a mixture of white fish, seafood and vegetables in a quick white sauce, topped with a golden turmeric potato pastry crust.

Serves 4

Preparation time 20 minutes,
  plus 15 minutes cooling

Cooking time 25 minutes

POTATO PASTRY

1 cup all-purpose flour

1/2 teaspoon ground turmeric

1/2 cup mashed potato

100 grams (3 1/2 oz) margarine, chilled and diced

1 tablespoon 1% milk, to glaze

1 tablespoon dried breadcrumbs

FILLING

400 grams (14 oz) skinless white fish fillets

200 grams (7 oz) peeled shrimp or seafood mix

2 leeks, trimmed and thinly sliced

3/4 cup frozen peas, thawed

2 tablespoons chopped fresh flat-leaf parsley

leaves from 2 sprigs of fresh thyme

1 lemon, zest grated

1/4 cup cornstarch

2 cups 1% milk

VARIATION

• *Alternatively, top the pie with mashed potatoes flavoured with chopped fresh parsley or chives. Bake for 20 minutes at 400°F (200°C).*

1 First make the pastry. Sift the flour and turmeric into a bowl and, using a fork, mix with the mashed potato until blended. Rub in the margarine, then draw together into a dough, adding trickles of cold water if necessary to bind the dough together. Wrap the dough in plastic wrap and chill in the refrigerator for about 20 minutes.

2 Meanwhile, prepare the filling. Cut the fish into small chunks and put into a pie dish of about 1.25 litre capacity. Mix in the shrimp or seafood, leeks, peas, parsley, thyme and lemon zest.

3 Blend the cornstarch with a little of the milk in a bowl. Heat the rest of the milk until it is almost at boiling point, then stir it into the cornstarch paste. Return the mixture to the pan and cook, stirring, until the sauce thickens. Season to taste and pour over the fish filling. Set aside to cool for 15 minutes. Preheat the oven to 400°F (200°C).

4 Roll out the potato pastry between two large sheets of plastic wrap to about the size and shape of the top of the pie dish. Remove the top sheet of plastic and use the second sheet to help you lay the pastry on top of the filling. Remove the sheet of plastic wrap.

5 Press and trim the pastry edges to neaten, and make a small slash in the centre of the lid to allow steam to escape. Brush the pastry with the milk, then sprinkle the top with the breadcrumbs. Place the pie dish on a baking tray and bake for 10 minutes, then reduce the heat to 350°F (180°C) and bake for a further 15 minutes until golden on top.

EACH SERVING

46 g protein • 22 g fat of which 4.5 g saturates • 51 g carbohydrate • 5.5 g fibre • 601 Calories

Tomato and mozzarella polenta

Why not try something different? Here, ready-made pesto is spread on a savoury polenta base, then topped with melt-in-the-mouth mozzarella cheese, juicy grape tomatoes and crunchy pine nuts.

Serves 4

Preparation time 15 minutes, plus 20 minutes cooling

Cooking time 25 minutes

4 cups water

2¼ cups instant polenta

¼ cup canned or frozen corn kernels, thawed if necessary

2 scallions, finely chopped

2 good pinches of dried oregano

²/₃ cup sun-dried tomato pesto

175 grams (6 oz) mozzarella cheese

400 grams (14 oz) cherry tomatoes, halved

¼ cup pine nuts

a few sprigs of fresh basil

8 black olives

1 Bring the water to a boil in a large pot. Remove from the heat, then add the polenta in a slow, steady stream, stirring constantly with a wooden spoon. Put the pan back onto the heat and cook gently, still stirring, for 5 minutes, until very thick.

2 Remove the pot from the heat and stir in the corn, scallions, oregano and freshly ground black pepper to taste. Transfer the polenta mixture to an oiled Swiss roll pan or rectangular baking pan measuring about 30 x 20 cm, and spread out evenly, smoothing the top. Leave the polenta to cool for about 20 minutes until cool and firm.

3 Preheat the oven to 425°F (220°C). Spread the pesto evenly over the polenta base. Thinly slice the mozzarella, then cut into strips and scatter over the polenta.

4 Arrange the tomato halves on top, cut-side uppermost. Sprinkle with freshly ground black pepper, then scatter the pine nuts over the top.

5 Bake for 15–20 minutes until golden and bubbling. Serve hot or leave to cool to room temperature, sprinkled with fresh basil leaves and some olives.

EACH SERVING

24 g protein • 17.5 g fat of which 5.5 g saturates • 61 g carbohydrate • 8 g fibre • 515 Calories

Butternut squash tart with Parmesan

Butternut squash make any dish look and taste superb. Their sweet flesh is rich in beta-carotene, and contains vitamin C, folate and potassium. You can make this tart a day ahead.

Serves 4 Preparation time 25 minutes Cooking time 55 minutes

PASTRY

1¼ cups whole wheat flour

1 tablespoon sesame seeds

90 grams (3 oz) margarine, chilled and diced

¼–⅓ cup cold water

FILLING

1 butternut squash, cut into 3 cm dice

1 large red pepper, deseeded and cut into 2.5 cm dice

1 tablespoon olive oil

2 eggs

⅔ cup 1% milk

¼ cup grated Parmesan cheese

2–3 pinches chili flakes or freshly ground black pepper

1 Preheat the oven to 450°F (230°C). Put the vegetables into a roasting pan, drizzle the olive oil over them, sprinkle with freshly ground black pepper and toss together. Roast the vegetables for 30 minutes until browned. Remove and leave to cool. Reduce the oven to 350°F (180°C). Put a baking tray into the oven.

2 Meanwhile, to make the pastry, combine the flour, sesame seeds and a pinch of salt in a bowl, then rub in the spread with your fingertips. When the mixture resembles breadcrumbs, stir in the cold water, or as much as is needed, with a round-bladed knife, to form the mixture into a soft dough. Wrap with plastic wrap and chill for 15–20 minutes.

3 Unwrap the pastry and roll out on a floured work surface to a circle about 25 cm round. Lift it over a 21 cm flan pan and gently press the pastry onto the base and sides. Trim off the excess.

4 In a wide pitcher or bowl, combine the eggs with the milk and cheese. Season with the chili flakes or pepper. Spoon the roasted vegetables into the pastry case, mounding them in the centre, then pour over the cheesy egg custard.

5 Set the pan on the heated baking tray and bake for 25 minutes until just set, puffed and golden. Remove from the oven and leave to stand for 5 minutes before serving. Eat warm from the oven or at room temperature.

VARIATION

• *Replace the sun-dried tomato pesto with basil pesto, and top with thin rings of red pepper and halved Roma tomatoes.*

EACH SERVING

18.5 g protein • 27 g fat of which 6.5 g saturates • 46 g carbohydrate • 8 g fibre • 519 Calories

Greek spinach and feta pie

A deliciously light, crunchy, layered phyllo pastry bake, with a filling of spinach, feta cheese, tomatoes and pine nuts — a classic Greek combination.

Serves 6

Preparation time 15 minutes

Cooking time 40 minutes

2 tablespoons olive oil

1 large onion, roughly chopped

2 garlic cloves, crushed

200 grams (7 oz) frozen spinach

3 ripe tomatoes, finely chopped and drained

1/2 cup ricotta cheese

100 grams (3 1/2 oz) feta cheese, drained

1/4 cup pine nuts, toasted

pinch of grated nutmeg

6 sheets phyllo pastry

COOK'S TIP

• The filling can be made up to 2 days ahead and kept chilled. When ready to serve, bring the mixture to room temperature, then complete the recipe.

VARIATION

• For a non-vegetarian pie, add 150 grams (5 oz) chopped bacon with the onion in step 1 and cook for 10 minutes. Continue with the recipe, omitting the feta cheese and adding 1/3 cup grated Parmesan cheese instead.

1 Preheat the oven to 375°F (190°C). Heat 1 tablespoon of the oil in a frying pan, then add the onion and garlic. Cook gently on a low heat, stirring occasionally, for about 8 minutes, until softened. Add the spinach and tomatoes and continue cooking for about 6 minutes. Tip into a large bowl and allow to cool slightly.

2 Stir the ricotta and feta cheeses into the spinach mixture together with the pine nuts and season to taste with a little salt and pepper and the nutmeg.

3 Lightly oil a shallow baking dish measuring about 28 x 20 cm. Use two of the phyllo sheets to line the base and sides of the dish, overlapping if necessary. Leave the excess pastry to hang over the edges of the dish. Cover with half of the spinach mixture, spreading it out to the edges in an even layer. Cover with two more sheets of phyllo, then another layer of the spinach.

4 Fold the excess phyllo in over the top, then place the remaining two phyllo sheets on top, folding the edges under neatly. Brush the top lightly with the remaining oil and bake for 25 minutes or until crisp and golden.

EACH SERVING

10.5 g protein • 16.5 g fat of which 5.5 g saturates • 13 g carbohydrate • 3.5 g fibre • 247 Calories

Vegetable pies with cheese and herb pastry

There is always something appealing about individual pies. These are filled with vegetables in a parsley sauce and topped with a tasty shortcrust pastry.

Serves *4*

Preparation time *20 minutes*

Cooking time *35 minutes*

PASTRY

1¼ cups all-purpose flour

90 grams (3 oz) margarine, chilled and diced

¼ cup finely grated aged cheddar cheese

2 tablespoons snipped fresh chives

2–3 tablespoons cold water

FILLING

2½ cups diluted salt-reduced or homemade vegetable stock (page 29)

200 grams (7 oz) broccoli florets

1 leek, trimmed and sliced

1¼ cups shelled fava beans (fresh or frozen)

¾ cup shelled fresh or frozen peas, thawed if necessary

8 cherry tomatoes, halved

2 teaspoons cornstarch

1 tablespoon cold water

2 tablespoons chopped fresh flat-leaf parsley

VARIATIONS
* *Use any selection of fresh, seasonal vegetables. Tomatoes add a splash of colour, but you could use corn or diced red pepper instead.*
* *For meat-eaters, add 4–6 diced strips of lean bacon to the vegetable filling.*

1 Preheat the oven to 400°F (200°C). Put the flour in a bowl and rub in the margarine with your fingertips until the mixture resembles fine breadcrumbs. Stir in the cheese and chives, then add enough cold water to bind to a dough. Wrap in plastic wrap and chill, while you make the filling.

2 Heat the stock in a large pot until boiling, then add the broccoli, leek, beans and peas. Bring back to a boil, cover and simmer for 5 minutes. Drain, reserving 1¼ cups of the stock.

3 Divide all the vegetables among four 1½ cup pie dishes. Mix the cornstarch with the water and stir in the reserved stock. Pour into the pot and stir over a medium heat until thick and smooth. Add the parsley. Pour over the vegetables.

4 Roll out the pastry and cover the pie dishes, sealing the rims with a little water. Cut a small vent in each pastry lid. Place on a baking tray and bake for 20–25 minutes until the pastry is firm and golden brown. Serve hot.

EACH SERVING

15 g protein • 18 g fat of which 4.5 g saturates • 42 g carbohydrate • 9 g fibre • 409 Calories

Goat's cheese and cranberry strudel

An impressive centrepiece for a festive vegetarian meal, this crisp phyllo pastry ring is filled with mushrooms, hazelnuts, vivid, tart cranberries and cubes of tangy goat's cheese. Serve with cranberry sauce and a mixed leaf salad.

Serves 4
Preparation time 25 minutes
Cooking time 50 minutes

2 tablespoons olive oil

2 red onions, finely chopped

200 grams (7 oz) button mushrooms, quartered if large

2/3 cup bulgur

3 cups cold water

3/4 cup hazelnuts, toasted and chopped

1 cup frozen cranberries, thawed

1 tablespoon fresh thyme

150 grams (5 oz) firm, medium-fat goat's cheese

6 sheets phyllo pastry

VARIATION

• *You can replace the cranberries with roughly chopped dried apricots, if you prefer.*

1 Heat 1 tablespoon of the oil in a medium frying pan. Add the onions and stir well. Cover the pan with a lid or press a circle of baking paper on top of the onions, and cook very gently for 10–15 minutes until the onions are very soft. Uncover the onions and add the mushrooms. Cook, stirring frequently, for a further 5 minutes.

2 Meanwhile, put the bulgur into a pot with the water. Bring to a boil, then reduce the heat and simmer gently for about 10 minutes until just tender. Drain thoroughly.

3 Tip the bulgur into a bowl, and stir in the onions and mushrooms. Add the hazelnuts, cranberries and thyme, plus seasoning to taste and mix well. Cut the cheese into small dice and set aside.

4 Preheat the oven to 375°F (190°C). Unwrap the phyllo pastry and arrange four of the sheets, slightly overlapping, to make a rectangle about 50 x 30 cm, using a little of the oil to lightly brush between the phyllo sheets.

5 Spoon the filling along one long end of the pastry, 6 cm from the edge. Scatter the cheese over the mound of filling. Fold the border over the filling, then carefully roll up the strudel, like a Swiss roll. Seal the ends together to enclose the filling, then carefully transfer to a large greased baking tray and shape into a horseshoe. Lightly brush with olive oil.

6 Cut the reserved phyllo sheets into wide strips using kitchen scissors, then scrunch up and drape over the strudel (this will also cover up any cracks). Brush with the remaining oil. Bake for 25–30 minutes until the pastry is golden and crisp. Serve warm.

EACH SERVING

15.5 g protein • 32 g fat of which 6.5 g saturates • 28.5 g carbohydrate • 8 g fibre • 477 Calories

Carrot tart

Carrots make a great filling for a tart because they are sweet and colourful. Here the smooth and creamy filling is made with low-fat ricotta cheese, plus cashew nuts for extra protein. The oats provide a nutty flavour.

Serves 4

Preparation time 15 minutes, plus 20 minutes chilling

Cooking time 50 minutes

PASTRY

¾ cup all-purpose flour

½ cup rolled oats

75 grams (2½ oz) margarine, chilled and diced

2–3 tablespoons cold water

FILLING

500 grams (1 lb) carrots, peeled and sliced

¼ cup reduced-fat ricotta cheese

1 egg

1 orange, zest grated

⅓ cup unsalted cashews, chopped

1 To make the pastry, mix together the flour, oats and a pinch of salt, then rub in the margarine with your fingertips. Add enough of the cold water to bind to a soft dough. Wrap in plastic wrap and put in the refrigerator for 20 minutes.

2 Preheat the oven to 350°F (180°C), with a baking tray inside to heat up. Roll out the pastry on a lightly floured work surface to a round large enough to line a 23 cm flan pan. Gently push down into the edges of the pan and trim the edge. Prick the base with a fork, then line the pastry case with baking paper and fill with baking beans or uncooked rice.

3 Put the pan on the tray; bake for 20 minutes. Remove the paper and beans; bake for 3 minutes.

4 Meanwhile, put the carrots into a pot of water, bring to a boil and simmer for 8 minutes until very soft. Drain and transfer to a food processor. Purée until smooth, then add the cheese and pulse to combine, scraping the sides occasionally. Add the egg and zest and pulse a few times to mix. Season.

5 Pour the mixture into the pastry case and sprinkle with cashews. Bake for 18 minutes. Serve warm.

EACH SERVING

11.5 g protein • 23 g fat of which 5 g saturates • 40 g carbohydrate • 6.5 g fibre • 425 Calories

Goat's cheese and red pepper quiche

A colourful vegetarian quiche with a filling of juicy roasted peppers and red onion in a tangy goat's cheese filling.

Serves 4 Preparation time 15 minutes, plus 30 minutes cooling before serving Cooking time about 1 hour

PASTRY

1 cup all-purpose flour

½ cup rolled oats

½ teaspoon dried thyme

100 grams (3½ oz) margarine, chilled and diced

2–3 tablespoons cold water

FILLING

280 ml jar roasted peppers

1 red onion, halved and thinly sliced

leaves from 1 small sprig of fresh rosemary, finely chopped

1 teaspoon balsamic vinegar

100 grams (3½ oz) goat's cheese, crumbled

2 tablespoons snipped fresh chives

2 eggs

¼ cup ricotta cheese

⅔ cup skim milk

1 Mix together the flour, oats, thyme and a pinch of salt, then rub in the spread with your fingertips. Add enough of the cold water to bind to a soft dough. Wrap with plastic wrap and chill for 15 minutes.

2 Meanwhile, drain the oil and juices from the jar of peppers into a small pot. Add the onion, rosemary and vinegar and cook gently for about 10 minutes until soft. Remove from the heat. Chop the peppers into small pieces.

3 Place a baking tray inside the oven and preheat to 400°F (200°C). Roll out the pastry on a lightly floured work surface to a round large enough to line a 21 cm flan pan, 3 cm deep. Gently push down into the base of the pan and trim the edge. Prick the base with a fork, then line it with baking paper and fill with baking beans.

4 Put the pan on the hot tray and bake for 15 minutes, then remove the paper and beans and bake for a further 3 minutes. Reduce the oven to 340°F (170°C).

5 Spoon the peppers into the flan pan along with the cooked onions. Sprinkle with the goat's cheese and scatter with the chives.

6 Beat together the eggs, ricotta, milk and seasoning. Carefully pour the mixture into the flan pan. Bake for 25–30 minutes until the filling is just firm. Remove and allow to cool for 30 minutes before serving.

EACH SERVING

16.5 g protein • 27 g fat of which 8 g saturates • 42 g carbohydrate • 4 g fibre • 481 Calories

COOK'S TIP

• *The pastry case can be made up to 1 week in advance. Once cool, double-wrap in plastic wrap, then keep chilled. Allow the pastry to come to room temperature, before baking blind, as described in step 3.*

Index